State Crime on the Margins of Empire

State Crime on the Margins of Empire

Rio Tinto, the War on Bougainville
and Resistance to Mining

Kristian Lasslett

PLUTO **PRESS**

In loving memory of Susan Lasslett

First published 2014 by Pluto Press
345 Archway Road, London N6 5AA

www.plutobooks.com

British Library Cataloguing in Publication Data
A catalogue record for this book is available from the British Library

ISBN   978 0 7453 3503 2   Hardback
ISBN   978 0 7453 3504 9   Paperback
ISBN   978 1 7837 1229 8   PDF eBook
ISBN   978 1 7837 1231 1   Kindle eBook
ISBN   978 1 7837 1230 4   EPUB eBook

Library of Congress Cataloging in Publication Data applied for

This book is printed on paper suitable for recycling and made from
fully managed and sustained forest sources. Logging, pulping and
manufacturing processes are expected to conform to the environmental
standards of the country of origin.

10   9   8   7   6   5   4   3   2   1

Typeset by Stanford DTP Services, Northampton, England
Text design by Melanie Patrick

Contents

State Crime
Series Introduction

With this book we launch an exciting new series dedicated to understanding state crime, a series which showcases the best of new state crime scholarship. This is work which challenges official and legal definitions of crime, but on any reasonable definition (whether based on national and international law or a concept such as social harm) crimes condoned, committed or instigated by states dwarf most other forms of crime. Genocide, war crimes, torture, and the enormous scale of corruption that afflicts nations such as Papua New Guinea make everyday crimes against the persons and property of European citizens appear almost trivial. This series grows out of the International State Crime Initiative's work on advancing our understanding of state violence and corruption and of resistance to them. The series is driven by a new and sophisticated wave of state crime scholarship; one in which theoretical development drawing on a variety of social scientific traditions is informed by courageous and rigorous empirical research.

A major area of state crime scholarship, to which this book contributes, is that concerned with the interaction and collusion between states and corporations. In *State Crime on the Margins of Empire*, Kristian Lasslett provides a compelling narrative of capital, empire and resistance on the island of Bougainville, Papua New Guinea, which endured a brutal civil war from the late 1980s into the 1990s.

On this one small island was visited almost every form of state and state corporate crime including forced displacement, mass-destruction of property, internment, torture, extrajudicial killings and a lethal sanctions regime. Lasslett demonstrates the necessity of understanding the complex layering of formal and informal power structures through a detailed study of clan relationships, patronage networks, patrimonial political relations and the asymmetrical interaction between mining capital and the states of Papua New Guinea and Australia.

The theoretical perspective from which Lasslett views these developments is an interpretation of 'classical Marxism', which draws on the works of Marx, Lenin and Trotsky as well as less celebrated figures such as the Soviet philosopher Evald Ilyenkov. When Lasslett's theoretical map places Papua New Guinea 'on the margins of Empire', the Empire in question is that of global capital. It is an Empire without a sovereign; if it has an Emperor, it is the impersonal logic of capital, which the governments of nation-states serve as more or less obedient viceroys. Although global in reach, its effects can only be understood in relation to the dynamics of local political and economic conjunctures.

Within this framework, the study of state crime starts from a recognition that states cannot rule for long by naked coercion alone. State crime occurs when economic and political pressures lead states to violate the norms on which their legitimacy depends, arousing processes of resistance, exposure and censure which may, in different circumstances, curb criminal activities or provoke an intensification of violent repression. The regional articulations of capitalism embody certain criminogenic potentials, but they become actualised only under specific historical conditions which Lasslett chronicles in meticulous detail. There is nothing crudely reductionist about Lasslett's version of Marxism.

While not every state crime scholar is a Marxist, classical or otherwise, Lasslett's Marxism is deployed partly in order to critique some other well-established approaches to state and corporate crime. We are delighted to launch the series with such a powerful and innovative contribution to state crime scholarship and hope this book will provoke a healthy debate within the field, to which other books in the series will also contribute.

Penny Green and Tony Ward
Series Editors

Abbreviations

ABC	Australian Broadcasting Commission
ABG	Autonomous Bougainville Government
ADF	Australian Defence Force
ADoD	Australian Department of Defence
AGA	Applied Geology Associates
AusAID	Australian Agency for International Development
BCF	Bougainville Copper Foundation
BCL	Bougainville Copper Limited
BIG	Bougainville Interim Government
BLF	Buka Liberation Front
BMWU	Bougainville Mining Workers Union
BRA	Bougainville Revolutionary Army
CIS	Corrective Institutions Service
CRA	Conzinc Riotinto of Australia Limited
DFA	Papua New Guinea Department of Foreign Affairs
DFAT	Australian Department of Foreign Affairs and Trade
DIB	Defence Intelligence Branch, Papua New Guinea
DPMC	Australian Department of Prime Minister and Cabinet
HBSS	Hagens Berman Sobol Shapiro
HC	Australian High Commission, Port Moresby
NEC	National Executive Council
NPLA	New Panguna Landowners Association
NSA	Bougainville Copper Limited National Staff Association
OPLA	Old Panguna Landowners Association
PLA	Panguna Landowners Association
PMD	Papua New Guinea Prime Minister's Department
PNG	Papua New Guinea
PNGDF	Papua New Guinea Defence Force
RPNGC	Royal Papua New Guinea Constabulary
RMTLTF	Road Mining Tailings Leases Trust Fund
RTZ	Rio Tinto
SOE	State of Emergency

Acknowledgements

A large project such as this is always indebted to a wide network of people. When I began the research back in 2004, evidencing the state-corporate decisions and motivations that underpinned the crimes on Bougainville seemed an impossible task. I was fortunate, in this respect, to have received much encouragement and guidance from activists and advocates involved in the Bougainville anti-war and independence movement, including Max Watts, Rosemarie Gillespie, Vikki John, Marilyn Havini and Moses Havini, to name just a few. Their steers led me first to Seattle where the law firm, Hagens Berman Sobol Shapiro, afforded me generous access to their case file. Then, when I arrived in Papua New Guinea during 2006, and faced the challenge of locating senior state officials, I was grateful to have the assistance of Effrey Dademo, Almah Tararia and Graeme Kunjil.

I owe a special debt of gratitude to my colleagues at the International State Crime Initiative (ISCI) including Penny Green, Tony Ward, Alicia de la Cour Venning, Tom MacManus, and Fatima Kanji. I have also benefited enormously from the support of ISCI's Honorary Fellows John Pilger, Noam Chomsky, and Richard Falk, all of whom have proven so generous with their time and guidance over the years (in addition to being unyielding beacons for truth and rigour). As a result of these collective efforts, ISCI has become a vibrant hub for state crime research, and without its support this book, and book series, would not exist. Equally, I have benefited greatly from the supportive and collegial environment at the University of Ulster's School of Criminology, Politics and Social Policy & Institute for Research in the Social Sciences, and before that at the University of Westminster's School of Law.

Also, it would be remiss not to note, with thanks, the many inspiring scholars currently working in the area of state crime studies. A special nod, in this respect, goes to Scott Poynting, Dave Whyte, and Steve Tombs, all of whom have lent a hand along the way. Furthermore, given the strong Marxist currents that underpin this volume, I must gratefully acknowledge members of the Historical Materialism World Development Research Seminar Group. Over the years our meetings and discussions laid the tracks for many profound adventures into Marxism.

Thanks also goes to Anne Beech and the entire Pluto Press team. One cannot emphasise enough what an important role they have played in supporting critical research, including this volume, over the decades. The scholarly terrain is so much the richer because of Pluto's efforts.

To finish I would like to acknowledge a few special individuals who have been an intrinsic part of this project since its inception – my colleague, Penny Green, who has acted as a mentor, intellectual collaborator and a pillar of support over the last decade, she is a selfless champion for new and emerging scholars, a tireless ambassador for the field, and a wonderful comrade; the entire community at the Bismarck Ramu Group – they are one of Papua New Guinea's great unsung treasures, and their support over the years has been truly amazing; my wife, Sandy Micik – through the ups and downs of the research process, and the prolonged time in the field and office, she has been there as a loving partner, and a cherished friend; and, of course, my father, Gordon Lasslett, not only for turning his house into little Bougainville when needed, but for the many stimulating hours of vibrant political conversation we enjoy.

Finally, I would like to thank Theonila Roka, and the Bougainville Students Association (Divine World University). They recently reminded me that behind all the data are real people – with lived experience of trauma and loss – who have a proud history, and unyielding commitment to the cause of social justice.

1

State Crime and the Empire of Capital

In the final, celebrated section of *Capital* (volume one) Marx (1976: 874) breaks from the preceding theoretical discussion to debunk liberal mythology on the 'idyllic' origins of capitalism (to be exact, Marx calls it a 'nursery tale'). Capitalism's *real* prehistory, he argues, is written in 'letters of blood and fire':

> The spoliation of the Church's property, the fraudulent alienation of the state domains, the theft of the common lands, the usurpation of feudal and clan property and its transformation into modern private property under circumstances of ruthless terrorism, all these things were just so many idyllic methods of primitive accumulation. (Marx 1976: 895)

The violence meted out at home in Western Europe, Marx observes, was replicated abroad in even more searing forms:

> The discovery of gold and silver in America, the extirpation, enslavement and entombment in mines of the indigenous population of that continent, the beginnings of the conquest and plunder of India, and the conversion of Africa into a preserve for the commercial hunting of blackskins, are all things which characterize the dawn of the era of capitalist production. (1976: 915)

Yet as David Harvey (2003) has argued, these 'idyllic methods' that helped mould a world in capital's image, are not confined to capitalism's prehistory. Rather, 'ruthless terrorism', 'conquest and plunder', 'undisguised looting', 'forcible expropriation' 'stock-exchange gambling', etc. (Marx 1976: 873–940), have proven enduring features of actually existing capitalism as its combustible dynamics mature and operationalise in a socially diverse range of regions. And like the historical hothouse in which capitalism was born through fits and starts, the state remains a key organiser of the less sanguine enterprises on which reproduction hinges.

That said, the annals of capitalism are not only written in letters of 'blood and fire'. Etched into its history with equal vigour are important struggles of solidarity and resistance. Indeed, in diverse regions global social movements, in their various complex constellations, embark upon vocal campaigns designed to challenge, censure and punish state actors responsible for dispossession, expropriation, and terror (see Marfleet 2013; Patel 2013; Stanley and McCulloch 2012b). This organised, social reaction – underpinned by evolving normative frameworks – imbue certain state practices with an illegitimate and deviant character. Indeed, rather than being an imposed intellectual category, state crime has in fact come into existence through the iron forge of history,[1] and upon its fault-lines new and important struggles over truth, impunity, and justice have emerged.

Historically, criminology has turned its back to this emerging reality. However, on its margins a growing number of scholars have begun to take this evolving relationship between state practice, popular condemnation, and struggles of resistance as the basis for a critical field of inquiry. Not surprisingly, given the dialectic this relationship presupposes, many scholars concerned draw their primary inspiration from Marxism (see Green and Ward 2004; Kramer et al. 2002; Michalowski 1985, 2009, 2010; Pearce 1976; Tombs and Whyte 2002). This would seem a comfortable marriage.

Indeed, making sense of, and responding to, state crime hinges on the careful application of Marxist concepts to interrogate critical social foci, including class, contradiction, crisis, resistance and revolution. On the other hand, explaining why criminal state practices are a constitutive feature of really existing capitalism, and grappling with the complex struggles they engender, is fundamental for a revolutionary tradition that both wants to concretise understandings of the present mode of production, while engaging with and buttressing political movements capable of engendering transformative change. In this sense, Marxism is well tailored to solving the theoretical and methodological dilemmas facing state crime studies, while state crimes studies has the potential to deepen Marxist understandings of those illicit practices and subsequent struggles that lie at the forefront of capitalism's recent, tumultuous history.

This volume is constructed on the latter presuppositions. Speaking at the most general level then, it is a study of the complex range of exploitative forms, socio-cultural arrangements and political systems through which capitalist relations of production function, and the historical conditions under which criminogenic potentialities embedded within particular regionalised articulations of capitalism, become actualised. However, speaking more specifically, this general focus will be operationalised through an in-depth study of the Bougainville conflict. This civil war, which consumed the South Pacific nation of Papua New Guinea (PNG) for most of the 1990s, was punctuated and exacerbated by a range of illicit state-corporate practices including forced displacement, mass-destruction of property, internment, torture, extrajudicial killings and the denial of humanitarian aid.

At the conflict's heart was a conjuncture defined by clan structures, patrimonial political relations, a 'weak' state (PNG), an emerging sub-imperial power (Australia), and mining capital (Rio Tinto). Very few things about PNG conform to textbook models of capitalism, nevertheless if applied dialectically with due respect for empirical difference, Marxist categories remain an indispensable tool for understanding the social fault-lines of this conflict and the range of illicit state-corporate practices it engendered.

This introductory chapter traces in more detail the conceptual and empirical focus that frames this intervention. To that end, we begin by examining the particular features of capitalism, defined from a classical Marxist perspective,[2] which have provoked a peculiar form of empire that is global in reach, but administered through a fractured system of nation-states that observes an inherently capitalist logic of power. Understanding capitalism as an expansive, crisis-prone system operationalised through an often contradictory synthesis of international capital flows and an asymmetric nation-state system, provides an overarching framework in which to situate one of empire's specific regional articulations, PNG. With this global perspective as our backdrop, readers are introduced to the 'unconventional' forms of heightened class struggle that emerged out of PNG's particular path of immersion into empire, and the illicit state-corporate response this struggle provoked.

This introduction to the book's empirical focus is followed by a more in-depth look at its scientific method. Specifically, we tease out the peculiar relationship between facts, theory and approximation that distinguishes the classical Marxist approach. We also examine classical Marxism's critique of those scientific traditions built on variations of empiricism, which presently have a strong following within state crime studies. Out of this discussion will emerge a set of concrete aims, pitched at the level of criminology and Marxism, which this study will strive to achieve.

The Empire of Capital

Over the past three centuries capital has amassed an impressive global empire (herein Empire).[3] Only a few regions on the margins remain 'off grid'. Wood observes:

> There is nothing else in the history of humanity to compare with the kind of social system created by capitalism: a complex network of tight interdependence among large numbers of people, and social classes, not joined by personal ties or direct political domination but connected by their market dependence and the market's imperative network of social relations and processes. (2002: 180)

The foundations of this historical achievement, unheralded in its magnitude, lie in the dynamics of Empire's structure.

Unlike the social systems which immediately precede the rise of capitalism – where the application of sovereign power was critical to forms of exploitation – capital's valorisation is increasingly underpinned by household dependency on market based exchange. Marx (1976: 875) explains, under capitalism the worker – who has been historically 'freed' from the means of production – must *sell* their labour-power in order to obtain the means (money) for *purchasing* household necessities.[4] This historically constructed double-dependency on capitalist markets (which must constantly be reproduced), in turn, *forces* the propertyless worker into a productive context where surplus value can be extracted by an appropriating class,[5] while at the same time upholding the appearance of 'free' exchange between buyer and seller.[6] 'He who was previously the money-owner [during exchange] now strides out in front as a capitalist', Marx (1976: 280) observes, 'the possessor of labour-power follows as his worker. The one smirks self-importantly and is intent on business; the other is timid and holds back, like someone who has brought his own hide to market and now has nothing else to expect but – a tanning'.

What is being pinpointed here then is the emergence of a new *generalised medium and lever*, that is market and market dependency, which with the transition to capitalism mediates the extraction of surplus from the immediate producer and its distribution to an appropriating class seeking to augment the value they have invested. Importantly, the emergence of this lever, and the class forces it presupposes, when coupled to a historical process of struggle and political upheaval, deprives sovereign power of the function it possessed under feudal and absolutist regimes. 'The moment of coercion' and the 'moment of appropriation', have now become, Wood (2002: 172) suggests, 'allocated between two distinct but complementary "spheres"'. Out of this arrangement emerges a civil society that is ostensibly 'autonomous from the state' (Lacher 2006: 97), and 'a "purely political" state . . . abstracted from the exploitation of surplus' (Lacher 2006: 107). This new unity of opposites provokes a 'profound transformation' in the functionality of sovereign power (Lacher 2006: 97). Teschke argues:

> Since ruling-class power in capitalist-societies is based on private property and control over the means of production, 'the state' is no longer required to interfere directly into processes of production and extraction. Its central function is confined to the internal maintenance and external defence of a private property regime. This entails legally enforcing what are now civil contracts among politically (though not economically) free and equal citizens subject to civil law. This, in turn, requires a public monopoly over the means of violence, enabling the development of an 'impartial' public bureaucracy. Political power and especially the monopoly over the means of violence now come to be pooled in a deprivatized state above society and the economy. (2003: 256)

However, in an intervention often overlooked in the Marxist literature, Foucault significantly advances this argument in a way that helps explain the rise of Empire. It is not simply that legal, administrative and coercive technologies have retired from the immediate process of production to assume a public form, they have, Foucault suggests, become organised around a new modality of power. Indeed, facing the emergence of an 'autonomous' civil society endowed with its own economic and social rhythms – a process which is bulwarked by significant and powerful class forces – Foucault (2007: 352) argues that states can no longer rule through 'systems of injunctions, imperatives, and interdictions' (see also Foucault 2003: 249). Rather, he claims, they must learn to 'respect these natural processes, or at any rate to take them into account, get them to work, or to work with them' (Foucault 2007: 352; see also Foucault 2007: 351).

From this perspective states operate strategically by shaping the regulatory, built and social environments through which these 'natural processes' intrinsic to civil society operate, in order to stimulate desirable ends conceptualised at the level of 'the population' (full employment, economic growth, reduced crime, stable currency, etc.) (Foucault 2007: 105). Accordingly, different technologies of government – taxation, duties, capital controls, public investment, criminal codes, monetary policy, service provision, infrastructure investment, policing, military intervention etc. – become tactics for affecting, with a definite end in mind, the economic and social rhythms of civil society.

As a result, with the transition to capitalism, the instruments of statecraft become what Foucault calls, *governmentalised*. However, simply because the instruments of statecraft no longer form a direct device for extracting surplus from the immediate producer, and feuding with rivals, it does not follow that they are exterior to capitalist relations of production. Rather, what changes is the character of these instruments, the rationality with which they are applied, and the particular way states intervene in the processes through which surplus is extracted from the immediate producer. For instance, technologies of capitalist statecraft influence, manage and shape, the quantity and quality of social labour available to individual units of capital, the intensity and conditions under which labour is used, the way in which value embeds in the built environment, the velocity and trajectory of flows in investment and credit, the dynamism of different markets, society's capacity to consume, etc. Governmental power also, of course, constantly secures and reproduces the vital social oppositions which capitalist relations of production presuppose, relations it might be added that are infused with potentially self-annulling antagonisms. The organisation and application of governmental power, therefore, forms a crucial part of capitalism's interior.

However, governmentalised states do not exist in the generic singular, nor do they exist in abstraction from each other. Rather, as Wood (2003: 141) observes, 'the very essence of globalization is a global economy administered by a global system of multiple states and local sovereignties, structures in a complex relation of domination and subordination'. The government of Empire, therefore, functions through an asymmetric, international state-system. The constitutive units of this system, states, act as central nodal points, in which governmental regimes embed themselves, through a process of struggle (see Jessop 2007). When these nationally organised governmental regimes operate internationally, they confront two realities. First, they are sovereign over a specific region of the capitalist world economy that is of a certain size and significance. Second, this global economic system does not function entirely of its own accord, mediating its rhythms are the actions of other nation-states. Consequently, specific governmental regimes must carefully register both their peculiar position within the world economy, as well as the relative impact other governments are having on the international flows they are seeking to affect.

In this light, it could be argued that international political struggle is over security, but in the very precise sense Foucault gives it. That is, unlike the geopolitical rivalries of the dynastic era, capitalist states do not seek to accrue sovereign power as an end in itself; capitalist states aim to accumulate sovereign power and strategically project it more effectively than rivals – be it in bilateral or multilateral forums – because this puts them in a position of having a greater impact on the regional and global milieus which mediate critical economic and social flows. By shaping these milieus, they are better able to stimulate flows of people and wealth, essential to achieving 'specific finalities' at a national level (Foucault 2007: 99). The aim of foreign policy then is not to outweigh rivals, rather it is to out-govern rivals.

Of course, in a govermentalised system of states marked by significant imbalances in power, and contradiction, imperial rivalries and conquest is an enduring reality, which at its very height engenders armed conflict, perhaps the most extreme tool states can employ to reconfigure the social landscape through which capitalism functions.[7] Nevertheless, despite the regularity of violence, this governmentalised inter-state system has created a framework for the facilitation, regulation, and safe passage of people and wealth on a world scale. Under these conditions, Rosenberg (1994: 129) argues, 'it is now possible, in a way that would have been unthinkable under feudalism, to command and exploit productive labour (and natural resources) located under the jurisdiction of another state' (see also Wood 2002: 31). As a result, Bukharin (2003: 24) observes 'the labour of every individual country becomes part of that world social labour', from which surplus is increasingly appropriated by globalised capitals.

Consequently, the transition to capitalism, and the social dynamics this transition has engendered – surplus value extraction mediated by market exchange, an 'autonomous' international civil society, governmental-ised nation-states, and an asymmetric inter-state system – has created a framework for Empire to emerge on a global scale. However remarkable (and unintentional) this achievement is in historic terms, it has not shepherded an enduring peace: to the contrary, Empire's intensive and extensive growth has been punctuated with social rupture and the loss of human life and dignity on new and unimaginable scales. Behind these catastrophic events, are the contradictions structurally inscribed in the capitalist mode of production.

Contradiction, Empire and State Crime

Marx's famous inversion of Hegel's dialectical method,[8] acutely registers the important role material contradictions – i.e. structurally inscribed social antagonisms – play in stimulating the social ruptures, which give history its violent motion. In the French 'postface' to *Capital*, Marx observes:

> The fact that the movement of capitalist society is full of contradictions impresses itself most strikingly on the practical bourgeois in the changes of the periodic cycle through which modern industry passes, the summit of which is the general crisis. That crisis is once again approaching, although as yet it is only in its preliminary stages, and by the universality of its field of action and the intensity of its impact it will drum dialectics even into the heads of the upstarts in charge of the new Holy Prussian-German Empire. (1976: 103)

Given Marx's view in this respect, it is perhaps not surprising to note that his critique of political economy, frequently registers the role material contradictions play in planting the seeds of confrontation, conflict, crisis and revolution into the capitalist mode of production. For example, when examining the social mechanisms that compel capital to enhance the methods through which value is pumped from labour, Marx notes an important contradiction. This process, on one hand, enriches our social productive powers, while on the other, it impoverishes the immediate producer, whose physical and mental well-being is subordinated to economies in the use of constant (plants, machinery, buildings, raw materials, etc.) and variable capital (living labour). Consequently, Marx argues:

> If we consider capitalist production in the narrow sense . . . it is extremely sparing with the realized labour that is objectified in commodities. Yet

it squanders human beings, living labour, more readily than does any other mode of production, squandering not only flesh and blood, but nerves and brain as well. (1981: 182)

Capitalism's contradictory drives also impinge upon its commanding class. In his theory of capitalist crisis, for instance, Marx notes that the use of labour saving technologies to accrue higher than average profits, once generalised, provokes a gradual shift in the organic composition of capital (ratio of constant to variable capital), this ultimately manifests in a declining general rate of profit for capital as a whole (Marx 1981: 317). Marx (1981: 319) thus observes, 'the progressive tendency for the general rate of profit to fall is thus simply *the expression, peculiar to the capitalist mode of production*, of the progressive development of the social productivity of labour'. This structural contradiction, Marx argues, sparks spectacular episodes in 'speculation, credit swindles, [and] share swindles', by over-accumulated capital in search of profitable outlets, a process which foreshadows looming economic crisis (1981: 359).

Of course, Marx's critique of political economy is famously unfinished. Accordingly, those continuing Marx's work have teased out capitalism's contradictory mechanics at more concrete levels of analysis. For example, Istvan Mészáros (2001: 23) notes what he calls the 'weightiest contradiction' of capitalism. That is, while capital is able to circulate across political jurisdictions, creating what Bukharin (2003: 41) refers to as an 'ever thickening network of international interdependence', the central nodal points of governmental power tend to be organised on a national scale. This lays the ground for one of capitalism's most catastrophic ruptures, inter-imperialist rivalry and world war. Reflecting on World War I and its colonial prelude, Bukharin (2003: 159–60) remarks:

Imperialism has turned its true face to the working class of Europe. Hirtherto its barbarous, destructive, wasteful activities were almost entirely confined to the colonial subjects; now it thrusts itself upon the toilers of Europe with all the horrifying impact of a bloodthirsty elemental power let loose. The additional pennies received by the European workers from the colonial policy of imperialism – what do they count compared to millions of butchered workers, to billions devoured by the war, to the monstrous pressure of brazen militarism, to the vandalism of plundered productive forces, to high cost of living and starvation.

If there is a general point that may be extracted from the preceding examples, quite critical to this book's overarching thematic, it is the intimate connection between Empire, contradiction, social rupture, and what scholars call state and corporate crime (or, more simply, crimes of the powerful). That is, as Empire operationalises itself through diverse regional arrangement, its contradictory dynamics generates a range of tensions, which unevenly mature into more overt forms of rupture – for example, economic crisis, class conflict, war – that prove fertile environments for state and corporate crime.

Of course for state and corporate practices to be deemed criminal, presupposes there is a normative moment to this social equation, which there is. Put simply, a semblance of social stability, which is essential to all modes of production, demands the generation of customs and normative frameworks capable of regulating social practice (Mészáros 2011: 116–17). This normative terrain is always contested, and undoubtedly some classes are in a better position to shape which norms achieve hegemony (Lasslett 2010a). Be that as it may, those who command the economic and political engine house of Empire, cannot simply act as they choose (Marx 1976: 348). If they are to function with a modicum of consent, they must submit to certain critical norms. As Green and Ward observe:

> In any situation where the state's claim to legitimacy is accorded some degree of consent – and exactly what this 'consent' amounts to may be a very difficult question – there is likely to be some tacit understanding of the limits of legitimate conduct (which may be more or less closely related to legal norms), departure from which will attract some kind of censure or sanctions. (2000: 108)

Consequently certain deviant state and corporate practices, when exposed, can and have elicited mass-censure. As millions flooded Tahrir Square during the Egyptian uprising of 2011, it was the criminality of the political elite, which elicited particular condemnation (Friedrichs 2012; Marfleet 2013). While the ranks of Occupy were swelled by citizens demanding that banks and their political patrons be subjected, like them, to the rule of law. It is this evolving relationship between hegemonic norms, elite practice, and mass-censure, that provides a compelling conceptual foundation for a criminology of state and corporate crime, at least from a classical Marxist perspective (see Green and Ward 2000; Green and Ward 2004; Lasslett 2010a; Ward and Green 2000).

This foundation allows us to examine crucial questions. For example, why do the different social configurations through which Empire functions, generate historically specific balance of forces where state crime not only occurs, but becomes systematised? And, how do communities across diverse spatio-temporal terrains label these actions criminal, mobilise against perpetrators, and set about neutralising the structural foundation of these crimes through social movements of different complexions (see, for example, Stanley and McCulloch 2012b). In this sense, the questions being asked by criminology, probe the tender fault-lines at the centre of Empire, resistance and revolution. And it is these tender fault-lines which lie at the heart of this book.

State Crime on the Margins of Empire

'What the bourgeoisie . . . produces, above all', Marx and Engels (1973: 79) observe, 'are its own grave-diggers' (see also Marx and Engels 1956: 52). This statement, featured in the *Communist Manifesto*, elliptically articulates Empire's contradictory tendency to generate, in different degrees and shapes, mass movements disposed to its negation. Although Marx and Engels tended to identify this radicalised mass most closely with the industrial proletariat, there are good reasons to think capitalism's 'grave-diggers' is a more inclusive category. Indeed, one of the most general features of a world created in capital's image is structurally inscribed unevenness. That is, the social arrangements constitutive of Empire vary greatly between regions, owing to the very different conditions under which they enter, and then dynamically operate within Empire. The fault-lines of class conflict are, therefore, heterogeneous in character.

Comprehending these varied social arrangements, the complex forms of class struggle they engender, the national and international balance of forces which mediate struggle, and the forms of social rupture to emerge out of this process, is vital to any criminology seeking enriched understandings of state crime, and perhaps even more vitally, concrete resistance strategies. And it is on this footing that we turn to PNG, where a volatile balance of class forces came together through the focal point of a major mining operation, administered by Rio Tinto. In this example of really existing capitalism rural class conflict, mediated by a longstanding kinship system, engendered a landowner movement that came into collision both with a mineral dependent, patrimonial state and the interests of international mining capital, which were bulwarked by Australian imperial state-power (albeit, for specific geopolitical reasons that extend well beyond the region). Out of this complex social equation emerged an episode in state crime without rival in the South Pacific's post-independence history.

However, our regional focal point in this volume is more concentrated still; it is the island of Bougainville, which formed part of PNG's easternmost province – the North Solomons[9] – which forms the stage for this criminogenic collision of forces. Resting on the northern tip of the Solomon Islands archipelago, Bougainville was a late entry to Empire, annexed by Germany in 1886. Following a small armed incursion by Australia in 1914, Bougainville became part of a League of Nations 'C' class mandate over New Guinea, which was awarded to Australia in 1921. When the neighbouring colony, Papua, was amalgamated with New Guinea in 1949, vigorous attempts were made by the Australian government to stimulate the sort of economic and political practices that could eventually shepherd a stable transition to independence, for their closest regional neighbour. The colonial administration found willing local participants in this respect.

As a result, village life on Bougainville transformed as young men began cash-cropping, while the introduction of a local, provincial and national government groomed the first generation of political leaders. Yet these practices were not imprinted upon a blank canvas, rather they were mediated by rich kinship systems. Accordingly, the new interests, drives and challenges, inspired by PNG's gradual immersion into Empire, merged in significant ways with the Melanesian interface of clan, ethnicity and custom.

On Bougainville social change was hastened when an administration geologist noted a promising deposit of copper in the Panguna region of the Crown Prince Ranges in 1960 (Downs 1980: 341). Having secured the interest of mining multinational, Rio Tinto – organised through its PNG subsidiary, Bougainville Copper Limited (BCL) – production at Panguna began in 1972, just three years prior to PNG's independence. With new income streams flowing in from the mine, prominent local interlocutors – who had been at the forefront of negotiating the island's entry into Empire – began to entrench themselves in seats of economic and political power, often at the same time. With a burgeoning generation of youth coming to maturity during the 1980s, they faced a daunting social landscape. New cash-cropping practices had generated land shortages, while small-business opportunities and employment was seemingly monopolised by elders and mainland migrants. Guarding this process were customary leaders, provincial politicians and Bougainvillean businessmen who were its chief beneficiaries.

Under these antagonistic conditions a number of articulate youth leaders came to the fore in central Bougainville, where the contradictions of the island's social trajectory were most acutely felt. Drawing on the language of class to articulate their experience, these youth leaders challenged the lucrative roles elders had awarded themselves. In particular, the powerful Panguna Landowners Association's (PLA) executive, whom activists labelled 'self centred traditional landlords brainwashed by foreigners and minority elite nationals' (NPLA 1987a), was confronted by these young activists. The PLA was a landowner body set up to represent, and act for, village communities in the mine lease area.

When a number of youth leaders successfully deposed the PLA's executive through an election, they began laying the foundations for a historic social revolt. It began with a campaign of protest and civil disobedience, designed to raise awareness over the mine's social and environmental effects. It soon expanded into a more ambitious programme directed at expropriating local and international capital. Escalating acts of protest and confrontation culminated in a prolonged campaign of industrial sabotage which started in November 1988. The mine was the primary target, but local business also suffered. A heavy handed response from the Royal PNG Constabulary's mobile squad units – which included a series of assaults and village burnings – prompted young landowner activists to flee into the jungle, where they organised an armed resistance under the banner of the Bougainville Revolutionary Army (BRA). The BRA's leader, Francis Ona (1989), claimed 'we are the 'sacrificial lamb' for the few capitalists whose hunger for wealth is quenchless and unceasing'. Believing that the state's loyalties lay with 'traditional landlords' and BCL, the BRA looked to independence as the medium to free Bougainville from the contradictions of its modern history.

Given that Melanesia rests on the periphery of the world economy, this uprising was never going to send a shudder through the administrative and economic centres of global power. Yet for those in the immediate region responsible for defending the social arrangements constitutive of Empire, it represented a significant challenge. After a period of hesitation, the PNG state responded to the nascent BRA insurgency with a show of military force. To that end, during 1989 villages around the mine were assaulted with volleys of mortars, and grenades, dropped from Australian-supplied helicopters. Those displaced were rounded up by the security forces and put into detention camps, where physical and sexual abuse was commonplace. Young men were executed at the slightest suspicion of BRA involvement, a hairstyle was enough to condemn an individual (Amnesty International 1990a: 26). Women were also punished for the BRA's revolt, at times with grotesque violence. Ruby Mirinka recalls: 'One of the victims was a 24-year-old pregnant woman. Shot dead by the PNG soldiers, her abdomen was then cut open to remove the foetus. The dead foetus was then placed on the chest of the dead mother for all to see – as a warning' (2004: 102). All of this was achieved with significant material support from BCL and the Australian government, who willingly filled a vacuum left by defence force budgetary shortfalls.

However, rather than subduing the island revolt these armed incursions during 1989 in fact earned the BRA – which was increasingly out-manoeuvring government forces – status and support from villages outside their direct sphere of influence in central Bougainville. Nevertheless, having declared Bougainville's independence in May 1990, after successfully routing the PNG Defence Force earlier in the year, the BRA began to experience overreach as they struggled to govern a war-torn province, while lashing out at internal opponents. The PNG state responded to the BRA's loose grip on power, by amplifying internal tensions on the island – principally, through a military blockade that 'was total, including a blockade on any medical supplies, and was therefore tighter than that placed around Saddam Hussein's Iraq' (Spriggs 1992a: 13). The growing social schisms were then militarised by the PNG government, through the arming and financing of loyalist paramilitaries on Bougainville. Out of this counterinsurgency strategy emerged a theatre of war where village was pitted against village, as class, kinship and regional allegiances intermixed in complex and fluid ways.

In this sense, the crimes of the PNG state – which BCL and Australia share a large degree of responsibility for – helped manufacture the conditions for a civil war that 'represented by far the most long-running and bloody instance of violent political conflict in the South Pacific region after 1945' (Claxton 1998: xvii). By the conflict's cessation in 1997–98 between 10,000 and 20,000 people had lost their lives on an island whose population stood at 180,000 in 2000 (Alley 2003: 231). State crime could not have produced a more extreme outcome.

The following intervention will examine this prolonged period of state criminality, in order to understand how Empire's operationalisation in PNG not only inspired rupture but also a criminogenic state-corporate reaction that considerably amplified social volatility on Bougainville. This particular socio-historical focus is underpinned by a number of scholarly motivations.

First, a very basic commitment to truth demands this intervention; in the limited scholarly accounts to date on the Bougainville conflict, the crimes of the powerful are often ignored, obscured, rejected or attributed little weight (see, for example, Griffin 1990a; Griffin and Togolo 1997; May 1990; Ogan 2005; Regan 2003), with honourable exceptions (Böge 1995; Braithwaite et al. 2010; Gillespie 1996; Spriggs 1992a, 1992b).

Second, this study provides us with an opportunity to examine, through the lens of Bougainville, the criminogenic ways in which the organisational vehicles of capital and government – that is, corporations and states – react to, and jointly mobilise against, collective threats;[10] for reasons that have been alluded to in the Marxist and criminological literature, this process is not without its own tensions (see Callinicos 2009; Harvey 2003; Michalowski 2009). Third, when probing this state-corporate response to a collective threat, I want to explore how the calculations, social intercourse, and actions this necessarily involves, concretely express in dynamic ways, the drives, pressures and limitations of those relationships and processes around which production and rule are organised. This aim reflects, and responds to, a criticism of the state-corporate crime literature made by Tombs:

> With few exceptions, however, such analyses focus upon what are essentially forms of discrete joint ventures between corporations and state, either at specific moments or towards specific ends, thus abstracting these from a more generalized set of social relationships, which are ongoing, enduring and more akin, in fact, to a process . . . This is not to deny that case studies can be useful in advancing our understanding of state-corporate dynamics: but to do so, they must be generated as vehicles which are operationalized through both theoretical frameworks and their related, internally consistent, conceptual tools which ground such cases in more fundamental relations and processes of contemporary capitalism and its dynamics. (2012: 175; see also Slapper and Tombs 1999: 51)

Finally, and related to the previous point, this study looks to openly break with the scientific method informing those contributions alluded to by Tombs, principally by adopting a classical Marxist framework. Given the critical role this framework plays in both differentiating this account from a number of existing state crime interventions, and in informing the book's core focus, a brief explanation of the classical Marxist method, and its critique of empiricism, is needed. This will be made with particular reference to the state crime literature.

Scientific Method and State Crime

For over three decades radical scholars have argued for an approach to the crimes of the powerful, which draws on critical theory to illuminate the general features of the capitalist mode of production that contribute to, and reproduce, these crimes (Green and Ward 2004; Kramer et al. 2002; Michalowski 1985, 2009, 2010; Pearce 1976; Tombs and Whyte 2002; Young 1981). For example, in a defence of Marxist political economy, crimes of the powerful scholars, Tombs and Whyte, remark:

> The labour theory of value and the theory of surplus value, the necessarily antagonistic relationship between classes, the inherent tendency of capitalism to expand, destructively, whilst at the same time reproducing the contradictions upon which it is founded, all seem to be crucial tools for understanding and engaging with the trajectories of the world. (2002: 222; see also Young 1981: 324–5)

The methodological position adopted here by Tombs and Whyte – with which I agree – treats theory and theory building as a device for orienting consciousness to the elusive processes in which state and corporate crimes are submerged. Implicit in this approach, is a dialectical appreciation of the incongruence between appearance and reality,[11] and the important role knowledge production plays in bridging this divide. This perspective contrasts with key assumptions that underpin the strong empiricist tendencies which currently prevail within state crime studies.

Empiricism admittedly is a nebulous term. It is used here to reference strands of criminological scholarship which primarily study state/corporate crime events in order to inductively identify sets of causes that bring about organisational deviance. In this respect, once an accumulated body of empirical research begins to reveal certain causative patterns, these patterns are given a general conceptual form, and elevated to a theory of state crime. Theoretical debate tends to consist of arguments over the saliency of certain general causes, and the identification of causative lacunas, which need redress. As these theoretical models are refined and developed, they form the basis for strategies of resistance and control.

A notable example of an intervention framed from this vantage point is Mullins and Rothe's *Blood, Power and Bedlam: Violations of International Criminal Law in Post-Colonial Africa*, and subsequent articles by the authors. Employing a number of case studies, Mullins and Rothe (2008) propose building a theoretical framework that identifies the causes behind violations of international criminal law in Africa. They explain:

> By exploring the sociohistorical context and the enactment patterns of the Rwandan genocide of 1994, the 20-year war between the Museveni government and the Lords Resistance Army (LRA) in Uganda, the complete collapse of social order following the Second Congolese War in the Democratic Republic of the Congo, and the Darfur genocide in the Sudan, we have provided rich narratives of atrocity-producing events. Although the descriptions has value in and of itself, the main drive for examining the four cases in this volume is the attempt to build a criminological theory that is capable of explaining the phenomena. (Mullins and Rothe 2008: 191)

The 'atrocity-producing events' referred to here, are in effect the raw materials for generating sets of theoretical categories that encapsulate the common causal mechanisms behind these events. Borrowing heavily from earlier models developed by Kramer et al. (2002), Mullins and Rothe schematise these criminogenic factors across a vertical and horizontal axis, which they order according to sociological levels (international, macro, meso and micro) and catalysts for action (motivation, opportunity, constraints, and controls). State crime events occur, when these multi-level catalysts unify, through certain nodal points, to create a criminogenic balance of forces. Mullins explains: 'Crime events are produced by a combination of motivation and opportunity elements influencing social actors decision making processes, those processes are then further influenced by extant constraints and controls before an action is or is not committed. These four catalysts can function at all levels of analysis: international, national (macro), meso and micro' (2009: 19).

Despite having reservations over the explanatory potential of theoretical schemas modelled in this way, I have acknowledged elsewhere that interventions like Kramer et al.'s (2002) integrated theoretical model make an important contribution to the field (Lasslett 2010b). However, that said, the conceptual content of such schemas does not offer a means for bridging the divide between appearance and reality, that is by orienting consciousness to the empirical richness of offending contexts. This limitation is fundamentally grounded in the scientific method that these contributions are rooted in (i.e. empiricism), and the assumptions it gives rise to. While I have articulated the classical Marxist critique of empiricism elsewhere, it is worth recapping, in summary, certain key points (see Lasslett 2010b).

Arguably, the most critical limitation empiricism faces – at least in its criminological form – is of an ontological and epistemological nature. In particular, empiricist scholarship fails to acknowledge that the 'factual events' which form the basis of their conceptual work, are in fact definite theoretical interpretations. That is, the notions and concepts we use to articulate the empirical world, are not simply vessels for reflecting what we see, feel and hear; rather, they are the medium through which meaning is given to the data of sense-perception. As Ilyenkov (1982: 40–1) puts it, 'each separate sensual impression arising in individual consciousness is always a product of refraction of external stimuli through the extremely complex prism of the forms of social consciousness the individual has appropriated'. The richer the concepts we employ, the richer are our potential empirical understandings. As Bukharin observes: 'From the primitive idea of the sun as a round, shining disc hanging from the firmament, people have advanced [through theory] to a highly sophisticated understanding which reflects a huge and very diverse complex of objective properties of the objective body and of its relationships and mediations' (2005: 75).

From this critical perspective, Mullins and Rothe's descriptions of 'atrocity-producing' events, are tempered in significant ways by the concepts they appropriate to give empirical reality meaning. The implication here being that the facts used to build empiricist theories, are themselves theoretically mediated interpretations; but without recognition of this critical point, empiricist works are hostage to the categories they employ to make meaning, which can constrict as much as they illuminate, given the lack of method.

In light of this critique, classical Marxism assumes a very different stance when it comes to the relationship between theory and empirical understanding. Indeed, theory and theory development, in the classical Marxist tradition, involves what Lukács (1978: 33) calls 'thought experiments', where intellectual efforts are plumbed into constructing concepts that articulate increasingly more complex determinations, which through a process of intellectual accumulation gradually tease out in more detail the rich content of different natural and social realities. Bukharin remarks in this respect: 'We cannot see ultraviolet rays, but we think about them in profound terms. We cannot directly sense . . . the infinite number of alpha, beta, gamma, and other rays, with their enormous velocities and so forth, but we think about them and their velocities . . . The point is that our senses are limited, but that our cognition as a process is boundless' (2005: 94).

Accordingly, Marx employed thought experiments to study and think about the social processes through which surplus is extracted from the immediate producer; out of this study emerged concepts that help orient consciousness to different dimensions of the relations of production under capitalism. Of course, like Rothe and Mullins, empirical data formed the base of Marx's studies, however, he always treated first appearances as a deceptive basis for the interpretation of reality, as a consequence it needs to be transcended through theoretical work. This allows the thinker to return to the concrete, 'as a rich totality of many determinations and relations' (Marx 1973: 100). Bukharin (2005: 85–6) explains:

[T]he thought process returns to its starting point, that is, to the concrete. But this concrete (the 'second concrete') differs from the starting point (the 'first concrete') in that we now understand its essence, its laws, its universal nature as revealed in the particular and individual . . . There is nothing scanty here; on the contrary, compared with the first concrete we see a massive enrichment, since instead of indeterminate and arbitrarily selected aspects, the living dialectic of the real process is represented here.

Since empiricist approaches adopt a different stance with respect to empirical research and theory generation, their thought experiments are accordingly of quite a different nature. Beginning with unmediated data – that is, data which has yet to be enriched through the conscious application of theory – patterns are discovered by stripping away empirical detail, until a causative essence is discovered.[12] An example of this approach may be found in a celebrated theoretical intervention by Gross (1978), on the causes of organisational deviance. He argues: 'Some organizations seek profits, others seek survival, still others seek to fulfill government-imposed quotas, others seek to service a body of professionals who run them, some seek to win wars, and some seek to serve a clientele. Whatever the goal might be, it is the emphasis on them that creates the trouble' (Gross 1978: 209; see also Braithwaite 1984: 94–5; Braithwaite 1988: 628).

Having stripped a number of goals – detected through unmediated empirical research – of their specific form, Gross 'discovers' a critical cause of organisational deviance, it is a product of goal-seeking. We see here a methodological path that inverts the Marxist approach. It begins with data unmediated by theorisation, and moves from this problematic starting point into even thinner abstractions that only faintly express actually existing processes – which is regarded as a chief part of their charm. As Braithwaite (1988: 628) argues, 'to identify the causes of white-collar "crime" with the competitive pursuit of profit is . . . theoretically constraining'. Bukharin (2005: 83) bitterly rejects this approach, '[w]e do not want these abstractions, the dead plucked peacocks, out of which you have pulled all the luxuriant plumage!'. Gramsci offers explanation why:

The so-called laws of sociology which are assumed as laws of causation (such-and-such a fact occurs because of such-and-such a law, etc.) have no causal value: they are almost always tautologies and paralogisms. Usually they are no more than a duplicate of the observed fact itself. A fact or a series of facts is described according to a mechanical process of abstract generalisation, a relationship of similarity is derived from this and given the title of law and the law is then assumed to have causal value. But what novelty is there in that? The only novelty is the collective name given to a series of petty facts, but names are not an innovation. (1971: 430)

The innovations which Gramsci refers to in the final line, and to which Marxism devotes itself, are concepts capable of articulating more fully the range of interconnected processes – that are always only hinted at on the surface – which form the content of complex social realities. Classical Marxism, in opposition to empiricist frameworks, treats empirical reality as the point of departure and the point of return for science, while theory and theory development mediates this journey by strategically drawing on thought to gradually help bridge the divide between appearance and essence.

With that approach in mind, this book will not trace the 'enactment patterns' underpinning the crimes on Bougainville, in order to abstract a causative theory of state crime. To the contrary, my aim is to understand more fully the criminogenic potentialities inherent in actually existing capitalism, by applying classical Marxist theory to illuminate in greater clarity the different mediated processes that condensed in Empire's socially volatile Melanesian trajectory. So, for example, the landowner revolt which sparked a campaign of industrial sabotage at the Panguna mine, it will be argued, cannot be fully understood without Trotsky's theory of uneven and combined development, which helps illuminate the way Empire merges with pre-existing social formations, engendering diverse spatio-temporal paths of capitalist development and historically specific contradictions and ruptures. Similarly, a proper understanding of BCL's criminogenic reaction to landowner protests cannot be achieved in abstraction from Marx's theories of value, surplus value and capital. While any attempt to comprehend the militarised response of the PNG and Australian governments, must pass through the conceptual lens of governmentality, hegemony and imperialism which orient consciousness to critical processes that mediate state practice. Accordingly, the aim here is constant, to articulate more fully the interplay of forces that underpin the crimes of Empire, as they emerged in the concrete specificity of Bougainville.

Data Collection and the Crimes of the Powerful

While theory, and theory development, offers a path for developing progressively enriched understandings of social phenomena, this important mediatory step nonetheless always presupposes the existence of compelling raw data, which must form the necessary point of departure for scholarship. In the area of state crime studies obtaining the sort of quality raw materials needed to produce cogent, theorised accounts is a particular challenge, owing to the secrecy that often hangs over elite deviance (see Tombs and Whyte 2003). In the case of Bougainville quite extreme efforts were devoted towards stemming the flow of information (see Lasslett 2012a). For example, all communications and travel between Bougainville and neighbouring regions was forbidden by the PNG state. Those wishing to break the embargo, had to find their way past a military blockade that operated under shoot to kill orders. Many died making the treacherous crossing into the Solomon Islands (see Sirivi 2004). The key organisational actors – Australia, PNG and BCL – were equally fastidious about breaches within their own agencies. On the whole, managers, civil servants, politicians and military officers, kept to a strict script during the war, with only the odd break in discipline.

Nevertheless, attempts to control information always take place within a contested power terrain (Lasslett 2012a). Indeed during the Bougainville conflict an international anti-war movement emerged; employing a range of tactics activists engaged in numerous interventions designed to pierce the veil of state-corporate secrecy surrounding the criminal events on Bougainville. Through these efforts a number of information coups were achieved. Arguably, one of the most significant involves a class action against Rio Tinto in the United States organised under the Alien Tort Statute, and prosecuted by the law firm Hagens Berman Sobol Shaprio (HBSS). This action – which now appears to have failed on jurisdictional grounds – has brought to light a large cache of internal documents from BCL including meeting minutes, memos and letters, in addition to a range of detailed affidavits composed by company executives and senior PNG state officials.

My research into the Bougainville conflict began here. Indeed, having been granted access to HBSS's case file, I flew to their Seattle office in 2005 where a room of records awaited me. I then continued the process of documentary research in Australia, where a number of anti-war activists had kept personal archives, which contained human rights reports, dossiers of victim testimony, leaked documents, transcripts from parliament, press clippings, documentary footage and transcribed data broadcasted from Bougainville through VHF radio. This paper trail was added to using a range of publicly available records, including parliamentary inquiry transcripts and submissions, state of emergency reports, budget hearing transcripts, budget statements, parliamentary Hansard and departmental annual reports. Unfortunately, though not surprisingly, freedom of information requests were denied. Nevertheless, the alternative avenues pursued permitted a vivid picture to emerge of state-corporate offending on Bougainville. This, in turn, put me into a position where I could begin to direct probing empirical questions at senior state and corporate officials from the period, assuming of course access could be secured.

In this respect the timing of my fieldwork was fortunate (2006–07). Many of the senior officials involved in the Bougainville crisis were in retirement, or semi-retirement, as a result the socio-legal restraints they operated under were no longer as palpably felt. And with the war having been obscured for so long by a veil of secrecy, many former state-corporate agents displayed a genuine desire to transcend the 'spin', and make sense of what had happened 'warts and all'. Consequently, I was able to conduct 46 interviews with former officials from BCL and key Australian/ PNG state agencies, including: the National Executive Council (PNG),[13] the Department of Defence (PNG), the Department of Foreign Affairs (PNG), the Prime Minister's Department (PNG), the PNG Defence Force, the Royal PNG Constabulary, Cabinet (Australia), the Department of Foreign Affairs and Trade (Australia), the Department of Defence (Australia), the Department of Prime Minister and Cabinet (Australia), the Australian Defence Force, and the Australian High Commission (Port Moresby). Nearly all interviewees were in senior organisational positions charged with direct responsibility for managing different dimensions of the Bougainville crisis.

During interviews I was privy to often startling admissions, which in many respects rewrite the conflict's official history. This is a testament to the documentary groundwork laid by the anti-war movement which permitted probing empirical questions to be asked, and of course the interviewees themselves who often demonstrated humility and empathy when discussing matters that shone poorly on their organisational past. However, these interviews offered something else also – an intimate window into the inner workings of Empire at a moment of crisis and revolt. Accordingly, I was in the fortunate position of being able to construct this criminological account employing primary materials that related strategies, processes and events so often denied to researchers.

Book Structure

The book continues, in chapter 2, by surveying the uneven and combined course PNG steered as it became gradually immersed within Empire, focusing in particular on the contradictions this engendered on Bougainville in the 1980s. Chapter 3 examines how BCL's incendiary response to early signs of social rupture in 1987–88, was shaped both by its value composition (as an articulation of mining capital), and the particular class practices it employed to affect government policy and bulwark stability. In chapter 4 we look at how the PNG government and BCL reacted to a campaign of industrial sabotage initiated by landowners in

November 1988; particular attention will be given to the social mediations which conditioned the often tumultuous state corporate relationship between BCL and PNG during this period.

Chapter 5 moves on to consider the first major military offensive launched by the PNG government to re-open the Panguna mine. Rather than being a knee-jerk reaction to BCL demands – although this was an important factor – it is suggested that this offensive was a complex condensation of certain power shifts which were occurring within the PNG state which shall be conceptualised using the theoretical works of Gramsci (1971), Poulantzas (1978) and Foucault (2007). These power shifts, it is argued, were also affected in important ways by Australia's intervention. Having examined some of the serious atrocities committed by government forces in 1989, chapter 6 traces the BRA's sudden accession to power, following the retreat of the PNG Defence Force during March 1990. Particular attention is paid to the internal fractures this accession to power provoked on Bougainville, in addition to the strategic efforts deployed by the PNG government to amplify and militarise the resulting tensions. It is suggested that this configuration of forces laid the groundwork for a brutal transformation in the war.

With this case study as our evidentiary base, chapter 7 looks at the different features of the conflict which classical Marxism was able to tease out, and the important implications this has for both how we understand, and respond to state crime. The book concludes by enumerating a number of general methodological and theoretical innovations, which could be usefully applied to help frame future state crime interventions.

2

The Specificities of Papua New Guinea's Development

Introduction – The Heterogeneity of Empire

It is sometimes argued that Marx's analysis of capitalism's global expansion was diminished by certain Eurocentric assumptions (see Anderson 2010). For example, the Pacific scholar Terence Wesley-Smith (1989: 308) suggests, 'there is an assumption in Marx's work that the transition to capitalism in Western Europe (from the sixteenth century onward) would eventually be replicated in other parts of the globe' (see also Wesley-Smith and Ogan 1992). Certainly passages can be found in support of this criticism. For example, in *The Communist Manifesto* Marx and Engels write:

> The bourgeoisie has through its exploitation of the world market given a cosmopolitan character to production and consumption in every country . . . All old-established national industries have been destroyed or are daily being destroyed . . . It compels all nations, on pain of extinction, to adopt the bourgeois mode of production; it compels them to introduce what it calls civilisation into their midst, i.e., to become bourgeois themselves. In one word, it creates a world after its own image. (1992: 6)

Yet to allow matters to end here would be problematic. In his mature writings, Marx offered a more complex portrait of Empire's spatio-temporal development. For example, when examining whether Russia was destined to replicate the path of Western Europe, Marx observes:

> In analysing the genesis of capitalist production I say: 'The capitalist system is therefore based on the utmost separation of the producer from the means of production . . . The basis of this whole development is the

expropriation of the agricultural producer. This has been accomplished in a radical fashion only in England . . . But *all other countries of Western Europe* are going through the same process.' Hence the 'historical inevitability' of this process is *expressly* limited to the *countries of Western Europe.* The reason for this limitation is indicated in the following passage of Chapter XXXII: '*Private property* produced by the labour of the individual . . . is supplanted by *capitalistic private property,* which rests on the exploitation of the labour of others, on wage labour.' In this development in Western Europe it is a question of the *transformation of one form of private property into another form of private property.* In case of the Russian peasants one would on the contrary have to *transform their common property into private property.* Thus the analysis given in *Capital* does not provide any arguments for or against the viability of the village community [in Russia]. (Marx and Engels 1982: 319–20)

As this passage suggests, Marx was aware that Western Europe's path into Empire would not, and could not, be replicated in a schematic fashion.[1] Indeed, he recognised that capitalism expands selectively, and in multiple ways, while those civilisations on the 'new frontiers', who are similarly diverse, actively resist, negotiate and shape their specific passage into Empire (see Anderson 2010).

However, arguably it was Trotsky (2005) who articulated this process with greatest conceptual clarity (albeit employing uncomfortably modernist phrases). He writes:

A backward country assimilates the material and intellectual conquests of the advanced countries. But this does not mean that it follows them slavishly, reproduces all the stages of their past . . . Although compelled to follow after the advanced countries, a backward country does not take things in the same order. The privilege of historic backwardness – and such a privilege exists – permits, or rather compels, the adoption of whatever is ready in advance of any specified date, skipping a whole series of intermediate stages. Savages throw away their bows and arrows for rifles all at once, without travelling the road which lay between those two weapons in the past . . . The development of historically backward nations leads necessarily to a peculiar combination of different stages in the historic process. Their development as a whole acquires a planless, complex, combined character. (Trotsky 2005: 26–7)

Trotsky, therefore, concludes:

> The laws of history have nothing in common with a pedantic schematism. Unevenness, the most general law of the historic process, reveals itself most sharply and complexly in the destiny of the backward countries. Under the whip of external necessity their backward culture is compelled to make leaps. From the universal law of unevenness thus derives another law which, for the lack of a better name, we may call the law of *combined development* – by which we mean a drawing together of the different stages of the journey, a combining of the separate steps, an amalgam of archaic with more contemporary forms. (2005: 28)

As Trotsky acknowledges, here the term '*combined development*' only partially captures what he is in fact trying to conceptually articulate. Trotsky is not suggesting that as Empire expands into 'backward' territories that it necessarily combines two modes of production to form a hybrid; rather, he is arguing that as Empire expands it merges in different ways with existing social formations, creating diverse trajectories of *capitalist* development. This process does not necessarily demolish existing customs, social institutions, cultural frameworks, or productive practices. Nevertheless, as they are submerged into Empire these different determinations acquire new meanings and impulses. That said, they also stamp their own indentation on capitalism, mediating how its tendencies and processes work themselves out concretely.

This is especially true in PNG. Here communities were not battered by over-accumulated capital, seeking a profitable outlet abroad. Instead, PNG's ethnically diverse rural population faced rather skeletal colonial administrations imposed by Germany, Britain, and Australia. Although differing in shades, all three imperial powers focused their limited resources on establishing the 'rule of law', coastal settler plantations, and mining enclaves. Even after World War II, when the Australian government significantly increased its subsidy to PNG, it was not colonial profits that *most* concerned the administration, but rather, forging an uneventful path to independence, in a country that would continue to be of importance for Australian security planners in the post-colonial era. As a result, while the different rural communities spread across the PNG mainland and its satellite islands, may not have been able to negotiate their entry into Empire, they could to an extent influence the terms and conditions under which it occurred. This historical advantage has accorded the customary structures of PNG's clan-communities a key mediating role with respect to introduced economic and political practices. While this has not dissolved the contradictions inherent in capitalism, it has shaped the specific way in which they emerge and are managed.

This chapter examines those aspects of PNG's 'combined development' that are most critical to an understanding of the events on Bougainville during 1987–98. To that end, we will consider how the pre-colonial social arrangements in PNG merged with the economic and political practices introduced by the colonial powers, and the forms of rural development and patrimonial politics this inspired. We will then analyse the specific tensions that emerged from this particular path of capitalist development, and how a large injection of mining capital in central Bougainville amplified their effects. The chapter concludes with an account of the emerging form of social rupture these tensions inspired on Bougainville during the 1980s, which will lay the foundation for an analysis of the criminogenic events that prompted and punctuated the war.

Papua New Guinea's First Settlers

PNG's social history begins with migration from Asia approximately 50,000 years ago. 'These settlers', Connell (1997: 13) observes, 'reached most of the coasts, the outer islands and the highlands more than forty thousand years ago'. During the subsequent 10,000 years they continued their spread, reaching Bougainville around 28,000 years ago (Oliver 1991: 1).

The natural terrain that greeted the settlers was uncompromising. Treacherous mountains, enclosed valleys, dense jungle, large swamps, etc., made mobility difficult. Accordingly, Griffin et al. (1979: 1) argue, human settlement 'has been dominated by New Guinea's geography, unique for the natural barriers which it placed in the way of human movement'. Given these natural barriers: 'Papua New Guinea's [pre-colonial] population consisted almost entirely of small, largely independent communities of subsistence cultivators. Within these communities social, political and economic relationships were generally close and fairly well defined. Between them, notwithstanding some extensive trade networks and enduring political alliances, relations tended to be limited' (May 2004: 40).

These small settler communities that spread out over PNG's rugged landscape at first survived through a mixture of hunting, gathering, and harvesting semi-cultivated root crops. However, archaeological evidence suggests there was a shift towards sedentary forms of agriculture around 10,000 years ago (Connell 1997: 3; Oliver 1991: 6; Wesley-Smith 1989: 311).

Organising production was the family-household, which generally consisted of a husband, wife or wives and children (Ogan 1999: 2; Ogan and Wesley-Smith 1992: 40–1). For these households, the kinship/ clan system was of vital importance.[2] Indeed, it was clan lineages, not individuals, which held property over the land. Therefore, membership in a landholding lineage assured the household usufructuary rights over a tract of land, as well as providing them with a distinct social identity (Oliver, 1991: 104; Turner 1990: 23). Consequently, as Regan (2005: 420) observes, 'the continuity of the clan lineage as a corporate landholding or cooperative group' was of collective importance.

Leading the clan community was the Melanesian form of chieftain, the big-man. Big-men generally achieved prominence competitively through ceremonial exchange, trade, containment of the spirit world, managing intra-community relations and by being a successful warrior (see Connell 1979; Rynkiewich 2000). Indeed, Rynkiewich observes:

> A big-man aggressively and continually worked to arrange his group's relation with spirits, allies, exchange groups and trade partners so that they would optimally benefit his group . . . The big-man system was an effective political order in a world where the spirits, enemies, and rivals could overwhelm a group and quickly then exterminate them. (2000: 21)

On this general social platform of kinship relations, subsistence farming and big-man leadership developed historical agents who had a deep knowledge of their clan heritage, a careful memory for genealogical fact, a strong connection with a particular geographical space, a sense of devotion to kin, and an overwhelming allegiance to the customs, culture and beliefs which fostered the higher unity of the clan community, on which their existence as producers and sovereign beings hinged. And it was this lens through which Empire would invariably have to pass.

Although European contact with Melanesia began sporadically more than 400 years ago, it was not until the 1880s that substantive efforts were made by the European powers to annex the region. To that end, Germany took possession of north-eastern New Guinea and the Bismarck Archipelago in 1884, while Bougainville and Buka were assigned to

German influence in 1886 under the Anglo-German declaration (Griffin 1990b: 72). This resulted in the Solomon Islands archipelago being carved in two.

The United Kingdom was a more hesitant entry to the region. Facing pressure from its Australian colonies, Britain claimed the south-eastern half of New Guinea as a protectorate in 1884 (see Nelson 2005). This move, however, did not dampen Australian anxieties over the security of its northern approaches. Consequently, following federation, Australia assumed formal responsibility for British New Guinea in 1906, which became known as Papua, while in 1914 they used light military force to occupy German New Guinea. The latter arrangement was formally converted into a League of Nations 'C' class mandate in 1921 (Nelson 2005: 8). Initially, Australia's two 'acquisitions' were administered separately as Papua and New Guinea, however, in 1949 they were amalgamated.

Under the eye of these three foreign powers, basic administrative rule and a scattered plantation economy, buoyed fiscally by isolated mining enclaves, was unevenly established across PNG. The initial aim of all three colonisers was 'pacification'. To that end, administration posts were incrementally constructed across PNG, from which colonial field officers, accompanied by indigenous police, would establish contact with villages. The field officer's first aim, in this respect, was to create a basic framework for collecting head tax, organising public works, recruiting labour and maintaining order (Dinnen 2001: 18; Griffin et al. 1979: 15–6 & 40–1).

Although colonial violence was not uncommon in PNG, Dinnen nevertheless notes that pacification,

. . . [W]as not achieved through the wholesale displacement or neutralizing of indigenous forms of social regulation. Neither were local actors merely passive subjects acted on in a top-down process of colonial imposition. Colonial peace could not have been achieved, even in the gradual and piecemeal fashion that it was, without the acquiescence and even open enthusiasm of many local leaders and groups. (2001: 22–3)

It should be added, none of the imperial powers were well positioned to *impose* radically new social arrangements, even were they so inclined (Denoon 1985: 121). Australia as a settler-colony itself, had very little in reserve for PNG (Denoon 1985: 121; Donaldson and Good 1988: 53; Fitzpatrick 1980: 57; Good 1986: 23), while German New Guinea was 'the Cinderella of the German colonial empire: her ugly sisters in Africa and the Pacific received much better treatment' (Denoon 1985: 121).

Consequently, colonial field officers relied heavily on local clan leaders to act as intermediaries for the administration; while clan leaders – even if on occasions eschewing the role of village official – were eager to use the opportunities this opened up to augment their influence at the village level (Anis 1977a: 92–3; Anis 1977b: 118; Donaldson and Good 1988: 49; May 2004: 209; Ogan 1972: 74; Oliver 1991: 49). This dialectic ensured customary structures were preserved, but dynamically so, as they merged with a new social order.

Through this system of a centralised administration, connected to local communities via regional posts, field officer patrols and indigenous intermediaries, basic colonial policy was implemented. In German New Guinea, Griffin et al. (1979: 39–40) observe, the colonial policy was notably lacking in 'benevolence':

> The Germans had the same aims in Melanesia as in Africa. They sought to create a colony for the white man, who should be able to survey his docile black labourers from the comfort of a plantation bungalow. The New Guinean's part in the scheme was to do what he was told, to abandon fighting and superstition and above all to sign a three year labour contract. (Griffin et al. 1979: 39–40)

Australia's administration of New Guinea during the inter-war period, did not depart fundamentally from the German approach, except for the fact that it was authored with fewer resources, and a less punitive attitude to rule.

British New Guinea, or Papua as it was later known, experienced a slightly different colonial trajectory. Initially, the first administrator, Sir William MacGregor (1888–98), 'looked to the indigenes as the main agents for economic growth and adopted coercion as the means by which commercial agriculture would be established in Papua' (Donaldson 1980: 65). However, by the time Australia assumed control of Papua in 1906, this approach had been deemed a failure. Consequently, under the command of Sir Hubert Murray (1906–40), the Australian administration instead promoted plantations, and 'plantation labour', as the means through which 'to integrate Papuans into the world economy' (Donaldson 1980: 65). It was thought, 'Australians could grow a variety of tropical crops and Papuans could supply the land and labour' (Dinnen 2001: 20). That said, 'Australian governments often spent a third of their revenues in debt servicing, and were reluctant to divert capital of any kind to Papua' (Denoon 1985: 121; see also McKillop and Firth 1981: 96). As a result, there was little in the way of government subsidies to aid this policy – indeed, the area under crop reached nearly 24,000 hectares in 1918, and stayed at that approximate level for the next 30 years (McKillop and Firth 1981: 97).

Consequently, for the indigenous population of Papua and New Guinea, early Australian administration offered little in the way of substantive benefits. As Turner (1990: 8–9) notes, 'derisory amounts of money were devoted to native health, education and economic advancement, as these . . . did not figure in the inter-war perception of what colonial administration should be about'.[3] Accordingly, by World War II, village life had only been affected in subtle ways by the imperial powers. For instance, big-men acted as local agents for the colonial administration (Anis 1977a: 92–3; Anis 1977b: 118; Ogan 1972: 74; Regan 2000a: 292); young men experienced new labour practices through tiring plantation work (Griffin et al. 1979: 62); missionaries modified traditional spiritual beliefs (Ogan 1972: 46–53); while villagers' consumptive and productive appetites changed through their exposure to international commodity circuits (Connell 1978: 238). These incremental changes did not spark major social transformation, that said, they did create the foundation for a more rapid integration into Empire during the postwar period, which was as much championed by local agents, as it was directed from above.

Rural Change, Petty Commodity Production and Custom

Following World War II, the Australian government implemented a more vigorous colonial policy. This was reflected perhaps most acutely in Australia's subsidy to PNG, which rose sharply from AU$8.7 million in 1951 to AU$18.9 million in 1957, reaching AU$50.5 million by 1964 (Hawksley 2006: 164). Guiding the increased expenditure, was an awareness that PNG's path to independence could be managed and even delayed, but not averted. Consequently, Australian strategic planners wanted to see these extra resources directed towards creating a stable mode of development, which would lay the economic and political foundations for independence, but in a way that did not upheave the country's 'traditional' structures (i.e. clan, custom, village) (Denoon 1985: 124 & 133). The emphasis would thus be on a calm stewardship towards independence, for a country lying at the centre of an area deemed by Australian security planners to be of immediate significant interest (Australian Department of Defence 1976: 10; Australian Department of Defence 1987: 2).

With respect to economic policy, the colonial administration began mapping PNG's natural resources in an attempt to attract injections of foreign capital. At the same time, efforts were also placed into promoting smallholder cash crop production attached to the village (MacWilliam 2005: 226–7). Accordingly, increased resources were plumbed into health, education and agricultural extensions services in the hope a skilled, healthy indigenous population would be better placed to participate in commercial agriculture (Connell 1978: 81; Connell 1997: 20; Donaldson and Good 1981: 144–5; Downs 1980: 98–101; Hawksley 2006: 164; MacWilliam 1988: 92; Thompson and MacWilliam 1992: 137–9).[4] Following World Bank advice, these resources were gradually channelled towards those regions in PNG judged to have the greatest commercial potential (McCasker 1966: 5–8). In effect this meant that the administration's agricultural extension services, credit policy, and land legislation, would amplify existing spatial inequalities, by focusing on already privileged regions (Donaldson and Good 1981: 163; Donaldson and Good 1988: 76–8 & 83; Good 1986: 88; Ogan and Wesley Smith 1992: 53–4).

As with initial European contact, PNG nationals were not passive players in an imposed process. Indeed, ethnographies from the period evidence villagers were active instigators and authors of their integration into Empire (Connell 1978: 113–4; Donaldson and Good 1981: 150; Rynkiewich 2000: 23). In this respect, big-men were often most adept at instrumentalising this process, employing their customary power to channel cash cropping and 'progressive values' into the village, which at the same time served to amplify their social esteem. However, in many cases the redistributive norms that governed positions of clan leadership, limited the capacity of big-men to bulwark economic transformation (Connell 1978: 244–5; Grossman 1983: 61–2; Ogan and Wesley-Smith 1992: 47). Consequently, it was commonly younger clan mates, who were free from the onerous obligations associated with 'traditional' leadership, but who nevertheless possessed standing in their community, that were best able to employ their access to relevant skills and inputs, to engage without inhibition in these new economic practices. For example, in the Siwai region of Bougainville, Connell (1978: 230) observes, '[t]he first businessmen had been mumis [big-men] but their place was eventually taken by younger men who had often benefited both from formal education and some kind of practical training'. These young men's interest, Connell (1978: 246-47) argues, 'was entirely centred upon the economic potential for cocoa and [unlike big-men] they were interested neither in demonstrating high status through the successful direction of group labour nor in acquiring prestige through ceremonial distribution of income' (see also Moulik 1977: 149). The initial accomplishments of these young entrepreneurs in cash cropping, business and local politics, created an important foundation and stimulus for other households, in need of cash for school fees, consumer goods, productive inputs and church tithes, to experiment in money generating activities (Connell 1978: 149).

On Bougainville this process effected a gradual generalisation of cash-cropping:

In the twelve-month period of 1963–4 production by 'indigenes' (i.e. Bougainvillian smallholders) totalled 174 tonnes of dry-bean cacao and 1935 tonnes of copra. By 1969–70 the figures on cacao had already risen to 1461; by 1979–80 to 10,151; and by 1988–9 to 13, 841 tonnes, with a value of just under K1,000 per tonne. (In 1977–8 Bougainvillian smallholders produced about 1.4 times as much cocoa as the province's plantations; in 1988–9 the relative amount had risen to three times.) Recent figures on copra production show that in 1980 22,565 tonnes passed through the two receiving depots of Buka and Kieta. In 1989 that figure had risen to 26,756 tonnes. In both years it is estimated that about two-thirds of the total was produced by smallholders.[5] (Oliver 1991: 162–3; see also Treadgold 1978: 16)

Accordingly, the North Solomons province went from producing 'one sixth of the country's copra and one quarter of the cocoa' prior to independence (1975), to producing, '45 per cent of the cocoa' in 1988, while also becoming 'the second largest producer of copra' (Griffin 1990a: 7; see also Thompson and MacWilliam 1992: 129). Indeed, in 1980 it was estimated that only 19 per cent of Bougainville's economically active population was engaged wholly in subsistence farming, two-thirds of whom were female (Oliver 1991: 161–2). Thus, Oliver (1991: 162) concludes, 'as time passed Bougainvillean men left it to their wives and unmarried daughters to do more and more of the food-growing, while they themselves turned more and more to money-earning, by cash cropping, wage labour, or *bisnis* (business)'.

As in other areas of PNG, on Bougainville the generalisation of cash cropping stimulated 'intra-village and inter-village socio-economic differentiation' (Connell 1997: 250–1). Ethnographies from the 1960s and 1970s reveal that households with larger smallholdings were beginning to diversify profits into business, while others who lacked access to the necessary resources for the household's reproduction (land, labour, capital), turned to temporal bouts of wage-labour to earn money (Connell 1978: 151 & 153; MacWilliam 2005: 237; Mitchell 1976: 112 & 142–3; Mitchell 1982 64–5; Moulik 1977: 154). Differentiation also had a definite spatial dimension. Those villages closer to essential infrastructure such as administrative posts, urban centres, roads, markets, ports, etc., often developed rapidly under the leadership of successful entrepreneurs, while in the more remote areas of Bougainville, communities observed with scepticism the changes in their coastal neighbours (Regan 2006: 7–8).

This process of social differentiation, of course, is not uncommon when subsistence communities of peasant proprietors are gradually immersed within global markets. While traditional practices and structures ostensibly seem to endure in these communities, but for diversification in crop output, the gradual commodification of productive inputs and outputs engendered by petty commodity production in fact excites significant new relations between households, the objective conditions of production, and their labour.[6] To that end, Bernstein (2000: 29) argues, petty commodity producers 'are capitalists and workers at the same time because they own or have access to means of production and employ their own labour'. As capital, households must competitively accrue a profit, which at the very minimum will allow reproduction of basic productive inputs such as tools and fertiliser, while as labour households must secure enough income to feed, clothe and care for the family. Accordingly, peasant proprietors face a double reproductive challenge – they must renew both labour and capital inputs. This creates what Bernstein labels the simple reproduction 'squeeze':

> *Poor peasants* are subject to a simple reproduction 'squeeze' as capital or labour, or both. Their poverty and depressed levels of consumption (reproduction as labour) express their intense struggle to maintain their means of production (reproduction as capital). Loss of the latter

entails proletarianization. *Middle peasants* are those able to meet the demands of simple reproduction, while *rich peasants* are able to engage in expanded reproduction: to increase the land and/or other means of production at their disposal beyond the capacity of family/household labour, hence hiring wage labour. (2000: 30; see also Bernstein 1988, 1994, 2010; Gibbon and Neocosmos 1985)

In PNG, as cash cropping generalised, the simple reproduction 'squeeze' began to generate quite significant forms of intra- and inter-community tension, that inscribed clan structures with new meanings. To once again use the example of Bougainville – in the pre-colonial period customary norms which emphasised the importance of reciprocation and balance, dulled the significance of temporal land inequalities between clan lineages. Land-rich kin would be obliged to support land poor relatives. However, the generalisation of cash cropping during the postwar period had certain individuating effects, which began to erode these redistributive norms. Moulik (1977: 149) notes, a 'successful young Buin [south Bougainville] entrepreneur, for example, remarked with a proper entrepreneurial distaste for the redistributive norms of wealth: "I have earned my money by my own hard work. I do not care what others say, but I will never share even a small part of it".'

With the weakening of those customary norms centring on reciprocity and balance, the social implications of differential land-holdings were transformed (Tanis 2005: 456–57). Regan (2006: 7–8) observes, 'members of small land-rich lineages had much greater access to land for cocoa than had those of large land-poor lineages. Indeed, by 1980 some members of lineages in the latter category were cutting down cocoa groves to provide land for subsistence gardens for newly married couples'.

On Bougainville these inequalities were magnified by rapid postwar population increases. Indeed, the population of the North Solomons province rose from 39,000 in 1939 to 59,250 in 1967; by 1980 it was 129,000, reaching 160,000 in 1988 (Lummani 2005: 242). So great was the overall increase, that in 1980 approximately 53 per cent of Bougainville's population was under the age of 18 (Griffin and Kawona 1989: 225–6). The existence of this expanding mass of young people caused Ogan (1972: 182–3) to warn almost a decade earlier that 'the present group of Nasioi children under ten years of age can look forward to an adulthood in which land for gardens and/or new cash crop planting will simply not be available' (Ogan 1972: 182–3).[7] Ogan's prediction was becoming a reality during the 1980s, as 'a considerable pool of semi-educated younger men with little opportunity or social status' emerged (Regan 2006: 8). Indeed, as tensions on Bougainville heightened during 1987–8, foremost among the grievances of young activists was 'the shortage of land' (NPLA 1988e).

As a result of growing inequalities, custom increasingly became a site of struggle for households facing the simple reproduction 'squeeze'. Tanis points to an example of this from the Nagovisi people in south Bougainville:

> Previously land had been used mainly for food gardens and hunting and there was plenty for everyone. Now, for the first time, there was real competition for access to land for cocoa gardens. Nagovisi society is matrilineal, the women 'owning' the land. Traditionally all land is inherited by the *Maniku* (female). However land can also be given by mothers and sisters to the *nugaa* (male) to pass on to children of the males as *vabui* (son's land). The *Maniku* (women) now became stronger in pushing the *nugaa* (men) into living on their wives' land. Sisters did not want to give land to their brothers to be given to the paternal nieces or nephews. This was called *voliwatawata* (chasing off children of males). While this did not happen uniformly, it created resentment between the *viumalo* (father's clan) and the *viulupo* (children's clan). This weakened the strong family ties that had once held our communities together, from time immemorial. (2005: 456–7)

Consequently, as custom and kinship became marked by new productive and consumptive pressures, Tanis (2005: 458) argues, 'the people started seeing each other not as brothers and sisters and clan mates with common ownership of wealth, but more as business competitors, with only the fittest to survive. This contributed to inequality, to social gaps and to hatred'.

Yet while petty commodity production may have laid the seeds for individuation, fragmentation, and communal conflict – which are potent forces for the disintegration of clan relations – the introduction of a state apparatus during the postwar period provided an important countervailing force. Therefore, we will now briefly examine how government has merged with the reproduction strategies of rural and urban communities, through the matrix of patrimonialism. Consideration will also be given to the impact patrimonial politics has had on the way state power is employed in PNG, with a particular emphasis on the natural resource sector.

'Neotribalisation' and Patrimonial Politics in PNG

The first tentative steps towards the construction of an apparatus that could support independent statehood in PNG began tentatively with a local council system in the 1950s. However, by 1976 – one year after PNG claimed independence – there existed an elected national government, 19 elected provincial governments, and over 140 elected local councils. Supporting these elected assemblies was a relatively sizable bureaucracy, consisting of 50,000 public servants, which accounted for around 40 per cent of formal employment (see Connell 1997: 279; Donaldson 1980: 70; Turner 1990: 136–7). Although the colonial administration hoped PNG self-government would mimic the Westminster model with the right amount of tutelage, in reality the country's trajectory of capitalist development inspired a very different form of democracy.

The source of this difference, in the first instance, can be traced back to the most elementary features of productive life in PNG. Facing a range of challenges associated with the simple reproduction squeeze, village households have strategically mobilised into social blocs, grounded in different forms of inter-class identity that centre around clan, language and region, in an effort to rally numbers behind particular patron-candidates running for office. These candidates, if elected, are expected to reward supporters by channelling state resources into their region for *divelopmen* (development) (Rynkiewich 2000: 32; see generally Moore and Kooyman 1998). Consequently, political leaders accrue prestige and build a following through the gifting of grants, development projects, infrastructure, public services, Agbank loans and other resources, to their constituencies, distributed through various personalised networks (Dinnen 2001: 190–1; Thompson and MacWilliam 1992: 68).

This system, Strathern (1993: 48) argues, has evoked a process of 'neo-tribalisation', that is, PNG's particular modality of democracy, tends to reinforce local forms of ethnic identity, for households hoping to attract much needed resources from the state. Accordingly, while the simple reproduction squeeze may engender forms of social tension, patronage politics affords leaders the opportunity to unite kin, clan, language group and region, around certain definitions of *divelopmen*, which allay the worst fears of the poor peasantry, while allowing the more 'progressive' class forces to continue their entrepreneurial activities unheeded.

As a result of this system, formal politics in PNG has taken a fragmented form consisting of rival MPs strongly bound to a localised support base. Political parties have tended to act as 'loose parliamentary support groups' (Regan 1997: 88–90; see also Ghai 1997: 315–7), organised hastily in what is known as the 'helicopter and hotels' post-election period, where party power brokers try to form governing coalitions by offering successful candidates Ministerial posts, and other incentives, which they can then tactically employ to fulfil their obligation to supporters (Turner 1990: 111). This, Regan (1997: 88-90) argues, has endowed influential Ministers with a high degree of autonomy, as 'political parties . . . have little interest in policy development, the main concern of party leaders and functionaries being the benefit of office'. Consequently, PNG has witnessed a small clique of successful coalition organisers monopolise senior Ministerial posts for much of the post-independence period – although their grip on power can be ended abruptly by the emergence of savvy rivals.

Complicating matters are the clientalistic networks – organised through the cultural rubric of 'wantokism' – that intersect with government. Traditionally, wantoks are people from a common language group (it translates as 'one talk') who share a form of ethnic solidarity that trumps allegiances to other social groupings. This solidarity must be regularly fertilised through reciprocal exchange (Okole 2005: 374). In PNG the wantok relationship continues to command considerable loyalty, however, its ambit has widened considerably over the past 30 years to include a range of relations including business partners, co-workers, fellow professionals, friends from university, to name but a few.[8] Fixers of fraud, misappropriation and swindles inside business and government employ this evolving customary institution as a framework through which to forge tightly-knit reciprocal networks that can circumvent due process and transparency with relative impunity. Through this framework procurement fraud, land grabbing, legal scams, the theft of public assets, etc., can be operationalised, thus allowing public flows of wealth to be diverted into private accumulation cycles. PNG's leading anti-corruption agency, Taskforce Sweep, estimates that half the government's development budget is stolen or squandered, as a result of these illicit networks (Blackwell 2012). We have thus seen over the past two decades, the vertical patronage networks between MPs and their regional supporters become gradually starved of resources, owing to the intensification of more powerful and absorbing relations between government officials and clients in the private sector.

However, it is important to keep in mind that although these different patronage networks condition how state power is applied, the content of the latter is a product of different historical forces. As we observed in chapter 1, state power undergoes a significant change with the shift to capitalism – it becomes governmentalised – which gives the legal, administrative and military apparatus that evolved in the epochs which precede capitalism new functions that significantly alter how they work. In short, these sovereign technologies are employed to stabilise, calibrate and stimulate the economic and social processes constitutive of the population – processes conditioned in a significant way by capital flows and the relations they rest on – so that certain desirable outcomes may be realised.

Of course, pre-colonial PNG lacked a state apparatus, it was built gradually over the course of the twentieth century by the colonial powers, in collaboration with aspiring local and national leaders. Out of this process emerged a Melanesian form of government. In this context, the patrimonial relations just mentioned, act as levers which intra-class networks, and regionalised class coalitions, can employ to influence how governmental technologies are applied. In the case of logging, for example, we have seen companies work with fixers inside the PNG state, to stimulate the flow of capital into the forestry industry, using an opaque legal mechanism known as special agricultural and business leases. This has facilitated a sizable resource grab punctuated with fraud (see Centre for Environmental Law and Community Rights et al. 2011; Filer 2011; Numapo 2013). These same horizontal patronage networks, have also employed one of the great incentivising levers of government, public infrastructure investment, to enrich client firms who provide services through corrupted procurement processes, at inflated prices, with often non-existent or sub-par results (see, for example, Auditor General's Office 2001; Auditor General's Office 2006; Auditor General's Office 2007; Public Accounts Committee 2003; Public Accounts Committee 2006a; Public Accounts Committee 2006b; Public Accounts Committee 2007). These are just a number of select examples; many others exist. All of which serve to show that in the absence of an organised labour or peasant movement, marginal class interests in PNG have been able to have disproportionate influence on how governmental technologies are applied, this has facilitated resource grabs, theft of public resources, and a haphazard implementation of development policy. As a result, the state's capacity to deliver critical services has been dulled (see Allen et al. 2005; Cammack 2009; Rogers et al. 2011), while in the absence of a diversified national economy with a strong multi-sector base, the country's fiscal dependence on the resource extraction industry continues (see Banks 2001; Fletcher and Webb 2012; Gouy et al. 2010). In this sense, the post-colonial PNG state continues to experience some of the dilemmas faced by its colonial predecessor (albeit for different reasons), that is, PNG's natural resources are heavily lent on as a means of encouraging foreign investment and increasing government revenues (Denoon 1985; Standish 2007). While at the same time, the state's absence from many rural areas has meant customary/clan structures continue to provide the foundation stones for stability in PNG (Bonney 1982; Dinnen 2001; Hegarty 2009; Morauta 1986; Morgan 2005).

Now critically, as far as the Bougainville conflict is concerned, the continuing role of clan communities in the regulation of rural social relationships, has opened up new opportunities for regional power blocs to extract patronage outside the electoral cycle, particularly when their customary land is the site of a major investment. Indeed, during the 1980s, the national government regularly faced challenges from rural communities who blockaded public and private investments, in order to secure compensation/rent (for land use) and other benefits (Claxton 2000: 265). In lieu of a viable alternative, the national government often succumbed to these demands (Strathern 1993: 55–6), 'thereby encouraging further extortionate claims backed by force' (Dinnen 2001: 184–5; see also Saffu 1998c: 486). However, with a series of major mining projects slated to start operation during the late 1980s and early 1990s, the PNG government attempted to manage these calls for patronage, by introducing development forums. These forums provided the national government, provincial government, landowners and resource operators with an opportunity to forge a negotiated agreement on the particular terms and conditions under which the mining project would operate. Banks explains:

> The outcomes of the Development Forum take the form of a series of three Memorandum of Agreement (MOA) between the landowners, the provincial governments and the national government. They typically cover issues such as the provision of infrastructure, the delivery of government services including local staffing, the breakdown of royalty

payments, funding commitments, and the provision of equity for local communities and provincial government. (2001: 79–80)

For local landowner representatives looking to alleviate the pressures and antagonisms associated with simple reproduction, such mechanisms have generally been welcomed. Nevertheless, they have not prevented landowners from also employing force to augment their bargaining power (Saffu 1998b: 473–4). In response, the state has increasingly relied upon reactive violence to channel disruptive communities back into more acceptable forums (see Connell 1997: 144). Responsibility for these displays of state authority has, in large part, fallen to the Royal PNG Constabulary (RPNGC). Formed in the 1960s, the RPNGC has developed what both Standish (1994: 62) and Dinnen (1994: 107) characterise as a 'para-military operational style'. Dinnen (1994: 107) notes that police are mainly confined to 'barrack-style quarters', consequently they respond to security threats through 'pragmatic and crisis driven' operations, which aim to restore order 'through a combination of force and numbers' (see also MacQueen 1993: 138–9).

In a bid to counter the particular threat posed by landowner blocs in mine areas, the national government set up a specialised police branch in the early 1990s, charged with deterring extra-legal actions in these critical regions of the country. According to Dinnen (2001: 119), 'the Minister [for police] envisaged a "quasi-military" role for the new police unit, with emphasis on mobility and weapons training'. Jointly funded and maintained by the national government and mining industry, the Rapid Deployment Unit (RDU), as it became known, began operating in 1992. Very quickly, 'the RDU . . . gained a reputation in the Southern Highlands and Enga Provinces as being the most indiscriminately violent of PNG police' (Standish 1994: 67). Indeed, Dinnen (2001: 126) writes, 'a Mount Klare landowner alleged that members of the unit and armed plain clothes officers had shot and killed several landowners'. He adds, 'the Premier of Enga Province called for the withdrawal of the Porgera-based unit, alleging that it was out of control . . . Members of the Rapid Deployment Unit allegedly shot and killed a man in a confrontation with villagers near the Porgera [mine] site in October [1992]' (Dinnen 2001: 126).

These reactive paramilitary style operations represented the violent 'other' to development forums. While the latter was a vital tool for stimulating foreign investment, (that is, owing to the added stability provided by MOAs), organised violence became a critical method for restricting the lobbying strategies of landowner blocs. Of course, that said, the Bougainville conflict broke out in late 1988, just as the national government was grappling with the maturing dilemmas associated with resource dependence and indirect rule. And in a sense, it was the first opportunity for the state to apply these emerging technologies. Indeed Bougainville, like other regions of PNG, had managed to dull the tensions associated with social differentiation, inequality and dispossession, through rallying households around forms of solidarity rooted in local, regional and provincial identities. As long as these blocs were bonded to a leadership subscribing to some form of capitalist development, local, regional and provincial demands for greater mining revenues could be pragmatically managed by the national government and BCL, through a variety of measures which would prelude development forums, and the RDU.

However, the North Solomons was one of the most dynamic provincial economies, as a result the tensions experienced elsewhere in PNG were more acutely felt on Bougainville, as social differentiation accelerated, and inequalities solidified. Accordingly, we see emerging in the mine lease area in particular – where these effects were amplified – young leaders radicalised by their historical experience of inequality, dispossession, land shortages, environmental harm, and racialised industrial relations. Rather provocatively, these leaders began to question the very basis on which their island had entered Empire. Out of these questions emerged an anti-capitalist movement that took hold of existing customary institutions in and around the mine lease area. The cooling effect of the patrimonial levers used to manage political power in PNG, presupposed customary blocs committed to some modality of capitalist development – thus, the growing hostility towards capital in central Bougainville created a dilemma the state was poorly equipped to tackle. On that note, we will now consider in more detail certain antecedents of this anti-capitalist movement, before conducting a brief sketch of its leaders. To begin, the origins – and social impact – of the Panguna mine is examined.

The Panguna Mine, Accelerated Development and Social Rupture

The Panguna mine, which would loom large in the rebels' critique, finds its origins in the colonial administration's postwar development policy. Mindful that PNG would need a sizable economic base to support independence – especially, if it was to be weaned off Australian subsidies – the colonial administration set about mapping the country's natural resources. To that end, in the early 1960s a colonial field geologist suggested that Bougainville's Crown Prince Ranges may contain a copper and gold deposit sizeable enough to support a large mining operation. These tentative finding were followed up by Conzinc Riotinto of Australia's (CRA) exploration arm (CRAE) in 1964 (Denoon 2000: 61–2).

CRAE's exploratory work revealed an ore body elliptical in shape consisting of 950 million tonnes of ore grading 0.48 per cent copper, and 0.55 grams per tonne of gold (AGA 1989: 3.5). The mineralisation of the porphyry extrusion was low grade, nonetheless, the deposit was judged to be commercially viable (Quodling 1991: 5).[9] Having attracted the necessary finance, CRA signed a formal agreement to develop the mine, which was ratified by PNG's House of Assembly in 1967 (see the *Mining (Bougainville Copper Agreement) Act* 1967) (Quodling 1991: 23).[10] A formal vehicle for the mining project, Bougainville Copper Pty Ltd (BCL), was set up and incorporated in PNG during 1969.[11] Downs (1980: 340) argues this initiated 'the greatest single event in the economic history of Papua and New Guinea'. Indeed, the expectation was that the mine would help fund PNG's transition to independence, following almost a century of colonial administration (Barnes 1969: 333–4).

Due to the economy of scales required, the project was a large one by world standards. Besides preparing the mine pit – which required the removal of 30 million tonnes of overburden – BCL also had to construct a town at Arawa (on Bougainville's east coast); a port at Loloho; a power station near the port; a major road from the port to the mine (Port Mine Access Road); a minor road to the tailings dump on the west coast; a concentrator plant; a town at the mine site; a dam on the Jaba river to provide water for the mine and concentrator; a water supply for Arawa town; and a limestone quarry (Denoon 2000: 146).

In order to implement this expansive project 22 different kinds of leases had to be negotiated under mining and land ordinances (AGA 1989: 3.1). The leases covered 13,047 hectares of land (mine lease area), of which only a third was actually utilised by the company (Regan 2003: 137). Landowners were remunerated for use of their land, through the payment of occupation fees. Compensation was also available for the destruction of cash crops, resettlement, nuisance, pollution of the local rivers and valleys, and for the loss of bush land (AGA 1989: 4.23).

With the legal, administrative, and technical building blocks in place, production at the mine began in April 1972. The ore body was extracted using conventional open cut methods (Vernon 2005: 259).[12] Approximately, 100,000 tonnes of waste rock was extracted per day (Vernon 2005: 259), and 'transported in 142 and 172 tonne capacity trucks or by conveyors to dumps in the headwaters of the Kawerong Valley. Soft waste comprising overburden and weathered waste rock . . . [was] selectively dumped within the hard rock dump' (AGA 1989: 3.2). Another 100,000 tonnes of ore rock was extracted daily and sent to the concentrator. Five per cent of this rock was turned into a concentrate slurry which was pumped to the east coast of Bougainville for export overseas, while the remaining 95 per cent formed a waste known as tailings, which was dumped in the Jaba river (AGA 1989: 3.2). Initially, it was thought that 80 per cent of the tailings would be transported by river to the Augusta Bay on Bougainville's west coast. This estimate proved optimistic, in actual fact the rate was around 60 per cent (Vernon 2005: 269).

Compounding matters, by 1988, 300,000 tonnes of ore and waste rock was being removed from the mine on a daily basis (AGA 1989: 3.2), thus multiplying the resulting volume of waste.[13] Consequently, the Kawerong Valley dumps 'filled up creating some 300 hectares of flat land, but totally obliterating the underlying terrain' (Vernon 2005: 269), while, 'the [Jaba] river . . . [was] now twenty times wider than in the pre-mine era' (Connell 1991: 67). These environmental costs were disproportionately borne by the surrounding communities, whereas BCL and the national government were the mine's principal beneficiaries. According to CRA figures, during the mine's life, the operation generated a total of K1.7 billion revenue (about US$2 billion), of which 32.8 per cent went to non-government shareholders, 61.5 per cent went to the PNG national government, 4.3 per cent went to the North Solomons provincial government and 1.4 per cent went to landholders (see Table 2.1).

However, households on Bougainville still enjoyed a number of relatively significant mine generated benefits (in addition that is, to compensation payments and occupation fees). For instance, by December 1988, BCL had 3,560 employees on the payroll, 83 per cent of which were PNG nationals, with preference being given to Bougainvillean applicants (Quodling 1991: 37–8). Although to this statistic we must add a caveat. According to Wesley-Smith and Ogan, 'only thirty-three Papua New Guineans occupied professional positions in the company, with a further thirty-five in assistant or subprofessional jobs' (Wesley-Smith and Ogan 1992: 258). This overlap

Table 2.1   Cash generated by BCL operations 1972–89

	K million
Papua New Guinea Government (61.5%)	
Corporate income tax	581.5
Group tax (PAYE)	120.3
Customs duty	104.1
Miscellaneous	10.1
Dividends	165.9
Dividends withholding tax	96.5
	1078.4
North Solomons Provincial Government (4.3%)	
Royalties (95% to North Solomons Provincial Govt)	61.4
Non renewable resource fund	1.8
Other taxes	12.0
	75.2
Landholders (1.4%)	
Royalties (5% to landholders)	3.2
Compensation	21.0
	24.2
Non-Government shareholders (32.8%)	
Dividends net of dividends withholding tax	576.7
Total	1754.5

Source: Conzinc Riotinto of Australia, 1990

of race, job status, and salary became a particularly heated issue during the late 1980s. Tanis (2005: 467) observes, 'after work I would listen to workers talking about their frustrations over what they saw as their low levels of pay as compared to their Australian counterparts, disparities in salaries for the nationals and details of personal problems with their white bosses'.

In addition to the generation of employment – albeit at lower rungs – the mine also opened up new opportunities for local businesses on the island. Wesley-Smith notes:

The Bougainville mining project . . . has spawned a significant number of locally owned and operated companies that supply its needs. By far the biggest of these, the Bougainville Development Corporation has become a multi-million dollar enterprise, with interests in engineering, catering, airline operations, and limestone mining. Its principals have become prominent members of Papua New Guinea's emerging bourgeoisie.[14] (1990: 16)

Then there was the rent and compensation payments made to landowners. BCL payments, in this respect, were made to primary right holders, who were expected to redistribute appropriate portions to secondary right holders. Though often this did not occur, which generated further tension:

> Rent and compensation payments were made to those listed as title-holders, in the expectation that they would distribute the money to those with links to the block who had any entitlements. In practice, there were often disputes about such entitlements and so about distribution of the money . . . Over the life of the mine, the population in the mine lease areas grew rapidly, and young children of the early 1970s grew to adulthood, so that by the late 1980s the numbers of adults seeking a share of rent and compensation payments had greatly expanded. (Regan 2006: 7; see also Wesley-Smith and Ogan 1992: 256)

Some scholars have viewed the failure to redistribute rent/compensation payments, as evidence of a critical breakdown in customary norms (see Filer 1990: 90). Following the example of Wolfers (1992: 247–8), I would argue to the contrary, this was an example of clan structures being transformed by members, to pursue a new range of interests opened up by rural capitalism.

Collectively, these direct and indirect benefits accelerated Bougainville's general integration into the national and international economy. However, for those villages in the mine lease area they assumed particular significance. Indeed, with the exception of villages in the north Nasioi region, these communities were relatively 'undeveloped' prior to the mine's construction. For instance, villages situated higher up in the Crown Prince Ranges, and near the headwaters of the Jaba river, critically lacked access to market centres and government services. Accordingly, plantation labour had historically been the primary source of income in these areas (AGA 1989: 2.5–2.6). Yet, as the mine developed, attracting greater government attention and resources to the mine lease area, access to markets, urban centres and public services improved (AGA 1989: 4.8; Regan 1996: 5). Complimenting this change, the mine offered new employment opportunities, while larger compensation payments provided a ready source of start-up capital for small business. Accordingly, Connell (1992: 34) observes: 'No households in the mine-affected areas are as dependent on the subsistence economy as they were before mine construction began and in some villages, especially Dapera, dependence on the agricultural economy in any form has almost ended because of the loss of village land'.

Yet the rapid introduction of market-centred economic practices also produced new tensions within villages in the mine lease area. Like the rest of PNG's more 'developed' areas, these households now faced pressures associated with simple reproduction. And invariably, custom and clan became vital determinates that mediated who had access to essential resources, and who did not. Additional competition over compensation payments, small business opportunities and choice positions at BCL, heightened the resulting extremes of social differentiation, and the antagonisms associated with noticeable inequalities in wealth and further resources. Complicating matters was the sizeable demographic shift that had been experienced on Bougainville, which produced a large youth population, who were coming of age during the 1980s. Facing distinct shortages in land, employment, cash payments, and small business opportunities, age and class began to overlap. One young villager complained: 'The company has created classes in our society, where there were none before . . . family disputes have now occurred over land, even within families and within villages' (AGA 1989: Appendix II; Filer 1990: 19). While another argued: 'Since Papua New Guinea gained independence, political independence, in 1975, the exploitation of our land, our resources and our people have increased rapidly. The process of exploitation of further social and economic disparities, that we see every day in our society, is encouraged by our leaders and elites, becoming instant millionaires by befriending foreign capitalists' (ABC Radio Indian Pacific, 14 October 1989).

However, if growing inter- and intra-village tensions were the negative expression of social contradiction on Bougainville, its positive content was a number of young activists, in command of concepts that could help critically dissect the island's experience of change. Two of the most vocal activists in this respect, were the cousins Francis Ona and Perpetua Serero. Both from Guava village, Ona was a truck driver for BCL, while his cousin Serero, was Bougainville's first female radio announcer (Oliver 1991: 205–10). Their critique was both pointed and complex. According to Ona (1989), 'the only significant development we have seen since independence is the widening gap between the few rich and the poor majority . . . Regional and provincial inequalities, as well as inequalities between urban and rural areas have widened dramatically within the fourteen years of political independence'. Ona and Serero argued, 'foreign capitalists', 'elite nationals', 'self centred traditional landlords', 'government officials', the state (which 'is the instrument for the few rich to accumulate wealth'), and 'the Australian government', were all historical agents who had fed this growing inequality (BCL 1988e; NPLA 1987a; Ona 1989, 1990a). Of course, BCL was singled out for particular condemnation, not only due to the sizable profits it had pocketed, but also for the environmental harm its operations had inflicted on the surrounding lands and waterways (AGA, 1989: 3.5; Connell, 1991: 67; Vernon, 2005: 269). Opposing this ruling class bloc, Ona (1989) claimed, are 'many frustrated landowners, public servants, intellectuals, youths, the unemployed and exploited workers', who have acted as the '"sacrificial lamb" for the few capitalists whose hunger for wealth is quenchless and unceasing'.

For these young activists, radicalised by their experience of marginalisation, differentiation, competition, and commodification, the island's social antagonisms could only be diffused by expropriating BCL and local 'capitalists'. This act, they believed, would pave the way for a new, egalitarian mode of development, one based on the 'equal distribution of society's resources and equal distribution of government services', and grounded in environmentally sustainable agriculture (Francis Ona, Archival Footage, 9 April 1999). Administering this economic foundation, would be a decentralised state, structured around a system of elders and chiefs, whose traditional role would be reinvented to regulate the new forms of social metabolism this trajectory of development inspired. While Ona's vision, in particular, was not necessarily married to Bougainville's independence, nevertheless, as the revolt matured he became adamant that a powerful class of national compradors and foreign capitalists would block the proposed transformation, thus secession was the only viable political mechanism through which change could be practically achieved.

In order to operationalise their social agenda, the young activists at the vanguard of this anti-capitalist movement challenged the Panguna Landowners Association's (PLA) leadership to an election during 1987. Formed in 1979, the PLA had acted as a representative body for landowners in the mine lease area (AGA 1989: 7.3; Okole 1990: 17). By impressing upon BCL the landowners' collective ability to mediate its access to the objective conditions of production, the PLA had won a new, more favourable compensation agreement (Okole 1990).

The radical landowner faction emerging in 1987 aimed to infiltrate the PLA and invert its character, co-opting the political power which their senior kin had used to extract rents and compensation, in order to both expropriate BCL and the local elite growing large at the expense of grassroots rural households. The struggle for control over the PLA, in this sense, was the start of a broader push to reconfigure the social basis under which Bougainville functioned within Empire.

Conclusion

It would be overly schematic, as Trotsky observes, to assume that as Empire expands, those newly immersed regions will replicate the trajectories of Western Europe, North America, or indeed East Asia. Instead, complex social equations develop as a range of forces merge through the agency of the coloniser and colonised. In that light, it would also be wrong to assume that class conflict in newly immersed regions will necessarily mirror Europe's experience, or that in the absence of an industrial proletariat, or Eurocentric forms of anti-capitalist struggle, class conflict fails to exist.

Indeed, on Bougainville a range of historical mediations gave class conflict quite distinct Melanesian features. In particular, spatially entrenched forms of customary organisation, bulwarked by rural production, clan, language and culture, became important spaces and frameworks in which hegemonic projects could be developed, established and challenged. Patrimonial state relations in PNG, served to reinforce, rather than challenge, this process.

The particular trajectory of capitalist development, and class conflict this prompted, created a complex, fragmented terrain in which an anti-capitalist movement could emerge (inspired by the amplified process of rural change experienced in central Bougainville), and then find expression through a radical reinterpretation of custom, culture, and community. Having developed within a customary space largely opaque to the gaze of capital and the state, this anti-capitalist movement had already gained traction when it openly challenged the latter two parties in 1988. Accordingly, its strength and depth came as a surprise to BCL and the PNG government, both of who struggled to understand, much less neutralise, the threat being posed by Ona, Serero and their supporters. Compounding matters, BCL and the PNG state were to an extent being tugged in different strategic directions owing to the contrasting pressures they respectively faced as expressions of capital and governmental power. This made a joint-response a tense affair. It is to the challenges they faced, and the response engineered, we now turn.

3

From Landowner Crisis to Industrial Sabotage

In the previous chapter we examined the particular way in which PNG was historically absorbed into the orbit of Empire over the last century. Taking Trotsky's theory of uneven and combined development as our starting point, we observed how this process laid some of the key foundations for social rupture in the mine area of Bougainville. In this chapter we examine the first overt signs of social rupture during 1987–88, articulated through the emboldened activism of young leaders. Though, as a study on the crimes of the powerful our focus will increasingly be on the reactions and strategic-response of BCL and the PNG state.

When assessing the latter phenomena, it is important to underline the relational character of the analysis being undertaken (Jessop 2007). The content and force of social rupture, in this respect, sets a gradient of difficulty for those organisations charged with defending existing social arrangements (Lasslett 2012a). The sophistication and depth of the strategic-responses to social rupture, will need to equal the intensity of the challenge being posed. To that end, the capacity of the state and capital to mend, suppress or defer social rupture will be conditioned by different characteristics of the institutional ensemble they work through, which is a very definite condensation – and a fluid one at that – of past social processes, practices, and struggles. Moreover, in cases where the state and capital engineer a joint response, we must also examine the nodal points that exist, if any, to mediate and coordinate inter-organisational action. The managerial temperament of key officials must also be considered; though like organisational structure, managerial temperament must be seen as the historical residue of class-situated practice and institutional culture. Indeed, to avoid overly voluntaristic assessments of history the deeper structural determinations that both limit, and empower, class responses need to be factored into the analysis. Accordingly, critical theoretical concepts must be applied in order to orient consciousness to the key relations and processes that enable, define and limit state-corporate practice.

With that in mind, we begin the chapter by surveying important features of the organisational context at BCL, and their relationship with deeper social processes engendered by the relations constitutive of capital. This analysis sets a conceptual platform for analysing the company's response to heightened demands emerging from the landowner community during 1987–88, which is dealt with in the second half of this chapter.

Class, Power and Personnel – A Generational Shift at BCL

During the mid-1980s, as tensions in the mine lease area matured, BCL underwent a number of important corporate changes that would have a significant impact on subsequent events in 1987–88. The first of these changes consisted of a generational shift in the company's senior management. To that end, in 1986 BCL's Chairman Don Vernon was replaced by Don Carruthers. While in mid-1987, BCL's Managing Director Paul Quodling stepped down and was replaced by Robert (Bob) Cornelius.

Both Vernon and Quodling had been involved with the mining operation since the 1960s, and enjoyed close personal relations with PNG leaders at a local, provincial and national level. Consequently, this change in senior management was particularly profound: 'So there had been a sort of quantum change that took place in the mid eighties, when most of the long term management staff for BCL, changed over. So guys like Paul Quodling, Jim Holt, these guys retired or moved on to other things, and a new group of guys came in, but most of those guys were fairly fresh to New Guinea, and most of them had not had any experience, nor could they speak pidgin etc.' (BCL official A, personal communication, 31 May 2006).

That said, BCL's new Chairman was considered within company circles to be 'one of the most logical men [you'll meet]' (BCL official B, personal communication, 13 September 2006), who 'understood history well and what drove societies' (BCL official C, personal communication, 9 September 2006). He was also regarded as a 'one hundred percent fair play man', and an 'ethical bloke' (BCL official D, personal communication, 7 June 2006). However, more conspicuously, Carruthers evidently adopted an 'abrasive' management style, he could be 'very harsh to judge', and when the situation demanded it, the Chairman had the potential to be a 'nasty bastard' (BCL official C, personal communication, 9 September 2006).[1] In the sensitive atmosphere of Port Moresby (PNG's political capital), where the parochialism and racism that had accompanied colonial rule remained fresh in people's minds, the temperament of BCL's new Chairman – which had a tendency to emerge at moments of extreme tension – would grate against PNG's nationalist politicians. As one BCL manager put it, 'Don and PNG, were oil and water' (BCL official B, personal communication, 13 September 2006). However, as Carruthers was based in Melbourne, his managerial style would not become an issue of importance until the campaign of industrial sabotage began in November–December 1988. Before the emergence of the crisis it was Robert Cornelius, BCL's new Managing Director, who was the company's most immediate and senior driver in PNG.

The transition from Quodling to Cornelius was relatively quick. A colleague remembers, 'I think he [Quodling] only decided [to retire] three months before it all happened . . . So Bob [Cornelius] only had a very short period of time to pick his brains' (BCL official E, personal communication, 26 October 2006). Complicating matters was the personalised character of Quodling's leadership. An accountant by training, he had been with BCL since 1966 (BCL official F, personal communication, 30 May 2006). Quodling took over the role of General Manager in 1977 and Managing Director in 1982. During his long tenure, Quodling utilised the company's integral place in the provincial and national economy to cultivate close personal relationships with politicians, bureaucrats, union leaders and clan elders (BCL official F, personal communication, 30 May 2006). Numerous Prime Ministers and Ministers were among his friends and close associates. Nevertheless, there was a sense among managers at BCL, that Quodling was unwilling to share his personal connections: 'Paul had been there from the time the mine was really conceived, he organised the finance, he did all the government contacts, he raised the money . . . he was involved right from day one and knew everything, and it was very difficult to get him to share that information' (BCL official E, personal communication, 26 October 2006).

Compounding the effects of Quodling's alleged political monopoly, was BCL's decision *not* to place senior managers in Port Moresby's political centre. This decision meant the company lacked agents who could, on a day-to-day basis, identify, monitor and build rapport with key power-brokers in government. As one senior manager at BCL puts it:

Cornelius couldn't ring anyone in Port Moresby . . . all they had was an office with two clerks with no authority whatsoever . . . It tells you about an attitude doesn't it. The head office was in Melbourne, Brisbane was a major office. And the company had a jet which flew Brisbane to Bougainville direct, to prevent from going to Port Moresby. (BCL official B, personal communication, 13 September 2006)

Echoing this critique, an official from the Chamber of Mines and Petroleum similarly recalls:

They [BCL] had a guy here [in Port Moresby], he was a nice bloke, but you might like to say he was a lightweight . . . he'd pick people up at the airport, he would get them to accommodation, he would get them back and forth to the airport, he would arrange the occasional government meeting they might have had, but he had no lobbying presence as such. Because that just wasn't their style. They didn't even see that as important. (Chamber of Mines and Petroleum official, personal communication, 2 July 2006)

This absence from Port Moresby was viewed by a number of senior BCL managers as deeply problematic in PNG's post-colonial environment. Indeed, in this sensitive context institutionalising personal rapport with the political elite was vital:

There was a term in Port Moresby, where people were referred to as 'blow-ins', because with all the overseas companies over there, the bosses would fly into Port Moresby, spend two days in the best hotel, they would then call into Waigani [political district] on the way to the airport, so that they could talk to the Prime Minister, whilst they looked at their watch so they didn't bloody miss the bloody plane and away they go . . . I spent a fair bit of time in Port Moresby when living in Australia, once I moved there it is extraordinary how the attitude changed, from the same people. They treated you differently. So I would get some bosses from Melbourne show up and I'd take them around to Waigani on the way to the airport, and they'd get the plane, and I'd go back home, and that created a different atmosphere. So the PM could ring me up and say what are you doing tonight, that sort of thing. You have to be there! (BCL official B, personal communication, 13 September 2006)

In this light, it can be argued that BCL as an organisation had failed to politically capitalise upon its central position in a provincial and national economy fundamentally dependent on the mine's revenues. The company, in effect, had relied on the cult of several personalities, who had steered BCL since its foundation in the 1960s. As a result, the loss of connected individuals, such as Paul Quodling, represented a significant dent in BCL's capacity to influence government policy – the significance of which should not be underestimated. While capital in general can influence the application of state power through certain structural levers (see chapter 5), for individual capitals institutional networks of influence, can be an effective medium for shaping how government power is applied. However in BCL's case, the magnitude of its economic significance in PNG encouraged a degree of organisational complacency, which meant these networks were neglected. As long as the provincial and national political environment remained serene, the impact of this decision was minimal. However, as the landowner campaign on Bougainville escalated during 1988, BCL's political impotence would be more acutely felt.

Making matters more difficult still, the company's new Managing Director tended to shy away from political engagements. A metallurgist by training, Cornelius felt somewhat out of water in Melanesian circles. Public relations duties were accordingly delegated to his Bougainvillean managers, whom Cornelius hoped might be more nimble in the local environment. A manager explains, '[Bob] was fairly new in dealing with Melanesian culture, and . . . [he] was relying very heavily on [two Managers] Joe [Auna] and Philip Mapah . . . because . . . [his] ability to communicate with the outside national world was a lot more limited because of . . . [his short] tenure. So it made it a bit difficult' (BCL official D, personal communication, 7 June 2006). Joe Auna was BCL's General Manager of personnel services, while Philip Mapah was the company's liaison and media services manager. While both men were indeed Bougainvillean, neither one was from a clan lineage in the mine lease area. Thus, while they may have had a better understanding of the cultural context in which BCL was operating, they were not going to necessarily find local acceptance in an area where they were perceived to be both outsiders and company men.[2] Consequently, during the course of 1988, BCL was poorly positioned to gather intelligence on political movements within the mine lease area (and in PNG more generally), much less shape their momentum.

World Copper Markets and BCL's Corporate Agenda

It was not only BCL's senior ranks that experienced change during 1986–87, the company's corporate goals were also facing realignment. A shift in strategic tact had been precipitated by certain developments in world copper production:

> Bougainville arose and prided itself on being a low cost producer by world standards, and they kept reducing their costs by a cent a pound every year or two. But in the mid-eighties they looked around, and they found with all the Arizona [copper mines] gone, replaced by the low cost Chilean mines, they [BCL] were actually [now] a high cost producer, even though they had been reducing their costs . . . Bob Cornelius is a technical guy, a metallurgist, and Bob's instruction was to get costs down. (BCL official B, personal communication, 13 September 2006)

The challenging international environment faced by BCL was formally registered in the company's 1988 *Annual Report*. In his Chairman's statement, Carruthers observed: 'It is clear that other copper mining operations around the world have significantly improved efficiency and labour productivity in recent years. This highlights the need for Bougainville Copper to increase its efforts in this regard, if it is to maintain its competitive position' (BCL 1989j: 5).

These comments register in a mediated way, the coercive effects of a social process articulated in Marx's theory of value. For Marx, value constitutes one of the most elementary features of the capitalist mode of production (Marx 1973: 100). When fleshing out its content, he begins with the observation that generalised production for exchange – which is a core differentiating feature of capitalism – brings into relation diverse forms of useful labour, cultivating a historical abstraction of sorts. Marx (1976: 135–6) notes:

> If we leave aside the determinate quality of productive activity, and therefore the useful character of the labour, what remains is its quality of being an expenditure of human labour-power. Tailoring and weaving, although they are qualitatively different productive activities, are both a productive expenditure of human productive activities, are both a productive expenditure of human brains, muscles, nerves, hands etc., and in this sense both human labour . . . More complex labour counts

only as intensified, or rather multiplied simple labour, so that a smaller quantity of complex labour is considered equal to a larger quantity of simple labour. Experience shows that this reduction is constantly being made. A commodity may be the outcome of the most complicated labour, but through its value it is posited as equal to the product of simple labour, hence it represents only a specific quantity of simple labour.

Accordingly, Marx (1976: 142) suggests that commodities as values are, in effect, congealed expressions of labour-time. He thus argues:

> What exclusively determines the magnitude of the value of any article is therefore the amount of labour socially necessary, or the labour-time necessary for its production . . . Socially necessary labour-time is the labour-time required to produce any use-value under the conditions of production normal for a given society and with the average degree of skill and intensity of labour prevalent in that society. (Marx 1976: 129)

With that in mind, in his theory of surplus value Marx argues that the source of capital's profit is the mass of value extracted from the worker during the productive processes, over and above what is returned to them in wages. However, Marx (1981: 267–8) notes an important paradox in this respect, while it is the mass of surplus value extracted from the worker, which constitutes the ultimate source of profit for capital as a class, nonetheless, intervening determinations exist that disconnect the surplus value extracted by individual units of capital and the rate of profit they realise (see Marx 1981: 257–80). That said, the social content of profit is still felt by capital in a number of different ways. One instance, of direct relevance to this case study involves the competition between rival producers. Marx observes that individual capitals in a specific sector can realise an above average share of the surplus value extracted by capital as a whole, through introducing labour-saving innovations. As a result of these innovations, less labour time is condensed in each commodity produced, but the commodity nonetheless still sells at a price determined by the social average – this accrues the beneficiary a temporal windfall. Nevertheless, Marx notes, this is only a temporal advantage, as 'the law of the determination of value by labour-time . . . acting as a coercive law of competition, forces his competitors to adopt the new method' (Marx 1976: 436).[3]

In the case of BCL, they had for a period established themselves as a low-cost producer; and indeed prided themselves on finding innovative ways to expend less labour time – expressed in variable and constant capital – on the extraction of each tonne of ore. However, they were ceding ground during the 1980s. Indeed, by 1987–88, it was BCL who was trailing behind its rivals. Consequently, the company responded by implementing, 'an enhanced cost reduction and control program' during 1988 (BCL 1989j: 7). Savings in this respect were made by utilising cheaper sources of fuel for the mine's power generators, replacing expatriate employees with nationals (who were on a lower wage scale), and by cutting excessive shipping costs (BCL official E, personal communication, 26 October 2006). BCL also embarked upon a reinvestment program to improve the efficiency of their mineral extraction processes. Beginning in 1987, the reinvestment program was expected to involve the expenditure of K300 million (US$354 million) over four years (BCL 1989j: 4).

One important side-effect of BCL's enhanced cost reduction and control program was,

> Things like community relations were not actually top priority . . . That was not to say ignore it. Under Don Vernon in the early days and then Paul Quodling, it was very much a priority, but under the instructions that Bob [Cornelius] was given it was still important, but it was lessening . . . he had less money to spend on roads, and bridges, and schools, and hospitals. (BCL official B, personal communication, 13 September 2006)

Of course, it would be problematic to assume that the delivery of further benefits to the local community could have diffused tensions. Given the social framework mediating distribution, in all likeliness increased benefits would have only amplified uneven accumulation, inequality, and inter/intra community conflict (although there is a possibility it may have provided the material for provincial and local leaders to consolidate a hegemonic bloc capable of quelling a nascent resistance movement).

That said, the cost-reduction/investment program did impinge upon how management responded to the first signs of landowner opposition during 1987–88. In particular, the company was increasingly sensitive to the potentially adverse cost implications that might emerge from taking pragmatic steps to diffuse tensions in the mine lease area. Indeed, BCL wanted to see all landowner demands carefully channelled through the existing legal frameworks established with the national government and the PLA; and to that end, it was particularly opposed to the granting of any extra-legal benefit that might be seen as a reward for rent-seeking behaviour. Consequently, as landowner activists embarked upon a wave of anti-mine protests during 1987–88, the company's management assumed an increasingly conservative posture that placed them at odds with their legally more flexible counterparts in the PNG state. Compounding matters, BCL fundamentally lacked levers of influence within local, provincial and national governing circles. They were thus poorly poised to impress their point of view on key political power-brokers, at a time when tensions were rising.

On that note, we will now trace the emergence of the anti-mine campaign – which began with the election of a new PLA executive in August 1987 – and the subsequent responses it engendered from those charged with defending existing social arrangements.

The Struggle for Control of the Panguna Landowners Association

The PLA, we observed, was founded in 1979 by landowner leaders who wished to see a greater share of the mine revenues enter local accumulation cycles (which they were active in).[4] This regional body quickly assumed a powerful monopoly over landowner relations with BCL and the state. The company was relatively happy with this arrangement. Indeed, the eleven primary land titleholders (as representatives for all primarily titleholders) who had signed the *Bougainville Copper Compensation Agreement*,[5] which governed payments to the local communities, were *also* members of the PLA Executive (Ewing 1989).[6] This direct overlap gave the PLA's monopoly over landowner negotiations cultural *and* legal legitimacy in the eyes of BCL's management, who were keen to ensure that their contracts were both watertight, and in accordance with local custom.

On the other hand, for marginalised youth and struggling rural households, this monopoly was interpreted through a class lens. These were not primary land title owners acting in the interests of all households, they were land title owners acting for themselves.[7] And to this end, they had successfully created a bottleneck of sorts on power, through an appeal to custom. As Dorney (2000: 105) notes, the PLA executive 'had never been formally elected', rather they had grounded their authority in 'traditional and birthright powers' (Old Panguna Landowners Association 1987). Francis Ona and Perpetua Serero hoped this bottleneck could be broken by challenging the original executive to an election – after all, there was no customary precedent governing the constitutional order of bodies set up to mediate landowner relations with mining capital. Therefore, it could be argued that selecting an executive through election was as legitimate as birthright. An election indeed took place, on 21 August 1987, at the Panguna gymnasium. It was witnessed by provincial and national politicians. According to Wiley (1992: 337), 'the people voted 98 to 12 to oust the old executive and elect a new one. The old members ran in the election but lost' (herein the original executive will be referred to as the Old Panguna Landowners Association or OPLA, and the new executive will be referred to as the New Panguna Landowners Association or NPLA). Perpetua Serero was elected 'Chairlady', Patrick Bano Vice Chairman, and Francis Ona Secretary. The new group's decisive victory, gave Ona and Serero a firm mandate to begin mobilising disaffected households in the mine lease area.

At this stage, BCL was unaware of the seismic changes occurring around them. Their focus remained on more practical dilemmas; principally, ensuring that their contractual arrangement with the landowning communities remained in place, and in accord with custom (indeed the contract's enforceability depended on its accordance with custom).[8] As a result, the company was now placed in a difficult position. Were they to recognise the NPLA officeholders, they would be undermining the customary authority of those primary titleholders they had contracted with, and thus the agreement's enforceability. However, failure to recognise the elected NPLA officeholders, would make it seem as if BCL was 'playing politics'.

The company hesitated as mixed signals from the local communities began to filter through (NPLA 1987a: OPLA 1987). This hesitant reaction was interpreted by the NPLA as tacit support for the OPLA. Accordingly, Serero demanded that BCL stop 'injecting their dirty ideology', and 'cease from interfering with a few self-centred traditional landlords brainwashed by foreigners and minority elite nationals' (NPLA 1987b). The North Solomons Premier,[9] Joseph Kabui, supported the new executive's position (North Solomons Provincial Government 1987). As a former industrial relations officer with the Bougainville Mining Workers Union, and a young secondary land title holder in the mine lease area, Kabui tended to sympathise with the populist component of the NPLA's platform (see Griffin and Togolo 1997: 377–8; Oliver 1991: 195–6) – while as the North

Solomons Premier, Kabui was keen to press any grievance that would see greater mine revenues accrue to Bougainville. Thus, during the NPLA's struggle for recognition Kabui placed his weight behind the new executive, as BCL's General Manager of personnel services, Joe Auna, was to later recall: 'Mr Kabui insisted that the election of the new PLA was democratically organised. Mr Kabui warned Mr Cornelius [BCL's Managing Director] and myself that unless BCL recognised the new PLA, the company would be "playing around with fire" and that we would have to be "prepared to meet the consequences"' (Auna 1989).

Despite these forceful communications, the company was reluctant to comply. Indeed, their legal arrangement was such that management were in effect bound to a certain ossified interpretation of custom – which granted OPLA leaders near despotic authority – that grinded against the more fluid, changing reality of rural social relations in Bougainville. Accordingly, BCL continued to support the OPLA, as 'legally the old group, they are the elected group looking after the landowner trust fund [RMTLTF]. And they have a legal document [1986 *Compensation Agreement*] which has their signatures on it, the legal document does not have this new group's signatures on it' (BCL official D, personal communication, 7 June 2006). As a result, BCL informed the NPLA: 'It is unfortunate that your Group has established itself in opposition to the long existing Panguna Land Owners Association Executive . . . In view of the apparent conflict the company has no other option than to continue recognising and dealing with the current executive which was selected traditionally by the landowners on the basis of traditional leadership and landownership custom' (BCL 1987).

While BCL's ongoing commitment to the existing legal framework was understandable from a commercial point of view, nevertheless, lecturing NPLA representatives on local custom and tradition was bound to be perceived as a provocative act, by a company intent on manipulating landowning relations for self-serving ends. The NPLA's reply was predictably pointed:

The Management['s] attitude [is to] establish divide and rule conquer tactic[s] [to] bring about [an] unhealthy state of affairs . . . to serve the . . . company's interest. The purpose of this letter is to warn your General Manager that it is not his business and responsibility to run the Panguna Land Owners Association as he is currently doing now. We would like to receive your response no later than 18 December, 1987 [with respect to recognising the NPLA]. Failure to [give a] positive response will result [in] serious political actions and protests to bring about . . . justice. (NPLA 1987c)

The North Solomons Premier again backed the NPLA, arguing that 'BCL should merely respect and accommodate the landowners' democratic decisions and choices' (North Solomons Provincial Government 1987).

Nevertheless, in the search for stability, unchanging traditional hierarchies had a continuing allure for BCL's management. Therefore, the NPLA's Chairlady was asked to provide the company with a list of the new executives, their land-holdings and the villages they represented, so BCL could confirm their traditional authority to speak on behalf of the mine communities (BCL official D, personal communication, 7 June 2006). BCL's Chairman later recalled, 'at no stage were we given any evidence that these people were legitimate land-holders or had the right to negotiate on behalf of the land-holders' (Joint Committee on Foreign Affairs, Defence & Trade 1990: 436–7). Thus, the opinion was formed that 'this was just a group that is going to be a try-on, to try and undermine some of the agreements that had already been agreed with the normal, the elected [sic] representatives of the people' (BCL official D, personal communication, 7 June 2006).

Nevertheless, at this early stage in the crisis, regardless of what BCL thought, these new 'try-ons' wielded significant support in the mine lease area (Connell 1990: 30), and they were backed by the North Solomons provincial government. Consequently, following a series of further polemical exchanges during February 1988, BCL resigned itself to *dealing* with the NPLA, without, that is, sidelining the OPLA with whom its agreements stood. This put the company in an uncomfortable position. Landowner negotiations were now being channelled through the NPLA, an organ with the power to disrupt BCL's access to the mineral deposit (that is, by denying them access to the land), while the binding legal agreements governing compensation were with the executive of the OPLA – who the company argued were the 'legitimate land-holders' – a group that had largely lost hegemony in the mine lease areas. As a result, the company's energies were being split between two organisations, as they attempted to pacify the NPLA, while protecting the legal agreements signed by the OPLA executive.[10]

The New Panguna Landowners Association Issues its Demands

During the course of 1988, as BCL grappled with its own economic problems, NPLA leaders drew upon their growing political support to agitate in the mine lease area. Their strategy at this stage was twofold. First, build broad-based coalitions with allied forces within the provincial government, BCL (local workers) and local communities. Second, graft a range of immediate goals, which address the reproductive demands of squeezed peasant households, to more substantive changes which can unpick the structural inequalities being experienced on Bougainville.

To that end, the NPLA began to stage public rallies, which were coupled to increasingly emboldened political demands. One of the first rallies held by the NPLA is described by BCL General Manager, Joe Auna:

> On the 11th [of March, 1988] approximately 300 or 400 people (largely male and largely comprising Bougainvilleans but with some non-Bougainvillean nationals) gathered in the Panguna township and marched up the road to the BCL central administration complex. The demonstration was quite peaceful. A number of the demonstrators carried placards demanding the resignation of myself and Philip Mapah . . . After the speeches had been made amongst much shouting and yelling I was presented with a petition signed by Perpetua Serero as chairlady and Francis Ona as secretary of the New PLA and by Damien Damen as Chairman of the demonstration. (Auna 1989)

Of particular note here, is the senior role given to local leader, Damien Dameng.[11] Dameng was from an 'undeveloped' mountainous region (Kongara),[12] south-east of the mine. During the 1950s he had utilised dissatisfaction arising from the region's uneven development (see Ogan 2005: 392–3), to forge a movement known as the Me'ekamui Pontoku Onoring, Daita Karakeni[13] (Tanis 2005: 450–1). Attracting followers in Irang, Pankaa, Mosinau and Poaru villages,

> Dameng and his supporters believed that customary social structures and ways were being undermined by the outside world . . . [His] opposition to the damaging impacts of the outside world also extended to the Panguna mine. He believed it destroyed land (the basis for social relations), introduced cash payment for use of land (thereby undermining Bougainvilleans' relatively egalitarian customary social organization), and

brought in large numbers of outsiders. (Regan 2002; see also Regan 2003; Regan 2005)

Dameng's involvement in the rally offered evidence that Ona and Serero were beginning to network with influential leaders aligned to their critique. Given that Dameng was reported to have a following of around 4,000 villagers (Oliver 1991: 180–1), this network would prove vitally important during 1989 when the PNG state deployed its security forces on Bougainville.

The petition handed to Joe Auna during the rally chaired by Dameng, included a log of claims. The log's content reflected the NPLA tactic of grafting immediate demands to more substantive social changes. For example, it requested increased compensation, employment/contracting priority for Bougainvilleans, the upgrading of community schools and centres, the provision of certain capital works, the relocation of villages adversely affected by the mine operations, and the establishment of youth groups, women's groups and community centres in the villages along the Port–Mine Access Road (NPLA 1988a). However, attached to the log was a declaration foreshadowing a more substantive agenda: '[The] landowners wish to stop the mine by stopping [the] national government, and BCL from renewing the BCL mining agreement . . . there is very little benefit to land owners and our provincial government from BCL copper mine' (NPLA 1988a).

Given the popular groundswell behind the NPLA – which was reflected in the March demonstration – BCL could not afford to ignore their demands. One senior manager explains:

I don't think there is any doubt at all, we took them as being serious, but you know when you reply, you have to be careful how you reply. You can't say yes I agree with you, we are going to deal with this issue. You have to say why it is like it is, and you have to say . . . we would appreciate talking to you further as soon as possible, and then suggest that the company representatives and your executive meet. (BCL official D, personal communication, 7 June 2006)

With this strategy in mind, BCL responded to the NPLA with a carefully drafted letter, which set out in detail the precise legal arrangements that governed land title, compensation, revenue sharing and public works – the sum result being, the company was legally unable to agree to any of the NPLA's requests (BCL 1988a). Nevertheless, a roundtable meeting was proposed for 29 March 1988, as an incentive it would include national government representatives.

The proposed meeting, however, was rescheduled to 12 April 1988, when the government representatives failed to appear (Ewing 1989). The rescheduled meeting featured over 150 participants, including representatives from the NPLA, OPLA, provincial government and Department of Minerals and Energy. At the meeting the NPLA tabled *new* demands: 'We the landowners demand that the Company pay for all the resources that you have destroyed on our land commencing in 1963 and up to 1988 in the sum of Ten Billion Kina' (about US$12 billion) (NPLA 1988b). If BCL agreed to this request, they would be allowed to continue their mining operation for five years, providing that 50 per cent of all profits were paid to the 'landowners and the government of Bougainville' (NPLA 1988b). Upon the expiration of this five-year period, the landowners would fully appropriate the company. The NPLA also requested that the national government return to the landowning communities 50 per cent of all moneys received from BCL since 1972, while the provincial government was asked to implement an expanded program of public works (NPLA 1988c, 1988d). These demands were perhaps the most overt indication to date of the NPLA's intention.

However, at this stage BCL was concerned, but not yet alarmed (BCL official D, personal communication, 7 June 2006). Claxton (1998: 83) perhaps best captures the mood prevailing inside the company: 'Such "outrageous demands are part and parcel of the Melanesian way of doing politics", and can be interpreted as bargaining rather than final positions'. That said, BCL managers were nonetheless forming the view that, custom aside, the OPLA was preferable to the NPLA for much more practical reasons. BCL's Company Secretary recalls: '[The OPLA had] greater commercial acumen than the new landowner group. They were largely composed of people involved in business with sound financial minds and there seemed to be a general feeling of embarrassment and of dismay at the [April] claims [of the NPLA]' (Ewing 1989). In effect, BCL knew their bond with the OPLA was more than just contracts, it was a reflection of sympathetic class interests. Nevertheless, BCL had few resources at its disposal to affect the balance of power in the landowning community; consequently, the company would have to wait for a more opportune moment before their preference for the OPLA could become more pronounced. In the meantime the NPLA's requests had to be dealt with.

Having tabled their demands, the NPLA gave the company 14 days to respond. BCL issued a formal response nine days later. Making no mention of the K10 billion request, the company informed the landowners, 'BCL has every intention of continuing to meet its [existing] obligations to make payments to Landowners and Government as defined in the Agreements under which it operates' (BCL 1988b).

The company's unflinching position was testing the new executive's patience. They entered their next encounter with Joe Auna and Philip Mapah – which took place on 28 April 1988 – in a more combative mood. Indeed, Serero began by complaining to the latter officials over the absence of BCL's Managing Director, 'when we put our demands we wanted someone who could make a decision on the spot to answer' (BCL 1988c). As the meeting continued, Ona reemphasised the NPLA's overarching aim, 'all we want is to close the mine', a view which was seconded by around 30 NPLA supporters (BCL 1988c). Serero added by way of explanation, 'one of our major concerns is pollution – money is of secondary consideration, compensation for these are insufficient' (BCL 1988c).

In response, Joe Auna conceded that changes could be made to the mining operation, but they had to be secured through the mechanisms formally set out in the *Bougainville Copper Agreement* (BCL 1988c). Auna was referring here to a provision in the contract, which permitted the agreement to be reviewed, and where necessary altered, on a seven-year basis (1988 was the date set for the second seven-year review). While the landowners were not signatories to this agreement – it was signed with the national government – the review nonetheless offered a chance to redirect some revenues from a national to a local level.

Having made little progress with BCL, the NPLA elected to ratchet up its struggle. To that end, on 16 May 1988, NPLA supporters set up a road block on the Port–Mine Access Road. It proved a short affair – the road block was removed after several hours by the North Solomons Administrative Secretary,[14] who agreed to organise a major roundtable forum for the end of May (Auna 1989). Nevertheless, news of the NPLA's actions reached Melbourne. In response, BCL's Chairman wrote to PNG's Prime Minister Paias Wingti, to press upon him the importance of implementing the seven year *Bougainville Copper Agreement* review:

I am sorry I was unable to see you personally about these matters during my visit to Port Moresby . . . I feel that I should draw your attention to the difficult situation which has developed in Bougainville . . . Landowners' representatives threatened to close the operation, and on Tuesday morning carried out their threat, bringing production to a standstill for several hours [BCL's Company Secretary claims the road blocks caused inconvenience but did not affect production (Ewing 1989)] . . . It seems to us to be of the utmost importance that the scheduled review of the BCA [*Bougainville Copper Agreement*] proceeds with the greatest urgency, and that the North Solomons Provincial Government be represented at these discussions. (BCL 1988d)

However, no more progress was made on the review under the Wingti administration, whose days in government were numbered.

A New Government and the Applied Geology Associates Review

PNG's Constitution, as it stood in 1988, allowed a change in government to occur 'on the floor of parliament via a vote of no confidence' (Turner 1990: 115). Turner explains: 'A motion of no confidence can be moved six months after the appointment of a Prime Minister. If it is successful, the alternative Prime Minister nominated in the motion – invariably the leader of the opposition – crosses the floor of the house to assume the reins of government' (1990: 115) .

On 4 July 1988, it was the leader of the Pangu Party,[15] Rabbie Namaliu, who was able to exploit internal divisions within the governing coalition, to form a new government under his Prime Ministership. Namaliu was part of a second generation of political leaders. This generation had generally received a better formal education, and a longer period of political tutelage, than had their pioneering predecessors. Namaliu, for instance, received a masters from the University of Victoria in British Columbia during the early 1970s, he then went on to serve as the Principal Private Secretary to Chief Minister Somare, and as Chairman of the Public Services Commission (Senge 1988).[16] After formally entering politics in 1982, Namaliu was also afforded the opportunity to assume responsibility for several Ministerial portfolios (Senge 1988). Thus, the new Prime Minister was well prepared for the rigours of his position. In addition, he was a looked upon with favour by PNG's main international benefactor, Australia (DPMC official, personal communication, 15 September 2006).

In terms of policy, Namaliu was a self-proclaimed liberaliser who 'said his Government would . . . open up its economy to foreign investment and give it a free hand . . . Namaliu said the government's role should be merely to create the right climate for investment and for real private sector growth' (Bromby 1990: 23). To that end, Namaliu promised to:

> [Bring about a] drastic reduction of the public service . . . the abolition of the National Investment and Development Agency (NIDA) [regulatory body for foreign investment] . . . increases in Papua New Guinean business involvement; a mortgage finance company to provide long-term housing loans; disposal of all surplus government land to businesses; a joint government business committee to simplify regulations; rural industry diversification, commercialise all agriculture extension services; eradicate compensation claims; change in visa fees and allow a permanent resident status to investors investing more than K250,000; a tax holiday to pioneer industries; remove duty on imports required by manufacturers for import creation; wage restraints and balance resource development and environmental protection. (Hiambohn 1990c: 17)

Married to Namaliu's programme of privatisation, public sector cuts, tax holidays, and deregulation, was a 'tough' law and order agenda. According to Namaliu (1995: 63), 'restoring law and order is as much about restoring respect for authority as it is about police efficiency, tougher penalties and ending the "revolving door" practice which seems to be universal in our prisons'. Consequently, in addition to introducing the death penalty, among other draconian measures (see Senge 1991), the Namaliu government also proposed expanding the state's security apparatus. The infamous RPNGC mobile squads received increased funding under Namaliu, while, as we observed in chapter 2, a Rapid Deployment Unit was created to provide 'para-military' style security for PNG's mining industry (Dinnen 2001: 119). The Namaliu government also increased the size of the PNG Defence Force from 3,050 to 5,200, and changed its principal strategic focus from external defence to internal security (May 1993: 44; see also PNG Department of Defence 1990; Woodman 1994).

In terms of the struggle in central Bougainville, Namaliu's accession to power significantly increased the government's resolve to assist BCL defuse tensions. To that end, on 31 July 1988, the Minister for Minerals and Energy, Patterson Lowa, and the Minister for Provincial Affairs, John Momis – who was Bougainville's regional Member of Parliament (MP) – visited the island to meet with the concerned parties. Francis Ona took this opportunity to brief the new government on the NPLA's position. He informed the visiting Ministers: 'We the landowners will close the mine . . . we are not worried about money. Money is something nothing. The operation is causing hazards healthwise. We don't want to talk anymore' (BCL 1988e). Additionally, Ona asked the Ministers whether the new government was 'working for money or the people' (BCL 1988e).

In an effort to soothe tensions, the Ministers' informed the NPLA that their government was committed to constructing a policy regime that delivered more benefits to landowners. However, echoing BCL, they maintained that the *Bougainville Copper Agreement* seven-year review, offered the most appropriate forum in which lasting changes could be made to the Panguna mining operation. Minister Lowa concluded the meeting by stating:

> The answer is 'yes' I am committed to take up and review your demands. Both Fr. Momis and I agree that Landowners must get a fair share of benefits from Mining and other Operations. I repeat once again that the timing for initiating changes is ideal now with the number of new Mines coming up in other Provinces and the support that will come from members representing those Provinces. An indication for my commitment to take interest in your problem is my attendance at this meeting. (BCL 1988e)

Upon their return to Port Moresby, Momis and Lowa made a policy submission to the National Executive Council – the submission proposed an independent investigation into the mine's environmental and social effects be implemented. The submission was approved, and the New Zealand firm Applied Geology Associates (AGA) was appointed to undertake the review (AGA 1989: 1.3–1.4).

When notified of this development BCL responded positively, they felt the review 'was an excellent thing to do' (BCL official D, personal communication, 7 June 2006). After all, from the company's perspective the mine was a world-class operation. The NPLA was also pleased that their grievances would finally receive an independent hearing. To that end in October 1988, the new executive sent AGA a log of mine-related grievances. The log listed concerns over the destruction of local tree and plant life, the pollution of rivers and creeks in the mine area, the loss of land, the reduction in soil fertility, the lowering of crop yields, the rotting of food crops, air pollution, the loss of wildlife, and the increasing level of skin diseases and unexplained illnesses among the local population (NPLA 1988e). A separate set of grievances was sent to the national government. This document alleged that 'people within the villages are no longer living . . . [a] harmonious life or in acceptable peace. There are constant disputes over . . . [the] land issue, because of the shortage of land' (NPLA 1988f). It also laments the loss of 'cooperative attitude[s]' which were 'common to our society long ago before CRA established . . . the mine in Panguna' (NPLA 1988f).

Having spent the first weeks of November conducting their review, AGA released its preliminary findings on 18 November 1988, at a public meeting in the provincial government offices (AGA 1989: 1.3.2). The mood in the mine area at the time was hinted at two days prior to the public meeting, when AGA consultants met with villagers in Guava. Led by Serero, villagers complained about the divisive effects of class conflict, in addition to the environmental damage being caused by the mine (AGA 1989: Appendix II). Also, prominent local businessmen such as Severinus Ampaoi and Matthew Kove were accused of having monopolised Bougainville's wealth, while BCL's Joe Auna and Phillip Mapah were charged with having abandoned their clan neighbours 'for the money' (AGA 1989: Appendix II). Villagers at the meeting demanded that BCL be turned over to the landowning community. They opined, 'we will never allow any more mining . . . we are planning how we can use force against the Company; if necessary we will die on our own soil. We don't want to finish up like the African Third World countries' (AGA 1989: Appendix II). Two days later, AGA made its preliminary findings known.

At the public meeting, AGA's consultants acknowledged to the audience, which included the mine's major stakeholders, that there certainly were problems associated with the mining operation. AGA singled out village relocation, the Bougainville Copper Foundation,[17] community liaison, compensation distribution, tailings management, and social disruption, as issues in need of redress. However, some of the more serious charges levelled against BCL were rejected. For example, AGA's consultant on health impacts, Ian Aitken, observed that health conditions in the mine lease area had actually rapidly improved over the past two decades (BCL 1988f). Increased rates of malaria and asthma, Aitken claimed, were province-wide phenomena. In addition to this, Mike Timperley, who addressed the mine's environmental impacts, informed the audience that while mine tailings was a considerable problem, nevertheless, there was, 'no evidence that chemicals from BCL have impacted on vegetables, flying foxes, diseases in sea fish. [The] problem may be over cropping and over population' (BCL 1988f). This conclusion provoked outrage from some of the villagers in attendance. Matters did not improve when AGA's Martin Ward concluded the meeting by noting that 'BCL has done good work' (BCL 1988f). An irate Ona stormed out of the meeting,[18] referring to AGA's findings as a 'whitewash' (BCL official D, personal communication, 7 June 2006).

Following AGA's controversial public presentation, a letter from the NPLA was hand delivered to BCL. The company was informed that the landowners would enforce an 'indefinite' stoppage of all mining operations on 21 November 1988 (NPLA 1988f). If BCL still failed to submit to the NPLA's April demands, the letter warned, then they would have to 'proceed to Stage 2' of their 'plans' (NPLA 1988f). A blockade at the mine's drainage tunnel exit was indeed erected on 21 November 1988, but was quickly removed following an appeal from the North Solomons Administrative Secretary, Peter Tsiamalili. Nevertheless, momentum towards 'stage 2' continued. While no concrete details had been publicly released on what 'stage 2' would involve, BCL was left with little doubt over its general content, when at 3.30 p.m. on 22 November 1988, three hooded men armed with axes and knives forced their way into the BCL explosives magazine, and removed a considerable quantity of boosters, detonating cords, delays and detonators (BCL 1988g).

Now that rallies, protests, blockades and an independent inquiry had failed to win benefits for the landowning community, BCL believed that the NPLA was preparing to employ force to achieve their demands. This serious change in the NPLA's strategic posture brought BCL's Managing Director and Chairman to the fore. The company immediately 'offered a reward of 10,000 Kina' for information relating to the break-in (Ewing 1989). Additionally, BCL's Managing Director made an 'urgent' request to meet in Port Moresby with 'Momis [the Minister for Provincial Affairs], and the Minister for Minerals and Energy at the minimum' (BCL official D, personal communication, 7 June 2006). A meeting was also arranged with Prime Minister Namaliu.

Both Cornelius and Carruthers hoped to use these meetings to formulate a joint response to the emerging landowner crisis (BCL official D, personal communication, 7 June 2006). In an internal memorandum to the Chairman, Cornelius was unequivocal on what the state's priority should be, 'I believe the above examples [recent disturbances at the mine] illustrate the importance of making Law and Order and Government authority issues high on the agenda for the 28th November meeting [which was to involve the Chairman, and Prime Minister Namaliu]' (BCL 1988g). It was on this footing that BCL's senior management flew to Port Moresby.

Conclusion

The first material signs of social rupture in the mine lease area had come at a difficult time in BCL's corporate history. Two towering senior managers, with a wealth of personal connections and historical knowledge, had departed and were replaced with new hands less attuned to the Melanesian context. Compounding matters, BCL faced an extremely challenging commercial environment where reducing costs and improving efficiency were foremost on the Managing Director's mind. As a result, the stability of the legal framework, which had served the company relatively well for the past two decades, remained a priority.

In this respect, BCL was aware that unlike their predecessors the NPLA executive lacked, for a range of reasons, commitment to the legal framework. Moreover, in light of the company's ossified interpretation of tradition, management also felt the NPLA was culturally illegitimate. Had the company been able to dictate events on Bougainville, they almost certainly would have opted to keep the OPLA in place. However, they could not, and following strong representations from the North Solomons Premier during 1987/88, BCL engaged with the NPLA, albeit not to the satisfaction of the latter's executive, who was laying the groundwork for a series of progressively more pointed political interventions.

Initially, the NPLA drew upon protest and civil disobedience to press home their agenda. Nevertheless, following the AGA meeting, industrial sabotage came to the fore. For BCL the apparent shift in landowner tactics was unwelcome news, but not wholly unwelcome. Naturally industrial sabotage was not something BCL intentionally courted, however, as we will see, once it started management was eager to instrumentalise the acts of 'terrorism', to have the NPLA's legitimacy scrutinised and its key members arrested – an opportunity that had been denied to BCL early in 1988 when the political tide was firmly against the company. Nevertheless, BCL's ambitions, in this respect, would continue to find resistance from power brokers within the national and provincial governments, who had formulated a very different interpretation of events.

4

Eight Days that Shook BCL, the First Mine Shutdown and its Aftermath

During 1988 social rupture on Bougainville remained only a possibility, albeit a likely one. Mediating its actualisation in part was the strategic-response of BCL and the PNG state. This worked into the mix a range of forces. For example, BCL's cautious stance served to heighten tensions with the NPLA, while unexpectedly perhaps the conciliatory step taken by the national government – i.e. the AGA investigation – had the inverse effect of triggering stage two of the landowners' campaign. This chapter will focus on the first concrete expressions of rupture – a prolonged campaign of industrial sabotage – and the intra and inter-organisational tensions it provoked as BCL and the PNG government organised a joint-response.

From BCL's perspective, now was the time to stand firm. Any attempt to placate the NPLA, they feared, would be perceived as a victory for extra-legal tactics. On the other hand, key PNG Ministers felt BCL had been the beneficiary of a colonial windfall, and that landowners deserved a sympathetic hearing. This was not mere difference in opinion. Indeed, it will be argued that this variance in perspective was a product of the different structural limitations under which BCL and the PNG state operated. As a specific articulation of capital, that is mining capital, with a value composition that binds it to a particular geopolitical region for a substantial period of time, BCL was acutely sensitive to indices of stability. In a period of heightened global competition, enforcing existing legal arrangements with landowners and the government remained critical. Accordingly, BCL married itself to a strategic-response that in effect advocated a political coup in the mine lease area.

The PNG government, on the other hand, operated under a different set of structural influences which invited a more sympathetic stance towards the NPLA. Indeed, as a *'strategic field'* where 'intersecting power networks' attempt to mobilise dominant classes behind specific governmentalised political projects, the state is an intense site of struggle (Poulantzas 1978: 136). In this light, the PNG government's response was mediated by the particular power networks within the state, their relative capacity to seize key seats of power, the specific political projects they were married to, and the relative capacity of these projects to win the support of dominant class fractions. During late 1988, a cautious operationalisation of neoliberal government that emphasised landowner participation in freeing up resources for capital assumed influence in the National Executive Council, a site in which significant power was accumulated. However, as we will see this stance was not without opposition, in particular, officials closely associated with PNG's security apparatus felt national stability and investor confidence demanded the NPLA be made an example of.

In this sense the present chapter examines how the structural possibility of intra-class contradiction inscribed into the intersecting social rhythms constitutive of capital and government was actualised through a moment of crisis, which found expression in intra and inter organisational tensions within, and between, BCL and the PNG state. Out of this dynamic emerged an inchoate response that sparked a significant qualitative transformation in the NPLA's character.

The 25 November Talks

When BCL's Managing Director arrived in Port Moresby on 25 November 1988, he expected a sympathetic reception from national government Ministers. After all, the company was 19.1 per cent owned by the national government, and had contributed over K1 billion (US$1.2 billion) to the state's finances (CRA 1990: 1; Quodling 1991: 23 & 34). However, upon stepping into the first meeting, Cornelius's expectations were quickly dashed. First, the Managing Director faced criticism from the Minister for Minerals and Energy over the mine's lapsed security. Then the Minister for Provincial Affairs, John Momis, took issue with BCL's 'segregation/ inequality approach' (BCL 1988h). Momis opined, 'the Landowners . . . are not given the same benefits as the expatriates in the mine . . . [yet] they have had their land taken by the mine' (BCL 1988h). Cornelius's reaction to his reception is captured in the Managing Director's meeting notes, 'when I came into the meeting, I fairly quickly gained the impression that it was

BCL more than the Landowners who were considered responsible for the problems that had arisen' (BCL 1988h).

While BCL did not expect this reaction from the PNG state, it should not have surprised them. At the time, the national government's principal source of information on Bougainville was the Minister for Provincial Affairs, and the North Solomons Premier, Joseph Kabui. In the past, both men had aggressively lobbied the mining company for greater revenues and benefits, often portraying BCL as the archetypal foreign monolith (see Quodling 1991). Indeed, on one occasion Momis labelled BCL a 'ruthless exploiter' with the 'ideology of a cancer cell' (Momis 1987a, 1987b; see also Quodling 1991: 51–2). With the company lacking a mechanism in Port Moresby to either monitor or neutralise hostile representations of its corporate practice, Momis and Kabui were able to project an unchallenged position, that 'corporate greed' rather than landowner 'recalcitrance', was the principal cause of the trouble over at Panguna. The rather different hue this gave the impending crisis in government circles, made formulating a joint position with BCL difficult.

Peter Tsiamalili, the North Solomons Administrative Secretary, recommended that an amnesty be granted to those who stole the explosives (BCL 1988h). He also suggested that BCL and the national government do something 'positive' to build rapport with the aggrieved landowners. Given that the company wished to make an example of the NPLA, Tsiamalili's approach was poorly received. Indeed, Cornelius rejected out of hand making a 'positive' move, as it 'indicates those involved in theft and in other pressure tactics have achieved what they wanted' (BCL 1988h). By the meeting's conclusion, the PNG government and BCL had failed to find appropriate middle ground. However, the day's deliberations would prove moot – in a few hours the emerging crisis would experience yet another qualitative shift.

Industrial Sabotage and the Fracturing of BCL – Government Relations

It was the small hours of 26 November 1988, when Bob Cornelius was awoken by a phone call from BCL's commercial General Manager, Ken Perry. The landowners, he was told, had just initiated a campaign of industrial sabotage. BCL's accounting office, executive guest house, and engineering drawing office were all damaged (Ewing 1989). Immediately,

Cornelius began preparing a coordinated response, he 'rang the Minister in the middle of the night', and suggested that they 'meet first thing in the morning' to discuss the 'crisis', and to examine 'security requirements in the first sense', and second, how they 'were going to redress the problems that were resulting' (BCL official D, personal communication, 7 June 2006).

As requested, key Ministers arrived the next morning to be briefed on the night's events. However, with the Prime Minister away in Wewak, and apparently unreachable, national government representatives were reluctant to agree a firm position. Tentative ideas, however, were tabled. The Minister for Minerals and Energy remarked, 'we could make an announcement saying that the Government and BCL would commence the BCL Agreement review prior to the end of this year' (BCL 1988i). Not surprisingly BCL's Managing Director 'rejected this on the basis that this would a) be seen as a victory by those who committed the acts of terrorism, i.e. condoning their actions; and b) raise expectations of some perceived benefit they may have in mind that is not achievable, hence resulting in [a] repetition of the lawlessness' (BCL 1988i).

Indeed, from the company's perspective, the overnight events offered tangible proof of what they had long suspected – the NPLA was attempting to grab a 'slice of the cake' using force (BCL official D, personal communication, 7 June 2006). Any attempt to negotiate with, or appease, the NPLA, it was feared, would only serve to institutionalise a rent-seeking culture. As one BCL manager explains:

> [We] didn't like to be pushed into doing things the Melanesian way
> . . . Because the Melanesian way is a little bit . . . you put pressure on
> someone, and the pressure results in a reward, and then there is an
> attitude, I wish I had asked for more, how do I get more. You then reapply
> the pressure, perhaps a little bit harder next time, and then you get a
> bigger reward, and eventually you're asking 'how can I stop this, they are
> bleeding the company dry'. (BCL official D, personal communication, 7
> June 2006)

Accordingly, on this occasion BCL felt a strong precedent needed to be set. To that end, Cornelius told Ministers this was an act of 'highly organised terrorism by the Landowner party under [the] directions of Francis Ona', accordingly it was necessary, 'to apply the law first, i.e. charge and deal with those involved; recover stolen explosives. Then, when things have quietened down, gradually resume normal discussions with landowner representatives'

(BCL 1988i). However, given that BCL had regularly expressed doubts over the cultural legitimacy of the NPLA, Cornelius added, the government also needed to establish who were the 'true representatives of the Landowners' (BCL 1988i). He concluded his policy pitch by emphasising, 'it is important they [landowners] are not given indication that increases their expectations and therefore vindicates their actions' (BCL 1988i).

Given that BCL was, in effect, talking about staging a political coup within the customary apparatus of the PLA, its strategy demanded a significant security force presence on the island. Bougainville's existing contingent of 170 RPNGC officers was regarded as insufficient (BCL official A, personal communication, 31 May 2006). Accordingly, Cornelius argued it 'was necessary to have at least two riot groups [mobile squad units] and special flight arrangements to get them to Bougainville' (BCL 1988i). The nature of this request was suggestive of the company's belligerent intentions.

Operating through 'weight of numbers and superior firepower' (Rogers 2002: 212), the mobile squads had a formidable reputation. A former Assistant Commissioner with the RPNGC explains:

> Basically the mobile squad people are semi-military, they are aggressive, they don't do what normal policemen do, they go in there and they beat a few heads in. I am talking frankly, they will knock a few heads in, burn a few houses down, shoot a few pigs, shoot at cars . . . That is not policing, that is not normal policing . . . The mobile squads operated with a modus operandi of frightening people. (RPNGC official, personal communication, 10 July 2006)

BCL executives were aware of the mobile squad's reputation. As one General Manager put it:

> We knew the riot squads were heavy handed, that was well known in PNG. That's how they worked. If you threw a rock at them you would get ten rocks thrown back. They were very heavy handed in the way they handled disputes in the Highlands [mountainous area on the Papua New Guinea mainland]. There was concern that that wasn't the right way of doing things in Bougainville, because Bougainvilleans are much more pacifist minded than Highlanders. For Highlanders fighting is part of their history, and the way they are brought up. If someone pokes their head over your side of the hill, you have a fight on your hands. Whereas Bougainvilleans are much more placid people, very different

in their temperament. We knew that the heavy handed thing wouldn't work if they were there long term. It was a case, somebody has to come. They were the only ones that could come, and put a lid on this thing before it got out of hand. (BCL official E, personal communication, 26 October 2006)

The Minister for Minerals and Energy agreed to BCL's request for two mobile squad units, promising they would arrive on the island by the afternoon of 26 November 1988 (BCL 1988i). However, the precise role which the mobile squads would play was still a matter for debate within cabinet.

The Minister for Provincial Affairs, John Momis, held considerable sway in this respect. Not only was his party, the Melanesian Alliance, central to Namaliu's governing coalition, as a Bougainvillean he was looked to by the Prime Minister for advice. 'We had Fr John Momis', one Minister from the period recalls, 'who was a member of the Cabinet, and we relied on him a great deal for his advice . . . he was a key member of cabinet. He also had strong links with the provincial government at the time' (PNG Minister A, personal communication, 5 July 2006). Given Momis' jaundiced view of BCL, he opposed the use of force to dislodge the NPLA from power,[1] a position with which the Prime Minister sympathised. Consequently, it was decided that the mobile squads would guard the mine, while the national government attempted to 'resolve the conflict through negotiation' (PNG Minister A, personal communication, 5 July 2006).

The PNG government presented its strategy to BCL's Chairman on 28 November 1988. The Prime Minister and the Minister for Provincial Affairs informed Carruthers that a special Ministerial delegation, led by the deputy Prime Minister, Akoka Doi, would be dispatched to Bougainville in order to hold peace talks with the rebel landowners. The mobile squad duties, the Chairman was told, would be limited to mine security.

Like BCL's Managing Director several days before, Carruthers was taken aback by the government's position – he believed nothing short of an authoritative response would suffice. To do otherwise, would only embolden an 'irresponsible handful of malcontents', as he characterised them, to employ similar tactics in the future (cited in Joku 1989; see also Carruthers 1990: 40). Consequently, BCL's Chairman reacted to the Prime Minister's proposal with characteristic force. Carruthers recalls: 'The PM's priority was to "appease" the landowners. I expressed the view that CRA would want to review its assessment of PNG as a place to invest. In all, it was an unsatisfactory meeting' (CRA 1988). At the time CRA was investing heavily in mineral projects at Hidden Valley in Morobe, and Mount Klare in Enga (*Post-Courier*, 29 November 1988, p.1).

It was, needless to say, regarded by cabinet as poor form for a 'blow in' – with little understanding of the national context – to arrive in Port Moresby and issue threats to the Prime Minister (PNG Minister B, personal communication, 9 July 2006). Worse still, Carruthers continued his criticism in the media. The Chairman told a reporter from the *Post-Courier*, 'there could not be anything more damaging to PNG's reputation as a place to invest than an attack on Bougainville Copper, which has been operating here for many years and always tried to do the right thing' (cited in *Post-Courier*, 29 November 1988, p.1). The Chairman's pointed attempt to dictate policy and publicly shame the government, resembled the worst forms of behaviour exhibited by Australian officials during PNG's colonial era. According to one influential member of the Namaliu government, Carruthers 'put himself in a situation where Melanesians couldn't trust him' (PNG Minister B, personal communication, 9 July 2006).

A part of the problem was that BCL's managers thought the company deserved greater input into the government's Bougainville policy than they actually had, given the mine's national significance (BCL official D, personal communication, 7 June 2006). Indeed, the company's Chairman felt successive PNG governments had failed to decisively act on BCL's concerns during 1988. In a memorandum penned several days after his meeting with the Prime Minister, Carruthers complained,

> The National Government . . . has largely neglected the deteriorating situation for most of this year . . . [and it now] seems unwilling or unable to assert its authority, and indeed is divided among itself. The Melanesian Alliance (represented by the Minister for Provincial Affairs and Minerals and Energy) which is strong in Bougainville, continues to show a degree of sympathy for the landowner militants. (CRA 1988)

This sympathy was something that BCL executives found particularly troubling – for them promoting a stable investment climate was an elementary responsibility of good government. One BCL manager uses a comparative case to demonstrate the challenges faced by mining companies in PNG:

It so happened on one trip I went to Indonesia, there was a couple of thousand illegal miners working up the creek, and they were going to start occupying our lease. So I went to the guys in Jakarta and said 'we have a problem, we are going to build a mine for four or five hundred million bucks, and these guys are getting in the road'. They said 'it will take us three months but we will fix it'. So they gave notice to these people that they had to be gone in three months, and they all were with a few exceptions, and the army moved the rest out. Having left Jakarta, I got a plane to Queensland and then up to [Port] Moresby, where we had founded this Mt Klare gold field, where there were thousands going up there and taking the gold. I went and saw the Minister for Mines, as I had done in Jakarta a week before, and in Port Moresby the guy said 'you have a problem don't you'. (BCL official B, personal communication, 13 September 2006)

Like in Indonesia, BCL expected that the PNG government would be sympathetic to the company's concerns as a matter of course, without any need to press its views through concerted political lobbying. Although BCL was correct in part, the national government indeed had compelling reasons to regard mining capital sympathetically, other important determinations came into play which affected how this sympathy was concretised in policy.

In this respect, it is important to note that during 1988–92 the Namaliu government broadly subscribed to neoliberal orthodoxy. However, that said, there were contrasting views in government on how the latter's prescriptions could be operationalised in a uniquely Melanesian context, where power was shared with customary authorities. With regards to the governance of mining in particular, there was an almost universal ambition to open up the country's natural resources to international flows of capital, but opinions were divided over how to best achieve this end. Key power-brokers in cabinet believed landowners could be prompted to open up their resources, through development forums (see chapter 2).[2] State violence would be reserved as a last resort device for channelling wayward communities back into acceptable legal channels. However, given that landowners on Bougainville had been excluded from the deliberations over the mine during the 1960s, the Namaliu government was prepared to stall on the use of such reactive measures, until such time as the NPLA had been given a reasonable chance to express their views on the mine's governance regime.

For reasons already stated, BCL viewed this strategic decision as fundamentally wrong. It would, they thought, validate the use of force, and cultivate an environment of rent-seeking. However, without social levers to impress their point upon the national government BCL was forced to rely on formal demands, coupled to bombastic threats. Carruthers' frustration at his company's relative impotence, showed in his 1990 appearance before an Australian parliamentary inquiry. 'The experience we have had in Bougainville', he claimed, 'is illustrative of the difficulty and complexity that a very primitive country has in trying to catch up quickly with the rest of the world' (Joint Committee on Foreign Affairs, Defence & Trade 1990: 432).

There was, of course, nothing 'primitive' about the situation in PNG. It was a wholly 'modern' crisis that was mediated through a cultural context which both BCL's Chairman and Managing Director tended to orientalise. Indeed, the wantok system used to engineer power centres in government – which BCL singularly failed to navigate – was not a throwback to traditional times. It was, and remains, an evolving modality of Melanesian class organisation, which allows diverse interests to mobilise and support each other through both vertical and horizontal patronage networks. BCL's failure to learn the language of power in PNG, cost it influence. As a result, the proposed Ministerial delegation went ahead, despite BCL's serious misgivings.

The Doi Special Ministerial Delegation

As the special Ministerial delegation prepared itself to visit Bougainville, NPLA activists escalated their campaign of industrial sabotage. Late in the evening of 1 December 1988, a high voltage transmission tower was toppled using explosives stolen from the BCL magazine, while the following day a radio repeater station was burnt down (Ewing 1989). The mine was now forced to run on its diesel reserve generators. As a result, the mine's concentrator could no longer function, and production stopped. BCL's Managing Director sent an urgent plea to Prime Minister Namaliu: 'My dear Prime Minister the present situation is one of an extremely severe deterioration of law and order. It would appear that this matter can only be dealt with by the National Government' (BCL 1988j).

While Prime Minister Namaliu was not prepared to abandon the Ministerial delegation, he did stiffen mine security. To that end, 49 mobile squad officers were sent to the island, bringing the total mobile squad contingent to 121 (BCL 1988k). The Prime Minister also issued a stern warning to landowner leaders: 'I will . . . use the full force of all internal security forces if those responsible for terrorism in Panguna do not cease their hideous activities promptly . . . My government will not tolerate wanton destruction of property, nor any threat to innocent lives . . . I will not withdraw the current police deployment in North Solomons until law and order is fully restored' (cited in Hiambohn 1988a: 1). To add teeth to the Prime Minister's warning, the Police Commissioner 'gave his men the order to "shoot to kill" anyone engaged in sabotage at the Bougainville Copper Mine' (cited in Hiambohn 1988b: 1).

It was in this tense environment that the special Ministerial delegation arrived in Bougainville on 4 December 1988. Included within its ranks were the Deputy Prime Minister, four Ministers,[3] four departmental secretaries[4] and the Police Commissioner. The peace talks were conducted over a period of four days. Negotiations proved tense, and by day three the Deputy Prime Minister was publicly ready to walk out on the process, claiming 'I seem to be wasting my time here' (cited in Rea 1988: 1). However, the next day an agreement was reached with the NPLA executive.

Following the breakthrough, a Ministerial party briefed the company. BCL was informed by the Deputy Prime Minister that, 'Ona and his group deny involvement in the sabotage and the explosion damage to the power poles . . . [however] Francis Ona and the youth have agreed to help the police recover the explosives' (BCL 1988l). In return for their assistance, it was explained, the national government had promised to review the *Bougainville Copper Agreement* and keep the mobile squads at bay. Before a shocked Managing Director, the Minister for Minerals and Energy proclaimed, 'I declare the BCA Review is started and [I] give the company time to rationalise their points and in the New Year we can commence discussions' (BCL 1988l). With matters now resolved to the government's satisfaction, the Deputy Prime Minister asked Cornelius to reopen the mine.

However, this was precisely the sort of result BCL had opposed since the 26 November attacks. Unsurprisingly, BCL's Managing Director 'expressed amazement at the outcome of the Ministerial party's actions over the past week or so' (BCL 1988l). Cornelius argued, 'the protested non-involvement of Francis Ona and his radical group in the acts of sabotage would seem highly questionable in the light of his offer to help Police recover the explosives and in his ability to guarantee no further acts against the company' (BCL 1988l). He added, 'the Government was virtually condoning [the militants'] actions' (BCL 1988l). Given the state of uncertainty surrounding the mine's security, Cornelius concluded his response asserting, 'BCL could not accept the assurances given, and certainly would not consider operating tonight' (BCL 1988l).

On this occasion BCL's Managing Director was not alone in his opposition. Indeed, there were sympathetic factions inside the police, and the PNG Defence Force (PNGDF), who felt rewarding law-breakers risked setting a dangerous precedent, at a time when PNG was trying to send the 'right' signals to international investors and other landowning communities (see Permanent Parliamentary Committee on National Emergency 1989a). One individual persuaded by this point of view was the Police Commissioner, Paul Tohian, who had accompanied the delegation to Bougainville (see Tohian 1990: 37).

Consequently, following the delegation's announcement, tempers simmered within the RPNGC contingent. These tensions reached boiling point when the North Solomons Premier made an impassioned speech at a function celebrating the peaceful resolution. According to ABC reporter, Sean Dorney (2000: 119), the Premier proclaimed, 'Francis Ona . . . "a contemporary hero" for Bougainville'. Kabui's remark evidently 'infuriated the police' (Dorney 2000: 119). Feeling the state had capitulated, the 'police then pulled the rug from underneath [the government] so to speak, and all hell broke loose' (PNG Minister A, personal communication, 5 July 2006). Fourteen landowners 'were arrested by the police on their way home from Premier Kabui's function' (Dorney 2000: 120). Early the next morning further police raids were conducted on four villages in the Guava region, where both Ona and Serero were from (Dorney 2000: 121).

One BCL manager recalls:

> The next morning [when] I woke up and went into work, there was a general state of alarm. We had been advised that during the night that Guava village had been raided, women had been molested, and Ona had gone bush. That's when the conflict started. The police went out on the hunt for Ona and shots were exchanged. Villages that were thought to be harbouring militants I think probably were torched. (BCL official D, 7 June 2006)

Francis Ona and his supporters took refuge from the police in the Kongara region of Bougainville, shielded by Damien Dameng's Me'ekamui Pontoku Onoring (May 2004: 279; Oliver 1991: 210).

Undeterred by the RPNGC's show of force, Serero, Ona and Dameng, distributed a communiqué to NPLA members on 10 December 1988.

It encouraged supporters to share the executive's revised position with villagers:

> BCL manipulates certain leaders . . . and bribes them at the expense of their people . . . The entitlements [from the mine] have been taken by a few land title holders . . . The system placed here will never go unchallenged . . . we demand here today that the mine be closed . . . with 28 days winding up time. (NPLA 1988h)

Just over a week later BCL and the national government also received a communiqué from the NPLA's executive, delivered through the former's internal mail system. It stated, 'we the landowners have recognised the Security personnel and the policemen who took part in raiding our village. We will kill these people' (BCL 1988m).

Now that the Doi delegation agreement was in pieces, and the militant landowners were threatening further action, Prime Minister Namaliu was anxious to see the company make a public show of confidence in his government. The Prime Minister informed BCL's Chairman that, 'while the final decision rests with the Company, in which the Government is a significant shareholder, my Government believes that you should seriously consider an early resumption of normal operations' (PNG national government 1988). In return for their cooperation, the Prime Minister assured BCL that the mobile squad contingent would remain on Bougainville.

BCL agreed to the Prime Minister's request, and reopened the mine on 11 December 1988. By then the mine had been closed for eight days. The cost of this closure, when combined with the damage caused by NPLA attacks, was reported to be K10 million (US$12 million) (Post-Courier 26 January 1989, p.2).

For the remainder of December security conditions on Bougainville were relatively stable. However, with several mobile squad units now stationed on the island, the mining company faced a new dilemma. One BCL executive recalls, 'when the riot police first arrived they had nothing. They just had their arms and a few clothes on board' (BCL official D, personal communication, 7 June 2006). As a result:

> It was expected that the company was going to feed, and house, and transport, these guys, and that added to the confusion. Is the police force acting for the company, ah, the company is feeding them, the company

is housing them, they are driving around in company vehicles . . . 'If you want us to drive around give us some fucking vehicles'. 'We are not going to be very effective if we are dying from hunger, we need to be fed'. So what do you do? (BCL official E, personal communication, 26 October 2006)

Some of BCL's managers were somewhat uncomfortable with the new arrangement. One General Manager remembers: 'These guys were ignorant thugs with guns, frightened ignorant thugs with guns, frightened ignorant thugs with guns a long way from home' (BCL official G, personal communication, 22 August 2006). While another senior manager notes: 'Basically the riot squads are thugs . . . Usually they were from other provinces, other tribes, who would come in and see it as an opportunity to come and beat up a few of these Bougainvilleans' (BCL official A, personal communication, 31 May 2006). That said, outside of the defence force, the mobile squads were the only unit equipped to prosecute the sort of measures BCL was asking for. Consequently, personal misgivings were put aside, as the company gradually became a logistic arm for the RPNGC on Bougainville.

To close off the year, BCL arranged a strategy meeting that included senior executives both past and present, to strategise a principled way forward. The executives agreed:

It is crucial for future investment in Papua New Guinea that the BCL Agreement be preserved as the basis for the long term, stable arrangements between BCL and Papua New Guinea. The Agreement should be made to work, and should not become an issue. It is important that additional money should not have to be paid over by BCL, as this would open the floodgates for the future erosion for all investment agreements. (BCL 1988n)

This, of course, mirrored the position of BCL's Chairman and Managing Director. Indeed throughout 1988 it was Cornelius and Carruthers' commitment to the existing legal infrastructure that had assumed priority, even to the point where they were prepared to support the deployment of 'ignorant thugs with guns'.

The depth of their commitment reflects, in part, the particular type of capital Cornelius and Carruthers were charged with responsibility of. Large-scale mining operations are distinguished by two critical features in this respect – the composition of capital it necessitates, and the temporal scale over which this capital-composition is valorised. On the former front, Marx usefully differentiates the value composition of productive capital using the terms constant capital and variable capital. The value invested in means of production is labelled by Marx constant capital, while the amount invested in labour-power, which productively consumes the means of production, is labelled variable capital. Marx explains the analytical basis of these categories:

> That part of capital . . . which is turned into means of production, i.e. the raw material, the auxiliary material and the instruments of labour, does not undergo any quantitative alteration of value in the process of production. For this reason, I call it the constant part of capital, or more briefly, constant capital. On the other hand, that part of capital which is turned into labour-power does undergo an alteration of value in the process of production. It both reproduces the equivalent of its own value and produces an excess, a surplus-value, which may itself vary, and be more or less according to circumstances. This part of capital is continually being transformed from a constant into a variable magnitude. I therefore call it . . . variable capital. (1976: 317)

However, because the rate of profit realised by individual capitals is not determined by the rate of surplus value they extract – other important mediations come into play here (Marx 1981: 258) – the precise source of surplus value is a matter of indifference. As Marx argues:

> Since the capitalist can exploit labour by advancing constant capital, and since he can valorize the constant capital only by advancing the variable, these are both one and the same in his eyes, and this is all the more so in that the actual degree of his profit is determined in relation not to his variable capital but to his total capital; not by the rate of surplus-value but by the rate of profit, which, as we shall see, may remain the same while expressing different rates of surplus-value. (1981: 133)

What matters then to individual capitals is that their investment – regardless of its value composition – is frugally applied to maximise returns (Marx 1981: 180).

With respect to large-scale mine operators, they function through a particularly high ratio of constant to variable capital, and are firmly rooted to specific geopolitical regions (in the case of BCL, the company had invested approximately K1 billion in and around Panguna (BCL official E, personal communication, 26 October 2006)). This large outlay of spatially anchored constant capital is productively consumed by living labour over a period of decades. The spatio-temporal dynamic of mining capital's valorisation, in this respect, means that those responsible for managing mining concerns must be sensitive to the political environments in which they will have to operate for an extended period. A sudden change of the political conditions – for example, a new taxation regime – could have a dramatic effect on the economy of their investment. As a result, mining concerns 'are looking for a stable mining legislation . . . and political stability' (BCL official E, personal communication, 26 October 2006).

In BCL's case, management realised from the very beginning that their investment in PNG required firm legal agreements which all layers of government – formal and informal – were committed to. As the company's first Chairman put it, 'there is no point in our starting an operation unless we are able to negotiate a reasonable and enduring agreement' (Sir Frank Espie cited in King, 1978: 100). This view continued to hold in 1988. Thus we find Carruthers and Cornelius taking a number of calculated risks – the threat of investment withdrawal, and a call out of the mobile squads – in an effort to force a political settlement sympathetic to the durability of the mine's governing framework.

Those present at the December meeting agreed with management's strategic priorities in this respect; given that the meeting included old hands like Paul Quodling and Don Vernon, this was perhaps not surprising. However, there was some criticism of how BCL had gone about operationalising these priorities. Those at the meeting argued, BCL needed to

> [S]trengthen . . . [its] liaison and communication with the National Government. The Chairman of BCL, as well as the M.D., will need to spend more time on this . . . [they also need to] improve relations with all the landowning villages in the vicinity of the operations (especially the younger generation), as well as other influential elements in the society. (BCL 1988n)

In other words, BCL needed to actualise the possibility of influence, inscribed in their economic position, by developing nodal points for influencing critical layers of political authority.

While backing this general strategy, BCL's Chairman remained doubtful of the company's chances. In a memorandum to Rio Tinto head, Sir Alistair

Frame, Carruthers' opined, 'right now I have a rather jaundiced view of the direction events are taking in PNG and of the erosion of the standards which were maintained for a number of years following the Australian administration' (CRA 1989a). This, of course, was the predictable reaction of a Chairman who had found his company increasingly in the political wilderness. Nevertheless, as we will shortly see, the political tide was not entirely against BCL.

The Formation of the Bougainville Revolutionary Army and the Murder of Deborah Dovonu

Back in November 1988, NPLA leaders had signalled their preparedness to 'die' in a bid to avoid the fate bestowed to 'African third world' nations. The December 1988 sneak attack had only served to reinforce the executive's resolve in this respect (see chapter 3). Consequently, during the early months of 1989, Francis Ona and his allies began to agitate for an armed struggle against both foreign and local capitalists. According to Regan (1996: 8), young Bougainvillean men, dispossessed of land and pushed onto the margins of the formal and informal economy, 'rushed to join' the militants (see also Regan 2006: 11). Additionally, Bougainvillean mine workers, aggrieved by the actions and attitudes of expatriate supervisors and managers, abandoned their post at BCL to take up arms with the rebels. A BCL worker from this period recalls:

> . . . [O]ne day an operator went missing. The next day he had joined the militants. Then a week later a colleague warned me not to come back to work on Saturday because the pay office was going to be burned. I caught a bus and went to my village and, true to his warning, the office was burnt. (Tanis 2005: 467)

However, militarily speaking the rebels most significant new recruits were a number of 'ex-soldiers and policemen [who] had come from all over the province to add their support' (Liria 1993: 74; see also May 1993: 29). One of these ex-soldiers was Sam Kauona. Kauona had joined the rebels after his cousin was killed by mobile squad officers in March 1989 (Liria 1993: 75). As a recruit training officer, and an ammunitions technical officer, he brought considerable military expertise to the rebel movement, and soon became Commander of their military faction (Liria 1993: 75–6). Under this leadership the rebels were moulded into an effective guerrilla force. With a broad spectrum of social actors now rallying behind the NPLA during the early months of 1989, Thompson and MacWilliam argue the conflict was proving to be much more than a 'landowner crisis':

> While many of the people [supporting Ona] were listed as being from Guava and Pakia villages (located within the mining lease of the Bougainville copper mine), many other villages from throughout the island were also represented, showing widespread support and representation for Ona's position. The broad representation, from the very beginning of the organisation, denies the contemporary popular mis-representation . . . [that the rebels were simply] a disenchanted landowner faction. The group drew support, albeit in a limited way, from a broad spectrum of landowners, peasants, workers and a significant lumpenproletariat. (1992: 14)

In a bid to signal their complex social composition and wider political aims, the rebels formally organised themselves under the banner, Bougainville Revolutionary Army (BRA). Francis Ona was appointed leader of the BRA, while he was closely advised by Damien Dameng, Sam Kauona, James Singko and Oscar Ampoi (BCL 1989i; Liria 1993: 74; Regan 1996). This Supreme Command, as it became known, based itself 'deep in the Kongara mountains' (Liria 1993: 76), and it headed a loose, pan-Bougainville organisational structure which consisted of a Northern, Central, Southern and Islands Command (Islands Command included Buka, Nissan and the Carteret Islands, just off Bougainville's coast) (Liria 1993: 76–7; see also Regan 1996: 9). Regional leaders reported to the Supreme Command, and in turn advised the village based militia units which lay within their jurisdiction.

Technically speaking, the BRA – which during 1989 was estimated to have between 200 and 500 'hardcore' members (Rogers 2002: 249) – was poorly armed. The rebels were initially forced to utilise .22 rifles, shotguns, homemade guns, fishing guns, traditional spears, bows and arrows, clubs and long handled axe (Liria 1993: 77; Rogers 2002: 250). However, as the insurgency grew, the BRA expanded its arsenal by capturing AR15s and SLRs from security force units, and through cleaning up stockpiles of weapons left on the island after the Second World War (Liria 1993: 44; Regan 2003: 149; Rogers 2002: 250). Counter-balancing the BRA's limited armoury was their guerrilla warfare training and the favourable fighting terrain, which consisted of steep, narrow ridgelines, covered in thick jungle, and heavy fog (Liria 1993: 71–2). This proved an ideal environment for the BRA to track security force patrols, and attack either the point-man or rear soldier, before blending back into the dense foliage (Liria 1993: 79; Rogers 2002: 250).

However, to survive in the jungle, and keep abreast of security force movements, the BRA needed civilian assistance. Supporting the rebels, in this respect, were 'the BRA's own [village] communities, whose economy of subsistence agriculture enabled them a ready food supply' (Regan 2003: 149). A PNG intelligence officer from the period recalls:

> The rebels . . . successfully manipulated the ordinary population, especially in the primary area of operation [central Bougainville], the PAO. Not only were they used effectively in normal guerrilla war tactics, that is, by the rebels hiding among them, using them as a source of information, food and general support, but also the people were convinced that the BRA was fighting for them. (Liria 1993: 84)

While the rebels organised themselves into a fighting force, they continued their attacks on mine property. However, BCL was not the only target. For example, vehicles and businesses owned by the prominent Bougainvillean entrepreneur, Severinus Ampaoi, were destroyed (Hriehwazi 1989a: 2), along with property belonging to Bougainville Forestry Limited, the Bougainville Development Corporation and the North Solomons Agricultural Foundation (CRA 1989c; Hriehwazi 1989a: 2). The rebels also began to target certain local leaders who had come out in opposition to the NPLA executive. For instance, during mid-January, Matthew Kove – who was a member of the OPLA, and the uncle of Francis Ona – was kidnapped from his home, 'the finest in Guava village', and then executed, presumably by BRA militants (Dorney 1998: 41; see also Okole 1990: 23).

In response to these events, the Namaliu government imposed a dusk to dawn curfew on 23 January 1989, which covered Kieta, Arawa, Loloho, Toniva, Aropa, Panguna and 22 surrounding villages.[5] Additionally, the island's mobile squad contingent was increased (Hriehwazi 1989b: 1). PNG's Police Commissioner warned the militants:

I am not here to play football . . . The time has come to take some very tough and stern action . . . I am asking the rebels to surrender immediately with all the stolen explosives. If they refuse to surrender and keep the explosives to use against police, property and innocent citizens, my men will shoot to kill . . . This is a special elite squad trained for everything and they will be walking around in plain clothes, and are armed to the teeth. (cited in Hriehwazi 1989b: 1)

Despite the Police Commissioner's belligerent posture, the rest of January and February were relatively uneventful.

However, the mood radically changed on 17 March 1989, when a Bougainvillean nurse, Deborah Dovonu, was stabbed to death while gardening. The suspected murderer was of Highlands origins (a mountainous region on the PNG mainland) (O'Callaghan 1989: 11), and part of a sizeable population of migrants who, since the 1950s, had travelled from the PNG mainland in search of work on Bougainville's plantations, and in its mining sector (AGA 1989: 2.7 & 4.6–4.7; Treadgold 1978: 14). Tanis explains:

Those living close to the established roads and cocoa plantations of the Tailings Lease [area] witnessed the arrival of *Ulugasi* (red skin) labourers (mainly from the Highlands and Sepik areas of the Papua New Guinea mainland). They came to work as truck drivers and plantation workers in the cocoa plantations owned by local people. Most of them got married to the locals and settled. When they married women they now became the *Motainala* (husband) with management responsibilities over the wife's resources. Often they confused their role as caretakers with the kind of authority they would have had in their patrilineal societies in their own provinces, thus wanting to be more powerful over their wives than is customary in Nagovisi society. At the same time they proved to be hard working and were soon controlling even the local food markets to the point that locals were buying food from them, and travelling in their PMVs (passenger motor vehicle). As soon as they settled they seemed to bring in their *wantoks* (people from their home area). As they grew in numbers they also grew in strength. In some cases they took over land without asking. This also threatened the security of the local people. By the end of 1988 most plantation owners were wishing that they had never recruited these labourers in the first place . . . Most of those who had bought vehicles in the late 1970s now had to ride on buses owned by *Ulugasina* (red skin) . . . During the 1988 provincial government elections one *Ulugasi* contested and won a seat in Arawa, where there was enough of a concentration of *Ulugasina* to vote him in to office. This was a grave shock to most Bougainvilleans. In the villages people worried that the *Ulugasina* were taking over government, and would control power, protect the squatter settlements and threaten customary land ownership. (2005: 458-9 & 466)

Indeed, with the pressures on Bougainvillean households intensifying during the 1980s, migrants from the mainland were increasingly seen as unwanted competition for Bougainville's finite resources, and thus became a popular outlet through which struggling villagers could vent their frustrations and fears (see, for example, Moulik 1977: 103; Tanis 2002). In this context, the murder of Deborah Dovonu ignited simmering racial tensions, triggering an intense episode of ethnic violence. 'All hell broke loose', recalls one mine manager (BCL official E, personal communication, 26 October 2006) – in revenge for the nurse's death a Bougainvillean man sprayed a rest house with bullets at the Aropa plantation, killing two Highland labourers, and injuring three others (Hriehwazi 1989c: 1). In response, migrant workers held a mass demonstration at Toniva on Bougainville's east coast, which descended into rioting and looting.

As the security situation deteriorated, the BRA began to step up its attacks on property. For example, on 21 March 1989, the Aropa Airport was burnt down, while at Buin on Bougainville's south coast a supermarket owned by Arawa Enterprises Limited,[6] and a police station, were destroyed. However, with the mobile squads now on 'shoot to kill' orders, the BRA sustained its first serious casualties – three rebel soldiers, reported to have been smuggling weapons (Second World War bombs), were shot dead by police, while seven others were injured (CRA 1989c; Hiambohn 1989b: 2).

According to *Islands Business* (March/April 1989, p.12), 'the troubles of March were a bad setback for Papua New Guinea in its attempts to shake away its worsening reputation as a place for investors to be wary of because of social and political instability and crime'. This argument was also being made in public statements issued by BCL and the Chamber of Mines and Petroleum (see Hiambohn 1989d: 2). There was, consequently, mounting pressure on Prime Minister Namaliu to act. With the prospects of a mediated solution now off the table, courtesy of the Police Commissioner, the Prime Minister ordered the security forces to arrest the BRA's leaders, in a bid to stem rising tensions (PNG Minister A, personal communication, 5 July 2006).

The Hunt for Francis Ona

With Prime Minister Namaliu now committed to the arrest of Francis Ona and his conspirators – almost four months after BCL's initial request – he announced on 21 March 1989:

> In recent days there have been unacceptable acts of violence which has resulted in loss of life, which fellow Papua New Guineans regard as most shameful and deplorable . . . All of these activities have created considerable uncertainty, bad feelings within the community, affected the nation's economy and harmed PNG's reputation and standing abroad . . . The National Executive Council views recent developments in the North Solomons province as being serious and has decided that firm action must be taken against those who have taken the law in to their own hands and threatened the lives of other citizens. (cited in Hiambohn 1989a: 2)

To help flush out the rebel contingent, RPNGC reinforcements were sent to the island, bringing the total police presence to around 300 (CRA 1989c). Additionally, on 26–27 March 1989, 200 PNGDF soldiers were deployed under section 204 of the *Constitution* (Rogers 2002: 215–6).[7] However, the Police Commissioner remained controller of operations, under advisement from a civilian committee (Liria 1993: 105). The army, therefore, initially played 'a subordinate role to the police on Bougainville, in keeping with the call-out provisions. Activities were on a small scale – patrols, roadblocks and the protection of key points – usually in the company of police' (Rogers 2002: 221).

Both the Police Commissioner and the Minister for Police exuded confidence before the press. In a joint statement they claimed, 'give us a month and we will get everything in order' (Hiambohn 1989c: 2). Underpinning the public bravado was a genuine belief that the RPNGC and the PNGDF would make light work of the BRA. Indeed, Rogers (2002: 245) claims, 'the PNGDF underestimated the militants, dismissing the rebel threat as little more than gossip'. This assessment is supported by a former PNGDF officer, involved in the operation: 'The main objective was to capture the militants, [but] no one had really given much thought to the implications. When we [actually] went in with the aim of capturing the militants, especially Francis Ona, we found out that it was not possible to achieve this aim' (PNGDF officer A, personal communication, 3 July 2006).

The initial over-confidence was perhaps not surprising given that the only other insurgency faced by PNG's security forces, was a secessionist uprising in neighbouring Vanuatu organised 'by the rag-bag forces of Jimmy Stephens' in 1980 (Turner 1990: 118–9). That insurgency had been put down through an 'operation [which] was a quick, inexpensive and a totally successful exercise of *force majeure* by the PNGDF' (MacQueen 1993: 137). However, neither Francis Ona or Sam Kauona were Jimmy Stephens, nor was the PNGDF the force it once was. A rapid process of localisation, continual budget shortfalls, the politicisation of its commanding ranks, a lowering in training standards and a failure to properly upkeep equipment, all meant that the PNGDF was in a poor state of preparedness for any significant contingency (Maketu 1988: 9; May 1993: 20; PNG Department of Defence 1989: 37; Rogers 2002: 127–8). As a former PNGDF officer explains:

> Bougainville was a test to the government, to the nation, to the defence force, and we were not trained, we were not prepared, both in training, in our *modus operandi*. We didn't have the logistics to go in, but when you have a call out, and the national government wants you to go, what do you do? You have to go. (PNGDF officer B, personal communication, 8 July 2006)

Compounding matters, the RPNGC mobile squads – which the PNGDF was supporting – had no experience fighting armed guerrillas. Indeed, with an operating strategy that hinged on numbers, firepower and fear, the mobile squads distinctly lacked the tactical capacity to counter elusive, well trained opponents.

Overconfident and underprepared, employing a strategy which was based on an overly narrow appreciation of the BRA's strength, the security forces 'suffered straight away' (PNGDF officer B, personal communication, 8 July 2006). While the BRA leadership eluded capture, loosely organised guerrilla bands used mobility and surprise to confront security force patrols. As a result, the PNGDF endured its first fatalities in the crisis on 6 April 1989, when Second Lieutenant Steven Yandu and Private Martin Romas were killed in a confrontation with around 20 BRA members (Callick 1989a: 3). Shocked PNGDF comrades were embittered by the deaths. Liria (1993: 66) recalls, 'we [the security forces] were now mercilessly committed against the BRA, the initial reluctance having gone the same day the two bodies were flown in from Aropa'.

Prime Minister Namaliu echoed the feelings of PNGDF soldiers in a statement to the media:

> Weapons meant to kill are now being used against other Papua New Guineans . . . No responsible government can allow this to continue . . . Those responsible for bringing in, and using, such weapons can expect no mercy or sympathy . . . Our nation depends upon the unity of all its people, all its regions and all its provinces, for its future . . . Unity is strength. Division can only lead to disaster. (cited in Hiambohn 1989e: 2)

True to his word, 'no mercy' was offered. Realising that arrest was now off the cards, the security forces were given the green light to conduct punitive, paramilitary style operations, which had become a standard government response to serious civil disturbances during the 1980s. A *Post-Courier* report signalled the new approach:

> The Defence Force has launched a full-scale military operation against militant landowners in North Solomons Province as trouble continues to rock the copper-rich Bougainville . . . At a news conference . . . Mr Marsipal [Defence Minister] confirmed that the soldiers had been ordered to 'shoot and kill' if they ran into guerrilla type attacks . . . He said the order was issued by the Force's Chief of Operations, Colonel Leo Nuia, on Friday – a day after two of his men were shot dead in an ambush. (Rea 1989a)

Operational efforts now focused on attacking villages suspected of supporting the BRA, using a tactical style known colloquially as 'destructions' (see Standish 1994: 72–3). 'Destructions' generally involve the burning down of village homes and crops, the killing of livestock and can escalate to the harming or execution of civilians (RPNGC officer, personal communication, 10 July 2006). Initially, this punitive technology was primarily used by the RPNGC's mobile squads, nevertheless, 'destructions' were also absorbed into the PNGDF's tactical cultural during the 1980s, following their participation in a number of combined security force operations (Rogers 2002: 251). Underpinning its use on Bougainville, was a belief that the militants were simply rent-seeking, consequently, the destruction of property, and the disruption of everyday life, would negate any perceived benefit that may accrue to landowners from the use of force (Rogers 2002: 252).

During April 1989, these 'destructions' took a heavy toll on villages in the mine lease area. An executive who surveyed the damage recalls, 'forty, fifty villages, and the crops [were destroyed]. The villages were varying from five or six houses to twenty or thirty houses' (BCL official A, personal communication, 31 May 2006). Explaining the security force approach, a *senior* PNGDF officer argues:

> I think that the aim of the burning down of houses, was for people to come back, and say look sorry I have done wrong, can you people [the national government] help ... They [the security forces] were not heavy handed, but they just went out and I think they were doing the right thing by burning down several [sic] houses. (PNGDF officer A, personal communication, 3 July 2006)

However, local residents did not respond to these attacks as predicted: 'In the case of Bougainville, you destroy the house, and people would be happy to stay in the bush, or go to another village' (PNGDF officer A, personal communication, 3 July 2006). Indeed, according to Forster (1992: 369), 'as the defence force destroyed villages they fed the ranks of the Bougainville Revolutionary Army, which became the new home of the youth from destroyed villages'.

Displaced villagers who chose not to live in the jungle or join the BRA, were forced into makeshift government camps, which became known as 'care centres'. Initially, these 'care centres' were a spontaneous result of security force destructions. However, during July 1989 they would become an integral part of the PNGDF's strategy to separate the BRA from its civilian support base. Nevertheless, in the interim, as more and more villages were torched, these camps were hastily put together in the town of Arawa to house and contain the displaced.

BCL, through its benevolent offshoot, the Bougainville Copper Foundation (BCF), assisted with the construction and administration of the camps. One manager recalls,

> The burning and desecrations was such that we had to construct evacuation centres for the refugees, and we had to feed the refugees ... they had no means of sustenance, nowhere to stay, men, women and

kids . . . [The government would say] 'you tell us how much you spend on feeding them, we'll reimburse you'. Bullshit, never did. (BCL official A, personal communication, 31 May 2006)

In addition to BCF donations, company staff also made personal contributions. One BCL executive recalls, 'my wife and I, together with dozens of other people, when villages got burnt around the mine, we went out and provided our blankets to them [in the care centres], and all sorts of things' (BCL official D, personal communication, 7 June 2006). So effectively the company's charitable arm and employees were aiding the displaced, while contrariwise BCL was logistically supporting the security force units destroying homes en masse.

Nevertheless, despite BCL's support, life inside the 'care centres' was reported to be harsh. Refugees were denied freedom of movement, and freedom of association. A local schoolteacher Marilyn Havini, recalls:

The care centres started when I was in Arawa and the first ones were in Arawa in 1989 . . . They roped off four [areas], market town, they roped off our church areas and they roped off the Independence Oval, our football field for the kids. They [were] herded, as they destroyed the actual villages around the mine to teach them a lesson, treating it like tribal warfare. To teach the people a lesson not to complain about the mine . . . They moved the people in behind those fences [around the 'care centres'] and we drove past them day in, day out, not at night because we were under the curfew. We were not allowed any contact through those fences. (1997: 31)

When two priests attempted to meet parishioners held inside the 'care centres', Havini notes, they were set upon by the security forces:

Fathers Tangin and Woerster, both German Catholic priests, had plucked up the courage earlier in the day to go together to the care centre (or detention camp) in Arawa and demand to visit their parishioners. No one in the community had been allowed access to these villagers, who had been incarcerated for weeks since being flushed out of their mountain-top villages. The soldiers had refused even these priests entry and, when they insisted that they had a legitimate right to check on the welfare of their parishioners, the soldiers attacked them most cruelly. Both priests were hit on the head with the butts of automatic rifles, blood was pouring out of their ears, and Fr Tangin was later evacuated to Europe for medical treatment to assist his recovery from trauma. (2003: 18)

The conditions inside 'care centres' would worsen considerably over the following years.

Village destructions and detentions camps, however, were not the only illicit component of security force operations during April 1989, the RPNGC and PNGDF also harassed prominent landowners, and young men suspected of supporting the BRA. Amnesty International documents a number of key examples from the April period:

Bernard Devata and his cousin Steven Ona were arrested during a police raid on Kobuan village in the evening of 8 April 1989. According to witnesses, the two men went with the police without resistance, but were punched and beaten with rifle butts a short distance from the village. Bernard Devata's jaw was fractured, reportedly as a result of a beating by police officers; Steven Ona also sustained an injury to the jaw. Bernard Devata was treated by doctors at the North Solomons Medical Centre who found that his injuries were 'consistent with the history of a heavy blow to the left hand side of the face'. (1990a: 28)

The day after this attack on Bernard Devata and Steven Ona, Amnesty International reports:

In an incident near Orami village on 9 April 1989, according to eyewitness testimony, a family of four including a two year old child, was surrounded by a unit of 15 to 20 soldiers, detained for several hours and subjected to verbal and physical abuse. The leader of the unit reportedly accused William Mungtu of supplying the rebels and, together with other soldiers, repeatedly threatened his life, while beating and kicking him. (1990a: 29)

Women were not exempt from the violence either. For example, Barbara Kinima, the wife of a prominent landowner Francis Kinima, was raped by mobile squad officers on 24 April 1989.[8] An angry North Solomons Premier, related this event to the national government the following day, stating 'members of [the] riot squads, with masks on their faces, held up Francis Kinima's family, and raped his wife' (PNG National Government 1989a;

Zale 1997: 21). The national government made no attempt to prosecute those mobile squad officers responsible for these crimes, indeed security force impunity would become an enduring theme in the years to come.

Trouble on 'Australia's Patch'

During the March–April 1989 period, as the violence escalated on Bougainville, the crisis began to attract the attention of Prime Minister Robert Hawke's government in Australia. Indeed, Australia had maintained a close relationship with its former colony with whom it shared enduring economic and political ties. This close relationship was reflected in the considerable financial,[9] and military,[10] support that Australia continued to provide PNG with. A senior Australian diplomat stationed in Australia's Port Moresby based High Commission (HC) during the period recalls:

> I often try to think of a relationship anywhere else in the world that was like that [with PNG], for example . . . [where a country has] a primary strategic interest; a major economic role, those days close to 30 to 40 percent of their [PNG's] budget was our budget support, and the trade was massive, so there was trade dependency; education [connections] w[ere] still quite strong. Where [else do] you have those connections, with the ex-colonial thing wrapped into geographic proximity, where else? (HC official A, personal communication, 25 August 2006)[11]

However, as the Bougainville crisis came to a head, the strategic significance of the Pacific region – and PNG – was evolving. Indeed, during this period the Australian government had embarked upon a concerted push to increase its international punch, in a bid to support a range of ambitious neoliberal reforms being implemented at home.[12]

To that end, the Foreign Minister at the time, Gareth Evans, argued his government could have a disproportionate impact on global and regional governance regimes by carefully targeting priority areas, using a range of tactics (Evans 1997: 18). Foremost among these tactics was 'coalition building with "like-minded" countries' (Evans 1993). 'The goal is constant', Evans claimed, 'maximising the influence that can be brought to bear by Australia and those countries which share interests with us' (Evans 1993).

To help engineer, and shape, these coalitions, the Hawke government drew heavily on its special relationship with the US. One of the more cerebral Ministers from the Hawke era, Kim Beazley, explains:

The key to understanding the Hawke Government's foreign affairs and defence policies lies in its handling of American alliance issue. The alliance was a reference point in the formulation of regional policies, and of its global agenda, particularly arms control, and a presence in the defence strategy of self-reliance. Even the efforts to link domestic economic reforms with reform of the international trading system saw the relationship utilised in some key initiatives, including a willingness to cite the valuable role Australia performed in the Western alliance in arguments with the United States over its farm support legislation as Australia began to assert leadership in the campaign for international free trade under the Cairns group. American involvement was an important part of the major Hawke initiative in the Asia/Pacific, for the creation of APEC, which combined overtly regional trade liberalisation policy and, more subliminally, a regional security objective. (Beazley 2003: 350)

Yet as Beazley notes here US patronage was not given freely, it depended upon Australia playing a productive role in the Western alliance. One way Australia contributed in this respect, was by shouldering the security 'burden' for 'its patch'. A senior Australian Department of Defence (ADoD) official notes, 'with the Americans we always made a big thing about our security support activities in Papua New Guinea and the rest of the South Pacific. We are looking after our patch, we are on the job' (ADoD official A, personal communication, 23 August 2006). However, by taking on this regional role, it was now expected that Australia would actively steward western interests and values in the region. Evans (1989) noted Australia's willingness in this respect, in an important Ministerial statement on regional security. He remarked,

Australia's interest will continue to lie not in resisting change [in the South Pacific] but in seeking to ensure that it takes place by peaceful means and within a framework of essentially, democratic political systems. It will also be in our interest that involvement by external powers, large or small, be constructive rather than disruptive. (Evans 1989: 45)

Albeit in the cloaked language of liberalism, this statement signalled to Australia's allies that the Hawke government was prepared to use its disproportionate military, politico-military, diplomatic, and economic capabilities, to strategically shape the domestic environment of its neighbours when the situation demanded it.

In this light, the crisis on Bougainville represented one of the first major tests for Australia, as it assumed the role of proactive sub-imperial power in a calculated bid to increase its leverage with key allies (principally the US). A senior official from Australia's Prime Minister's Department (DPMC) explains:

> Certainly there were concerns that this [crisis] might detrimentally impact on Australian citizens and capital, but once again this was a security concern, it was not going to break the Australian economy. What appeared significant was the fact that the South Pacific was Australia's patch, and a barometer of its credibility as an international force. (DPMC official, personal communication, 15 September 2006)

A senior Department of Foreign Affairs and Trade (DFAT) official concurs:

> This was our primary area of responsibility, and primary area of perceived responsibility. So if we were going to have credibility in the conduct of our foreign policy elsewhere, we pretty well had to have strong credibility to begin with in our own neighbourhood, in terms of having good policy, applied in a coherent and effective way, that won the respect of the locals and demonstrated a capacity on our part to deal with a situation that might arise, and not to require outside assistance to do so. That was that. (DFAT official A, personal communication, 11 July 2007)

Yet as important as PNG had become to Australia's international political strategy, the Hawke government had not predicted the troubles on Bougainville, nor was there much intelligence to hand on the key protagonists (HC official B, personal communication, 6 September 2006). A senior defence official recalls, 'it was as if a bunch of kids who didn't like the school headmaster had gone back to the school and trashed it' (ADoD official B, personal communication, 29 August 2006). In light of Australia's strategic interests in the crisis, it was incumbent upon the Australian High

Commission in Port Moresby to get its officials onto the island in order to gather more concrete data and advise expatriate resident.[13]

Initially, Australia faced some resistance in this respect, owing to a personal feud between Australia's High Commissioner and PNG's Foreign Secretary (HC official B, personal communication, 6 September 2006). Nevertheless, the replacement of Australia's High Commissioner in April 1989, soothed tensions. The new High Commissioner, Allan Taylor, proved an adept hand at managing relations with the PNG government. Under Taylor's stewardship the Australian High Commission was able to set up a mini-office on Bougainville and place intelligence operatives on the island. There were also dozens of Australian Defence Force (ADF) officers on loan with the PNGDF and stationed in the High Commission, closely monitoring the situation. A senior RPNGC officer recalls, 'their intelligence was better than ours. Their intelligence was much better and efficient' (RPNGC official, personal communication, 10 July 2006). The establishment of this beachhead on Bougainville placed the Australian government in a position where it was poised to become a more influential player in the conflict as the security situation worsened over the coming months.

Conclusion

The destruction of villages, the torture of civilians, the rape of local women, and the internment of displaced peoples, constituted a chaotic, but nonetheless systematic and in many cases sanctioned campaign of terror, designed to deter support for the BRA. For those in the primary area of operations, this 'policy . . . of terrorising the population of the North Solomons through random acts of brutalising innocent victims', generated fear, resentment and anger (The Bougainville Justice and Peace Committee cited in Hiambohn 1989f: 1). Indeed, one resident from the mine lease area recalls: 'The mobile riot squad burnt down villages, assaulted and harassed villagers, and some even raped women during raids. I was feeling cross, frustrated, angry and soon these feelings were becoming deeper and deeper . . . Instead of dealing with the militant landowners, the government attacked the people' (Tanis 2002).

In short, the Namaliu government had only succeeded in cultivating a social environment more receptive to the rebels' message. Indeed, this was not organised criminality or tribal warfare, the BRA was made up of motivated activists who over the period of years carefully laid the foundations for a substantive uprising. Therefore, the sudden application of violence did not scuttle the nascent rebel movement, to the contrary, it concentrated the resolve of BRA leaders, and reinforced the socio-ethnic bonds of solidarity being forged to brace the resistance movement.

As a result, by the end of April 1989 an insurgency was beginning to enter the ascendancy on Bougainville, courtesy, in part, of the crimes committed by the PNG state. Caught in the political whirlpool, of course, was BCL; the company, however, was by no means an innocent party to the April events. The blankets and aid given to displaced villagers, was small recompense for the logistic assistance being supplied to the security forces. This support would only intensify as the conflict entered into a new, more bloodier phase.

Indeed, by the end of April 1989, Bougainville was standing on the edge of a dangerous precipice. Back in August 1987, it seemed unlikely that a number of local activists from some of the more remote areas of the Crown Prince Ranges could ignite a movement of provincial significance; yet a range of explainable determinates fertilised growing tensions in the mine lease area, creating the possibility of such a substantive rebellion. That said, the depth and breadth of this rebellion was a matter still to be decided. A protracted war, in short, was by no means a certainty. Nevertheless, as we will see, the probabilities of tensions cooling on Bougainville were declining significantly as powerful new domestic and international forces began to intervene.

5

A Tale of Two Solutions – Counterinsurgency Warfare and the Bougainville Package

Following the acts of industrial sabotage during November 1988, the trajectory of events on Bougainville was increasingly informed by forces from within the PNG state. In this respect, a conciliatory political bloc had formed, spearheaded by the Minister for Provincial Affairs and the North Solomons Premier, both of whom were leveraging the tensions on Bougainville to achieve a better economic deal for their province. As we observed, this bloc's influence on the national government's strategic response, provoked a significant clash with BCL's management. However, during 1989 the political landscape within the state was beginning to fracture between opposing power networks. In opposition to the conciliators, was an emerging hawk faction as they became known who believed a zero-tolerance approach needed to be adopted.

At first, champions of this strategic perspective were based in the state's security apparatus. However, during May 1989 a carefully timed political ultimatum, delivered by a senior power-broker within the Namaliu coalition, launched two vocal hawks into senior cabinet positions. In contrast to the reactive paramilitary response of April 1989, this increasingly powerful hawk faction had formulated a coherent military strategy for bringing the BRA to heal. Nevertheless, that said, even after the events of April 1989, influential conciliators in cabinet still felt the BRA could be successfully isolated through political, rather than military, means.

Accordingly, this chapter focuses in significant part on these two blocs as they compete during mid-1989 to impress their perspective on the national government's strategic response. Mediating their relative influence, in this respect, were historically generated dependencies that tied the PNG state to mining capital. Indeed, while mining capital in the particular form of

BCL had initially proven impotent in the face of strong opposition within the PNG state, as we will see mining capital in general was more difficult to ignore.

Other social processes also conditioned the state's strategic response during this period. For instance, Australia emerged as a major player – indeed, having assessed the situation on Bougainville, the Australian government began to cautiously place its weight behind the hawk faction. This weight came in the form of high level diplomatic representations, a substantial package of military aid specifically designed to increase the offensive capacity of the PNGDF on Bougainville, and the influence exerted by ADF officers stationed at the Port Moresby High Commission and in line positions within the PNGDF. Additionally, BCL was far from an absent force. Indeed, as taxation revenues from the mine began to dry up, and the PNGDF became more reliant on BCL's assets, the company's management was given frequent access to Ministers and senior PNGDF Commanders, to voice their concerns and views.

The intersecting rhythms of these different social forces, as we will see, allowed the hawks to assume the temporal ascendancy during mid-1989, out of which emerged the first of a series of major military offensives that included graphic extra-judicial killings, the aerial bombing of villages, and the use of white-phosphorous mortar rounds.

However, to begin this chapter we examine the political strategy which had been engineered by the conciliators, in a bid to isolate the BRA in the immediate aftermath of the April 'law and order operations'. This strategy centred around an expansive peace package – the Bougainville Package – which would be formally presented to people in the mine lease area at the end of April 1989. The BRA's reaction to this strategy, as we will see, was an important initial trigger for the hawk's rise to power.

The Bougainville Package

During 1988, the NPLA had mobilised significant support through its quite vocal efforts to address the simple reproduction squeeze being experienced by struggling households in the mine lease area. BCL's opposition to any serious concession outside the formal seven-year review process, only served to confirm the company's reputation as a 'ruthless exploiter' (Momis 1987a). In this light, the Bougainville Package represented an ambitious attempt by the national government to win back some of the popular ground from the BRA, by addressing the immediate needs of rural communities in the mine lease area.

By any stretch, the package included a generous range of benefits. In return for their support, villagers in the mine lease area would be given an equity stake in BCL,[1] Arawa Enterprise Limited and the North Solomons Agriculture Foundation;[2] a one-off contribution of K20 million from BCL (around US$24 million); national government mineral royalties, which would be split 50/50 between the North Solomons provincial government and the landowners; an increase in the payment made by BCL into the Non-Renewable Resource Fund from 50 toea per tonne to K1.00 per tonne; employment, training and contract preference; the extension of water and electric supply to unserviced villages; and the upgrade of schools, health centres, hospitals and roads (Auna 1989; CRA 1989b; PNG National Government 1989a). One commentator valued the entire package at K400 million (approximately US$480 million) (Callick 1989d: 29). Its core features were presented to BCL on 17 April 1989, and approved by the National Executive Council on 21 April 1989 (PNG National Government 1989a).[3]

However, before it could be presented to communities in the mine lease area, the Namaliu government wanted to organise a powerful local lobby for the package – a unified PLA. Indeed, for the previous two years the PLA split had driven a wedge in the mine lease communities, as NPLA leaders employed concepts such as class, exploitation, inequality and greed to articulate social divisions. In so doing, the hegemonic function of 'tradition' and 'development', upon which the OPLA executive had been anointed, were thrown into question. The Namaliu government wanted to dull the resulting tensions, by co-opting moderate sections of the NPLA into a regional bloc with OPLA members. An undivided PLA, the government hoped, could then set about addressing the immediate needs of peasant households, while restoring to power leaders prepared to work within the existing order, and legal arrangements.

In an effort to launch this initiative, a roundtable forum was organised for 25 April 1989. In attendance were senior national and provincial government officials,[4] in addition to representatives from the OPLA and the NPLA.[5] However, the NPLA's Chairlady and Secretary were notable by their absence. Their view was articulated to the forum in a letter read out by the Prime Minister. Written by Perpetua Serero, it invited the Prime Minister to Panguna for face to face negotiations. As a show of good faith, however, Serero asked Namaliu to withdraw the security forces from Bougainville.

NPLA representatives present at the forum were keen to distance themselves from Ona and Serero's position. A former associate of Francis Ona, Wendelinus Bitanuma, informed the gathering, 'it is not the Premier's [Kabui] wish or our wish, but Francis Ona's own decision to resist and demonstrate' (PNG National Government 1989a). Of course, this was the sort of internal schism which the national government wanted to capitalise on. Indeed, the Minister for Minerals and Energy advised NPLA and OPLA representatives, 'let us not talk about the "old" and the "new" Association. We should talk about *one* Association representing the landowners' (PNG National Government 1989a).

Around seven hours was spent discussing the package's features with OPLA and NPLA representatives. By the end of the meeting, all parties noted their general approval. The Deputy Prime Minister concluded the forum stating, 'we hope the package can be explained to the people of Bougainville and to the people of PNG in general so that we have peace and harmony as we develop into the future' (PNG National Government 1989a).

This was a promising start for the Namaliu government initiative. However, the social divisions which had been building in the landowning communities for decades, could not be dulled overnight. For the government's plan to work, the NPLA and OPLA would need time and space to overcome historic frictions. Moreover, there was the additional complication of BCL. As it stood, the Bougainville Package would make significant changes to the mine's governing framework. For it to succeed, the government would need to win support from BCL's risk-averse management.

This demanded quite delicate diplomacy. Comments from the 25 April forum, however, indicated BCL would be approached in a more mercenary fashion. For example, the Minister for Minerals and Energy told the forum, 'we ought to sought matters out and *tell* BCL, this is the new arrangement agreed to by everybody, which it must accept' (PNG National Government 1989a). While the North Solomons Premier added, 'if we can get BCL to fund the whole lot, the better, as BCL has caused a lot of internal problems' (PNG National Government 1989a). However, when BCL was finally briefed on the forum's outcomes in a series of exchanges during late April and early May 1989, a more subtle tact was employed.

As a result, the company was generally supportive of the Bougainville Package. Indeed, BCL's Chairman wrote to Rio Tinto head office in London noting his approval of the government's strategy, which was to 'isolate the militants by offering a package of benefits to the genuine landowners and the Provincial Government' (CRA 1989c). Nevertheless, BCL still had a number of reservations. Principally, there was concern that the Bougainville Package altered some of the core principles upon which the mine operated. Specifically, since the mine's beginning the company had paid landowners restitution for the use of, and damage to, their land, while improved social services and public works ('benefits'), were to be delivered by the national and provincial governments, employing the taxes, duties and dividends they received from BCL (BCL 1989a; Cornelius 1989). If the company was to now shoulder some of the burden for delivering benefits to the community, this was something they believed needed to be addressed through the seven year review of the *Bougainville Copper Agreement* (BCL 1989a). However, before this important step could be taken the company continued to argue that the landowner uprising had to be suppressed. Indeed, in a memorandum to BCL's Chairman, Cornelius argues, 'further concessions ahead of settlement of the security problems is just not on. To do otherwise, would be irresponsible as it invites those demanding benefits to say it is not enough and just keep asking for more' (BCL 1989d).

Nevertheless, the general thrust of the Bougainville Package had obtained broad acceptance from some of the mine's key stakeholders, including BCL. A solid foundation had, therefore, been established for implementing a technology critical to the conciliators' political solution. However, there were clearly quite complicated conceptual, legal and political challenges which still needed to be resolved, before the package could be signed and implemented. This would demand multi-level negotiations between local leaders, provincial government representatives, national government officials, and BCL. Thus, above all else, what the Bougainville Package now needed was time – time for the PLA's unification, time for the finalisation of package details, and time for villages in the mine lease area to be convinced of the Bougainville Package's merits. However, time was not a privilege the BRA was going to afford the national government and their allies in the mine lease area.

Seceding From Papua New Guinea

Following a public statement announcing the Bougainville Package at the end of April 1989, the Namaliu government withdrew the security forces from offensive duties (Hiambohn 1989g: 2). Further violence threatened to undermine the groundwork being laid to unite the PLA and champion the peace package. Nevertheless, serious damage had already been done, and many on the island were attaching racialised meanings to the security forces' actions. Tanis (2002) explains, 'as the majority of the policemen and later the Defence Force were non-Bougainvillean, in the eyes of the people, Bougainville was being attacked by the *retskins* [redskins], who were using the power of the State' (see also, Lawson 1992). As a result, Regan (2003: 144–45) argues, the security force operations:

[H]ad little direct impact on the small but growing groups of 'militants' supporting Francis Ona, but provoked outrage and further violence among the general populace, many of whom until then had little reason to support Ona's nascent movement. Within weeks of being deployed, the almost entirely non-Bougainvillean riot squads became seen as the enemy by many. There was rapid mobilization behind Ona, who emerged as the central leader of a diverse coalition of actors and interests.

With a growing support base, on 28 April 1989, Francis Ona (1990a: 7–8) announced the BRA's alternative to the Bougainville Package:

Our only option now is . . . to break away from PNG. Only then we will be able to save the lives of our people in Bougainville . . . Please be united and walk side by side. Forget about your differences and struggle for only one goal: to save the lives of our future generations. Keep talking to the radio and newsmen. Tell the Government that the time for round-table talks is over. We want to break away from PNG so that we will rule our own lives and economy.

One immediate allure of secession, was that it offered a solution to the deep sense of racial insecurity provoked by security force violence. However, ethno-nationalism had deeper historical roots than this. Indeed, the goal of independent statehood for Bougainville received its first major articulation during the 1960s and 1970s by a formally educated generation of provincial leaders (see, for example, Hannett 1975), eager to carve out a powerful position for the North Solomons in PNG's state system (Ghai and Regan 2000: 244 & 251; Oliver 1991: 183). However, at this stage secession was primarily utilised to bend the stick towards decentralisation, rather than as a realisable goal in itself. As a result, when the national government granted constitutional protection to the provincial government system in early 1976, secession drifted off the immediate political agenda on Bougainville (Ghai and Regan 2000: 251).

Nevertheless, the formal articulation of this political project inspired the imagination of peasant households struggling to cope with the simple reproduction squeeze. Indeed, in a survey conducted by Moulik it was found:

> Both among Kieta and Buin respondents a large majority of those who desired an independent Bougainville were . . . generally very dissatisfied with their present lot and with their motivational and resource constraints they were unable to compete with the 'entrepreneurs' and 'peasant' farmers. Most were prepared to work in industry or in the mine as a way out. But here also they seemed to face severe competition from the privileged group of their own fellow-Bougainvilleans (entrepreneur and peasant farmer) and also from non-Bougainvillean Papua New Guineans . . . Consequently this is the group that makes elaborate demands for government assistance, for preferences to 'sons of the soil', for wage employment in Bougainville. The reasons for such a strong desire for a politically independent Bougainville was simple: a politically independent government would enforce a deliberate policy of preference to 'sons of the soil' for wage employment opportunities in Bougainville and would lessen the competition in the job market by excluding non-Bougainvillean Papua New Guineans. (1977: 176–7)

Given that the inequalities, grievances, and frustrations catalogued here by Moulik had only intensified during the 1980s (Tanis 2005: 269), the BRA's re-articulation of Bougainvillean ethno-nationalism, provided a popular mechanism for politically institutionalising the sort of radical social changes that the NPLA leadership had been championing since late 1987. Furthermore, an appeal to ethnic identity also had the potential to dull divisions within the broad inter-class, inter-regional coalition, secession necessarily involved.

However, the rebels' brand of nationalism was certainly not going to find universal acceptance. Indeed, the BRA's drive to expropriate capital and disengage from the PNG national economy, promised to negatively affect a broad range of actors including local businessmen, politicians, bureaucrats, wealthy farmers and workers. Those adversely affected could, in turn, employ familial allegiances to dissuade wantoks from banding behind the BRA. Therefore, while secession had the potential to institutionalise the BRA's agenda at a province wide level, local opposition could unpick their influence employing powerful kinship networks.

That said, secession was only one of several strategies which the BRA could employ to diffuse the threat posed by the Bougainville Package. Another, was to step up their attacks on the mine. As the national and provincial governments both depended on the mine's revenues, were the BCL operation to endure a prolonged closure, neither party could afford to engage in the long and delicate discussions needed to make the Bougainville Package a reality. The mine's vulnerability to attack was, in effect, the government's Achilles heel. Unsurprisingly, just a fortnight after the Bougainville Package had been formally announced, the BRA instituted a second major wave of attacks on the mine. However, this time both mine property and personnel were targeted.

The Second Shutdown of the Panguna Mine

The second round of mine attacks began at around noon on 15 May 1989, the same day that a provincial government select committee issued a report rejecting secession (North Solomons Provincial Government 1989: 5). The attacks started with a Toyota Hilux and bulldozer being set on fire, but escalated soon after when two contract grass-cutters received serious arrow wounds. Employee safety in the mine pit area was now compromised. Accordingly, the Bougainville Mining Workers Union (BMWU) and the Bougainville Copper Limited National Staff Association (NSA) immediately withdrew labour from the outer and inner pit areas. The unions then held a meeting with management. Cornelius recalls:

> The meeting lasted for some 30 minutes during which we attempted to reassure the Unionists about the security and safety of BCL employees and requested that the Unions reconsider their decision to withdraw BCL labour from mine operations. In response, Mr Tagornom [BMWU] and Mr Dumit [NSA] advised me that the recently concluded meeting of BMWU and NSA members had resolved to support their respective Union management's call for a cessation of work and that this stop work would remain until the conclusion of the night shift on Friday 19th May, 1989. (1989)

The unions' decision was confirmed the following day at members' meetings in Panguna, Arawa and Loloho. Furthermore, it was also agreed that unless BCL could 'guarantee total safety and security of Union members', then the 'company should consider a reduction in work volume to day shift work only' (Cornelius 1989).

These resolutions were immediately relayed to the Prime Minister (BMWU 1989). In response, Namaliu assured BCL that extra security had been organised for Panguna, Arawa, Loloho and the Port–Mine Access Road, to ensure a rapid return to work on 19 May 1989 (Cornelius 1989). Company management was not satisfied, they felt the national government was too far removed from the ground, and did not fully appreciate just how serious the security situation had become. Consequently, BCL's Managing Director wrote to the Prime Minister, stating:

> I believe it is important to realise that no matter how much security is provided in and around the work areas, the total safety and security of employees cannot be guaranteed. This is, of course, because the law and order problem has not been brought under control . . . No guarantee can be given [to the unions] nor can we be persuasive I believe, in a situation where out-of-control militants are still ranging free in the jungles immediately around our operations and communities . . . Protection for such a diverse operation as ours is virtually impossible against a determined militant effort and I believe [that we] can at best . . . [maintain] a holding position while the law and order problem is being addressed. I appreciate the efforts the Government is taking in endeavouring to resolve this extremely serious situation but I believe it is only proper that I point out the concerns we all have concerning the still well out-of-control lawlessness that pervades the Province. (BCL 1989b)

The Prime Minister responded to Cornelius the next day:

> I would like to reiterate the commitment and assurance given by my government to safeguard the safety of the personnel and all employees on Bougainville as contained in my letter of 23rd December 1988. As a further measure to this effect I have instructed the deployment of the security forces well in excess of 180 personnel to safeguard the security and safety of the workers and their families . . . I am more than satisfied, that this measure is adequate. (PNG National Government 1989b)

With a guarantee from the Prime Minister in hand, production at the mine restarted following the unions' stop-work period. Almost immediately the BRA resumed its attacks on the mine. Initially, a transmission pylon was toppled on 21 May 1989. The next morning a BCL bus convoy ferrying employees to the mine was ambushed, leaving eight people seriously injured (Cornelius 1989). After the ambush, another transmission pylon was brought down. A repair team sent to fix the damage was withdrawn, when BRA militants were found to be operating close by.

As a result of this new wave of mine attacks, management held a meeting on 24 May 1989. Cornelius (1989) recalls, 'I decided that BCL would not . . . be directing linesmen to work in the field again until BCL was satisfied that the law and order problems had been resolved'. On 25 May, the company determined that it would take approximately three to four weeks to repair the damage to mine infrastructure, once law and order had been restored. Accordingly, management elected to put all non-essential employees (around 3,500) on early leave. Only 700 workers remained at the mine, in preparation for repair work (CRA 1989d).

Now that the BRA's attacks were growing in intensity, scale and daring, those lobbying to politically isolate the rebels through the Bougainville Package, were finding that the timeframe which their approach demanded was chafing against material realities on the ground. Nevertheless, in a final effort to retrieve the spiralling situation, and create the necessary space for the peace package, the national government called a 15 day truce beginning on 25 May 1989. An influential Bougainvillean priest, Bishop Gregory Singkai, was sent to negotiate with Francis Ona (Oliver 1991: 215–6). According to Oliver:

> Ona was agreeable to the truce offer and the opportunity to negotiate . . . [providing] that the mine remain closed; that a referendum be held to decide whether Bougainvilleans wished to secede from PNG; and that Ona be granted, not only safety during negotiations, but immunity from prosecution later on. (1991: 216)

The Prime Minister would only agree to the last of these conditions, as a result the negotiations ended (indeed, it would be another twelve years before these conditions were formally accepted by the PNG government).

Consequently, by June 1989, six months after Namaliu had registered his preference for a negotiated solution – the events of March/April not withstanding – the government's conciliatory strategy was becoming less defensible before domestic and international audiences. Indeed with the mine shutdown indefinitely, the PNG state now faced an impending fiscal crisis. Moreover, the potential ripple effects of the uprising on other parts of the country and investor confidence were also becoming palpable concerns. In these fertile soils the hawks seized a significant foothold in cabinet during May 1989.

Ascending Hawks and the 'Delicate Flower' of Investor Confidence

Like his predecessor, Paias Wingti, Prime Minister Namaliu could not circumvent the volatile character of governing coalitions in PNG, where votes of no confidence are rarely off the agenda. In this respect, one particular member of Namaliu's government, the Papuan MP Ted Diro, had substantial influence over the coalition's stability (PNG Minister B, personal communication, 9 July 2006).

Diro began his role in public life during 1963 when he joined the Pacific Islands Regiment (PIR). At that time, PIR was formally part of the Australian army. Having received training in Australia, Diro was fast tracked up the officer ranks in preparation for PNG's independence. He became Commander of the PNGDF in 1975, at the age of 33. Diro remained at the post for six years, quitting as Commander in 1981 to pursue a political career. By the 1987 national elections, Diro headed the People's Action Party, which had successfully monopolised seats within PNG's Papua region (Saffu 1998a: 440). As a result, his support was a critical boost for any leader hoping to form a governing coalition.[6] Indeed Kolma argues:

> [Diro] has been a prominent figure . . . in determining the course of
> Governments . . . The man who now heads the Opposition, Paias Wingti,
> was put in power in 1987 by Diro and dethroned in July the next year by
> Diro. Current Prime Minister, Rabbie Namaliu, gained power with Diro's
> help. (1991: 8; see also Saffu 1998a)

Despite his political influence, Diro was forced to resign from Cabinet in November 1987, after the Barnett inquiry into PNG's forestry industry, 'alleged that he improperly granted timber rights, thereby gaining monetarily and had subsequently lied to the Commission of Inquiry' (Thompson and MacWilliam 1992 26–7). However, by 1989 Diro was eager to return. To that end, during May 1989,

> Ted Diro reportedly issued one of his familiar ultimatums: Namaliu
> should reshuffle and bring him back into cabinet by 4pm on Friday, 19
> May, or he would move his group out of the coalition . . . With sixteen

members, PAP [People's Action Party] was the third largest group in the
Parliament . . . Namaliu caved in. (Saffu 1998b: 477)[7]

The cabinet reshuffle was formally announced on 20 May 1989. Ted
Diro was appointed 'Minister of State with special responsibility for the
North Solomons crisis' (Kaputin 1992: 3.21). Accompanying Diro into
cabinet was another important addition, Ben Sabumei, who was made
Minister for Defence. Together they joined the Minister for Police to form
a powerful hawk faction within the NEC. They were backed by the Police
Commissioner, and the PNGDF's senior command.

This increasingly influential hawk faction was not opposed to the
neoliberal regime championed by Prime Minister Namaliu. The point
of contention lay over its implementation. Like the Prime Minister and
the Minister for Provincial Affairs, they accepted political rule needed
to be shared with customary authorities. However, unlike the latter two
leaders, the hawk faction felt when customary authorities crossed the
lawful boundaries set for coordinating rule, a strong example needed to
be set. This was a calculated nod to the instrumental role violence could
play in the government's development policy. As one member of the hawk
faction explains:

> See you have to understand the Melanesian psyche. You give them an
> inch, they will want a foot. You can't do it. The Germans, the British New
> Guinea Constabulary, as soon as they [the local population] step out of
> line which is not in conformity with the general administration policies,
> they banged them so hard, they hit them so hard, that they wouldn't do
> it again. (PNG Minister B, personal communication, 9 July 2006)

Applying the lessons of early 'pacification', they continue:

> The leader has to be open, he has to be benevolent, he has to empower
> the people to create wealth for themselves, to give them power, and allow
> them to use their initiative to get on with their job. At the same time
> you spell out the rules, and you say these are the rules, if you step over
> this mark, then I am going to clobber you. (PNG Minister B, personal
> communication, 9 July 2006)

This view was formally outlined by Ted Diro to parliament in July 1990:

> Any initiative that may be taken by this Government or any future
> government to promote economic development can have no lasting

impact if many of the forces which are tearing our nation apart are not dealt with firmly and with purpose ... It is ... alarming to see demands, threats and even confrontation becoming the main feature of discussions about resource development in this country. Why is it that our people resort to smashing down government buildings and properties just to gain public support or to press a demand for a grievance ... The serious law and order problems we are facing, can raise doubts about whether many of the major resource developments will actually materialise as we expect . . . I fully support policies that are being put in place by the Government to promote economic development . . . but as I have advocated for some time, those and many other policy initiatives must be strongly reinforced by efforts to promote a true sense of national unity and national purpose. Together with this, a much more aggressive campaign on law and order. (Hansard, 2 July 1990)

Applying this principle to Bougainville, the hawk faction believed that any form of concession to the militants risked setting a dangerous precedent, which may encourage other communities to emulate the BRA's tactics.[8] Indeed, the PNGDF Commander who would lead the first major strike against the rebels, argued: 'If the Bougainville militants are not effectively neutralised or eliminated so as to serve as a deterrent to would-be militant landowners in other parts of PNG, the whole of the Bougainville operation would have been a failure, setting a bad precedent' (Dotaona cited in Permanent Parliamentary Committee on National Emergency 1989a; see also Tohian 1990: 37).[9]

Adding to the urgency of the situation was the BRA's strategic use of secession to realise their political aims. National unity was an imperative the hawks were keen to guard. The loss of a crucial border region, and its potential domino effect on other 'wayward' regions of PNG, weighed on the mind of the hawk faction (PNG Minister B, personal communication, 9 July 2006). Accordingly, they proposed to cabinet that 'the weight of PNG' should be 'felt by Bougainville' (PNG Minister B, personal communication, 9 July 2006). It would appear BCL had finally found a strong ally in cabinet.

The conciliator faction, represented principally by the Prime Minister and the Minister for Provincial Affairs, and to a lesser extent by the Minister for Justice, opposed the hawks' militaristic perspective. Indeed, the conciliators remained committed to the overarching framework of the Bougainville Package, and to negotiations with BRA leaders. Also, they were more hesitant – though not strictly opposed – to embark upon the sort of brutal course of action making an example of the BRA entailed. However, now that the mine was facing a prolonged closure, immediate material realities began to intervene into cabinet politics. Indeed, by the beginning of June 1989 the mine had been shut for over a fortnight. With the security situation still a long way from being resolved, a closure measured in months, rather than weeks, appeared the most likely outcome. Given that 'the Bougainville copper mine was the single most important component of the [national] economy' (Connell 1997: 29), this prolonged closure spelt economic disaster for PNG. A senior official from PNG's Prime Minister's Department (PMD) explains: '[The closure] was going to have a great impact . . . there was no [other] mine opening at that time when this thing blew up. Lihir had just come on, but they were still going through the first stage of development. Ok Tedi was coming out, but was not generating revenue' (PMD official A, personal communication, 10 July 2006).

Accordingly, revenues from the Panguna mine were especially vital. As Rabbie Namaliu observed in 1995:

At the time of its closure, the Bougainville Copper Mine provided about 10 per cent of Papua New Guinea's GDP, 36 per cent of export earnings, and 24 per cent of total government revenue. Virtually overnight, a massive slice of the whole economy – a third of exports, and a quarter of revenue – was taken away. The situation was made even worse by the destruction of the North Solomons cocoa and copra export industries, and by the massive cost of the security force operations on Bougainville. (1995: 61)

However, the crisis on Bougainville not only endangered a vital revenue stream, it also threatened to significantly increase international perceptions of risk in PNG. Rio Tinto, for example, sold out of PNG's Lihir mine as a result of the crisis.[10] Other companies were also registering the effects of Bougainville – in notes compiled for its August 1989 board meeting Papuan Oil Search Ltd remarked:

The greatest danger to the Iagifu-Hedinia [oil] project is the effect Bougainville may have on the macro-economy of PNG and to investor/financier confidence at a time when we are attempting to raise project finance . . . Investor confidence is a delicate flower and we are concerned that the Iagifu-Hedinia financing may be damaged. (Papuan Oil Search Ltd 1989)

Given that the Namaliu government was relying on foreign investment flows to help PNG overcome poor economic growth rates (PMD official B, personal communication, 4 July 2006), the 'delicate flower' of investor confidence was at the forefront of the Prime Minister's mind. He was, 'very concerned, extremely concerned . . . that it [closure of the Panguna mine] would affect investment adversely' (PNG Minister A, personal communication, 5 July 2006). So were the hawks, 'well it [mine closure] was terrible. It could send the wrong signals around the country, and I thought that was going to be damaging for the investment climate here in PNG' (PNG Minister B, personal communication, 9 July 2006). In this sense the mine's closure was perceived as a double threat, it could cripple the state fiscally, while also drying up sources of foreign investment. This dual threat gave the hawk faction powerful collateral when pursuing a military solution in cabinet. Adding to their weight, was the intervention of the Australian government.

Australia and PNG's Bougainville Policy

During 1989 the Australian government had publicly signalled its preparedness, under certain conditions, to intervene in its immediate region when 'change' threatened 'democratic political systems' (Evans 1989: 22 & 45). In his important statement on regional security, the Australian Foreign Minister listed the 'instruments of policy' which his government could employ in this respect (Evans 1989: 15). At the very top was 'military capability' (Evans 1989: 15), indeed the Foreign Minister boasted: 'Australia's defence budget . . . [is] roughly equivalent to that of all the ASEAN countries combined (just as is our GDP). Australia's military expenditure in 1987 was US$4.98 billion, compared with Indonesia's US$1.37 billion, Malaysia's US$937 million, the Philippines' US$458 million, Thailand's US$1.66 billion, and Singapore's (1986 figures) US$1.01 billion' (Evans 1989: 17–8).

Yet just as democracy seemed to be buckling in PNG under the weight of an armed insurrection, the Hawke government adopted a curiously aloof public posture. Writing in 1990, the head of the Department of Foreign Affairs and Trade's (DFAT) Pacific, Africa and Middle East division, claimed:

'Our guiding principle . . . has been that the dispute is an internal matter for PNG, one that the Papua New Guinea Government should resolve for itself without outside involvement' (Smith 1990: 69). He continued, 'the Australian Government has made it absolutely clear that it would not intervene in the dispute, and has not been asked to do so' (Smith 1990: 69). Australia's Foreign Minister and Prime Minister reinforced this line in numerous public statements. For instance, Evans informed parliament in 1990 that 'Papua New Guinea's policy on Bougainville is an internal matter for the Government of Papua New Guinea and has always been regarded so by the Australian Government' (Hansard, 8 November 1990), while Prime Minister Hawke (1990) remarked to a Port Moresby press conference, 'it would not be proper for us to interfere in the way you manage your affairs'.

These statements belied geopolitical reality. The truth was Bougainville had significant implications for Australia's strategic interests (see chapter 4). Compounding matters, senior Australian security planners believed that PNG was materially unable to resolve the matter without outside assistance. Accordingly, PNG's Bougainville policy was very much a matter of direct concern for the Hawke government.

A senior Defence official recalls, 'when the shit hit the fan in 1989 it [Bougainville] was a fairly big part of one's life for a while there' (ADoD official C, personal communication, 31 August 2006). Inside the Australian High Commission, Bougainville's significance was even more pronounced, 'a huge amount of my time, and a huge amount of the High Commission's time [was devoted to Bougainville]. It was almost 24 hours a day' (HC official A, personal communication, 25 August 2006). Acutely aware that PNG's security forces were struggling to cope with the uprising, these officials had to assess the precise threat posed by the BRA and the appropriate balance of measures which Australia could deploy in response.

To that end, it was the potential strain which the secessionist bid could place on PNG's fragile state apparatus that was judged to be the most immediate and palpable threat to regional security. A senior Defence official explains:

[Would] the country tear itself to pieces in frustration at not being able to deal with the Bougainville problem? Would the army break? We were really worried about that. Would morale totally collapse? It certainly went through some low points. Would there be mutinies? There were a couple of little ones, but not really big and well organised ones. Would the army fight the police, and vice versa? (ADoD official A, personal communication, 23 August 2006)

According to this official such questions 'became more important than Bougainville itself, because the rest of the country was infected with this virus transmitted through Bougainville' (ADoD official A, personal communication, 23 August 2006).

Were the PNG state to indeed collapse it was feared that 'the logic of a region in turmoil . . . would apply' (DFAT official B, personal communication, 21 September 2006). Most immediately this would pose a significant danger to resident expatriates and Australian investment,[11] which stood at around AU$1.8 billion (approximately US$1.3 billion) (Evans 1990: 7). More generally, and arguably more significantly, Australia's regional leadership aspirations would be seriously compromised, at a time when its enhanced security role was being trumpeted in international centres of power. As a result, Australian officials 'never doubted that we had pretty strong interests in the situation' (ADoD official C, personal communication, 31 August 2006). Nevertheless, for a number of reasons, ADF intervention was deemed inappropriate:

> That was seriously discussed, but dismissed because we took the view that it would be incredibly costly in people, and it would put us in some very complex and ambiguous situations of shooting Bougainvilleans without really knowing whether we were shooting the right Bougainvilleans or not. This was 1990 and not 2006, and we were still very cautious about deployments, you know the post-Vietnam reluctance to deploy forces overseas was very high. (ADoD official C, personal communication, 31 August 2006)

However, as the rebels were unwilling to drop their demand for the mine's closure and a referendum over independence – which was a necessary presupposition for any mediated settlement with the PNG state – Australia's interest did warrant a large investment in a PNGDF-led military campaign.

To that end, senior-level talks were held with PNG's newly instated Defence Minister, Ben Sabumei. One member of the hawk faction recalls, 'a couple of weeks' after Sabumei's appointment the Australian government 'sent a jet up here, and I think that was a pretty serious move' (PNG Minister C, personal communication, 8 July 2006). 'Immediately they took' the Defence Minister down to Australia for 'long discussions' (PNG

Minister C, personal communication, 8 July 2006). In particular, Australia's preference for military force was made known to Sabumei. Indeed, a senior High Commission official recalls: 'We were certainly pushing them . . . to get more troops over there and that sort of thing. Ben Sabumei was the [Defence] Minister, and I used to see him all the time saying, "get your people over there"' (HC official A, personal communication, 25 August 2006).

The Hawke government had a variety of levers available to it to ensure that this advice was taken seriously, not least among them was Australia's considerable financial assistance to PNG. However, the PNG government was coming around to Australia's point of view by its own volition. Indeed, the economic consequences of the mine's closure, the recent cabinet reshuffle, the BRA's apparent stubbornness, and the existing security force contingent's weakness, as a whole ensured that by June 1989, political momentum was beginning to favour an increased PNGDF presence on Bougainville.

Nevertheless, Australian officials were still mindful that their growing role in the Bougainville arrangements had to be tactfully managed. A senior ADF officer explains:

I have been involved with PNG for ten or fifteen years, and we did have some bureaucrats who were, perhaps heavy handed is the wrong word, but who were a little bit dictatorial. And that does build resentment, particularly with some Papua New Guineans. I mean its natural, you don't want to be told what to do. (personal communication, 1 September 2006)

Consequently, a Socratic method was employed when pushing Australia's Bougainville agenda:

You would sit down, if you were with Ben [Sabumei the Defence Minister], you'd say 'gee things aren't going too well in Bougainville tell me about the problems'. 'Well we have been looking at that too. We wondered whether maybe a bit of extra training here [would help], and we noticed you have a limitation in equipment, would you think some extra this and that would help enhance your capability'. So you know you'd go through that, and by the time you had finished the discussions over a couple of days of gentle probing, you'd come up with a list and you could say at the end of it, 'well I reckon Ben that were we to do this, and contribute this, and make this happen, you'd probably be more comfortable about your ability to handle the Bougainville situation, is that right?' 'Yes'. 'Oh ok what do you reckon we try and organise a meeting between Ministers'. (ADoD official B, personal communication, 29 August 2006)

The package of military assistance negotiated through these carefully styled diplomatic interventions was delivered during 1989–91. It proved vital to the counterinsurgency efforts on Bougainville:

> I mean the logistic support that we supplied to the PNGDF during that time was very large and significant, without our support they couldn't have done what they did . . . We'd be training them at training camps, we'd be supplying them with weapons, we'd be supplying them with uniforms, everything. And then we'd say these companies are now fit to be used, let's send them now to Bougainville. We'd even fly them to Bougainville for God's sake, so we would facilitate everything. (ADF officer, personal communication, 1 September 2006)

Naturally, spending on Australia's Defence Cooperation Program (DCP) with PNG rose substantially during 1989–91.[12] For example, in 1988–89 the Australian government spent AU$27.4 million (US$21 million) on military assistance to PNG, this rose to AU$37.9 (US$29) in 1989–90, and AU$52.1 (US$41) in 1990–91 (Australian Department of Defence 1995: Appendix H). 'Oh yeah, it [DCP] was ramped up,' recalls a senior ADF officer. 'Oh yeah, we put a lot more money into it, we put a lot more advisors in there to train the companies, the logistic support was just sort of flowing over' (personal communication, 1 September 2006). Admittedly not all this extra expenditure was earmarked for the Bougainville operations. Nevertheless, a large part of it was. For instance, the increase helped to fund the delivery and maintenance of four Iroquois helicopters (including privately contracted Australian pilots); the training of 450 new PNGDF recruits (by the ADF); the replenishment of the PNGDF's exhausted arms/ammunition stock; and the provision of extra ADF personnel to help relieve the strain which Bougainville was placing on the defence forces' administrative/logistic systems.

This support came at a critical time for the PNG state. A Minister from the Namaliu government recalls:

So after they [PNG security forces] got there [Bougainville], within a few months [we thought] 'oh shit, now they are over there we better bloody find money to feed them, pay their allowance, pay for the fuel'. We looked around and said 'shit, we could be fighting these buggers for years, and we don't have enough men'. So it dawned on the defence force Commander and his people that we didn't have enough. (PNG Minister C, personal communication, 8 July 2006)

As a result of this dilemma, the Minister argues, 'we had to look towards Australia, we did not know where else to go for help, in terms of arming our people, getting our defence force better prepared, training our soldiers for combat' (PNG Minister C, personal communication, 8 July 2006).

Australia's willingness to engage, in this respect, ensured the PNGDF had the necessary resources, equipment and numbers, to launch a series of increasingly more aggressive counterinsurgency offensives during 1989–91; once, that is, the necessary political will had been cultivated. As one Minister from the Namaliu government put it, 'without the DCP, Papua New Guinea was not in the position to effectively carry out the war on Bougainville' (PNG Minister C, personal communication, 8 July 2006). Of course, it would be overstating matters to say Australia was solely liable for the subsequent crimes committed by the security forces on Bougainville, nevertheless, their actions and support were a critical determinate in facilitating and amplifying the latter deviant tactics, which it is important to add, the Hawke government was acutely aware of.

The Namaliu Government Declares a State of Emergency

With Australia's weight falling behind the hawk faction, the latter now had the means to operationalise a military solution. However, this solution still required cabinet assent, and strong opposition remained. On the other hand, the conciliators' indecision was provoking serious anxiety in the foreign investment community, whose allegiances was critical to the national economy's health. Speaking at a more general level, Block observes in this latter respect:

Those who manage the state apparatus – regardless of their own political ideology – are dependent on the maintenance of some reasonable level of economic activity. This is true for two reasons. First, the capacity of the state to finance itself through taxation or borrowing depends on the state of the economy. If economic activity is in decline, that state will have difficulty maintaining its revenues at an adequate level. Second, public support for a regime will decline sharply if the regime presides over a serious drop in the level of economic activity, with a parallel rise in unemployment and shortages of key goods . . . In a capitalist economy the level of economic activity is largely determined by the private investment decisions of capitalists. This means that capitalists, in their collective role as investors, have a veto over state policies in that their failure to invest at adequate levels can create major political problems for the state managers. This discourages state managers from taking actions that might seriously decrease the rate of investment. It also means that state managers have a direct interest in using their power to facilitate investment, since their own continued power rests on a healthy economy. (1977: 15; see also Callinicos 2007: 544; Harvey 1982: 153; Michalowski 2010: 6)

In PNG, the vertical (between MPs and supporters) and horizontal systems of patrimony (between wantoks), so critical to regional power blocs and bourgeoisie accumulation strategies, was coming to depend more overtly on foreign investment in the extractive industries. The loss of revenues from Bougainville, and the danger of a boycott from mining capital, thus threatened to throw PNG's political-economy into a state of crisis. Harvey notes in this respect:

[S]tates that stray too far from organizational forms and from policies that are consistent with the circulation of capital, the preservation of the distributional arrangements of capitalism and the sustained production of surplus value soon find themselves in financial difficulty. Financial crisis . . . turns out to be the means whereby the discipline of capital can ultimately be imposed on any state apparatus that remains within the orbit of capitalist relations of production. (1982: 153)

In the case of PNG, the threat of financial collapse placed the hawks in the temporal ascendancy, as they were the ones who offered the most direct method for routing the BRA and restoring investor confidence in the national government. In this strategic light, the Minister of State was able to obtain cabinet assent for a military solution in June 1989.

The news of this critical shift in the national political terrain was delivered personally to BCL by its principal engineers – the Minister of State, the Minister for Defence, the Minister for Police, the Police Commissioner and Colonel Lima Dotaona. The Minister of State did not mince words. The military, Diro claimed, was in the process of developing a plan to 'neutralise' the BRA utilising 'brutal firepower'; he added, 'the time for talking is over' (BCL 1989c).

The company, broadly speaking, was supportive of the news, indeed only weeks earlier BCL's Chairman had complained that 'at no stage was martial law, or even a state of emergency imposed' during the March/April 'law and order' operations (CRA 1989c). Moreover, the company's Managing Director had firmly stated throughout the second wave of mine attacks that no way forward could be found until the militants had been brought to heal. As the meeting concluded the Minister of State opined, 'it will take time, democracy' (BCL 1989c).

Following the BCL briefing, Prime Minister Namaliu publicly signalled that a major PNGDF offensive was afoot (Rea 1989b: 1). In response, Francis Ona warned the Prime Minister in a handwritten letter:

> You must be blamed for the loss of lives, harassment of people and destruction of their properties. Your security forces have passed the limits allowed in the international laws of justice and peace as stated in the Geneva Convention . . . We are going to try to defend ourselves from your well equipped security forces. We will use whatever we have on hand. (BRA 1989)

With the BRA standing its ground, the NEC declared a State of Emergency (SOE) (under section 228 of the Constitution), which took effect at 6.00 a.m. on 26 June 1989 (Hansard, 4 July 1989). The SOE declaration empowered the Namaliu government to make such laws, regulations and orders as was necessary to deal with the crisis, without however prejudicing the Constitution's human rights provisions.

The PNGDF's Counterinsurgency Strategy

With a SOE declared, the security forces' command structure changed. Formally, the Police Commissioner, stationed in Port Moresby, was the SOE Controller. However, now that the crisis was officially deemed a 'military problem demanding a military solution' (Minister for Defence, Hansard, 11 July 1989), actual control over security force operations was placed in the hands of the Deputy Controller, Colonel Lima Dotaona. A senior officer involved in the operation recalls, 'everybody understood, with no doubt in their mind, that police cannot go out into the jungle there and try to combat or capture the rebels, so it ended up the defence force coming to the front of the operation' (PNGDF officer A, personal communication, 3 July 2006).

To that end, Colonel Dotaona arrived on Bougainville in late June to take command of the security forces. Immediately Dotaona employed his emergency powers to order:

> All sea and air transport in and out of the province shall use the Buka or Kieta wharves and Buka or Aropa airports. Coastal vessels and the provincial air service provided by Bougair are exempted. Movement of all people, vehicles, animals and property on roads within the province shall be subjected to scrutiny or checks, by force if necessary. All organised gatherings or meetings except sport, church services and funerals have been banned unless approved by Colonel Dotaona. The 10pm to 5am curfew will remain in force until further notice. (cited in Hriehwazi 1989d: 2)

These emergency orders were the administrative preface for a series of counterinsurgency operations that the PNGDF had planned for July and August. Codenamed *Nakmai Maimai* ('lonely leader') (3–10 July), *Bull Dog*[13] (12–28 July) and *Kisim Dog* ('to catch the dog') (4–15 August), these offensives first aimed to clear the villages immediately around the mine site, beginning with communities along the Port–Mine Access Road (which connected Panguna to important urban and port areas on Bougainville's east coast). This would then be followed by a broader sweep and clear of all villages in the general mine site area. It was hoped that the evacuation of villages would prevent the BRA from operating near the mine site, which was an essential precondition for the initiation of mine repair work (Liria 1993: 47; Rogers 2002: 226). Once the mine site areas had been cleared, leaving the remaining BRA forces concentrated south-east in the Kongara region, a full-scale military assault would then be launched to rout the BRA – this was the goal of operation *Kisim Dog* (Rogers 2002: 233–4).

It is unclear how many troops were available for these three operations. Oliver (1991: 219) claims there were, '500 soldiers, 200 riot police, and an unspecified number of Correctional Service officers'. However, a national government SOE report, records a more modest contingency size of 265 soldiers, 276 riot police, and 100 Correctional Service officers (Namaliu 1989: Appendix 9). In support of the latter estimate is Liria's (1993: 24) observation that PNGDF numbers were 'frighteningly low' (Australia's military aid would only take effect gradually over the course of 1989–90). Regardless of exact numbers PNGDF soldiers, supported by mobile squad officers, were to conduct the three counterinsurgency operations, while RPNGC regulars and Correctional Service officers helped with static guard duties around the mine, in conjunction with BCL's unarmed security staff (Liria 1993: 106; Rogers 2002: 125).

Operation Nakmai Maimai

The day before operation *Nakmai Maimai* – which aimed to clear 16 villages along the Port–Mine Access Road – Colonel Dotaona announced to a press conference, 'if people refused to move [from their village], they would be forcefully moved' (Hriehwazi 1989e: 2). Despite the Colonel's warning, villagers failed to appear at designated pick-up areas the next morning (Liria 1993: 84). Some risked staying in their homes, while others fled into the jungle in anticipation of the military's arrival. As a result, the PNGDF was forced to manually clear each village along the twelve kilometre stretch of road. According to Rogers (2002: 224–5), any resident BRA troop was afforded ample time to slip away.

With the Port–Mine Access Road clear, on 6 July 1989, the PNGDF moved their Forward Tactical Headquarters from Aropa on the coast, to the heart of the mine, Panguna (Liria 1993: 68). This was an important strategic move, now the PNGDF could draw upon BCL's considerable logistic resources (Liria 1993: 68). According to Rogers (2002: 224) 'the long period of deployment and the growing numbers of contingent personnel had seriously strained the [military's] logistics system. Even before Bougainville, the defence system was not capable of supporting large numbers in the field, especially over extended periods'. Like with the mobile squads, BCL helped fill the logistic gaps. Indeed, one senior official from the Prime Minister's Department acknowledges: 'We relied heavily on some of the civilian facilities provided by the company. They did everything, I mean we spent lots and lots of money, to provide backup support services for the operation, but the defence force was not properly equipped at all' (PMD official B, personal communication, 4 July 2006). This assessment is supported by a counterpart in the PNGDF, who argues: 'The support of the mine was so significant, it augmented where the national government was lacking' (PNGDF officer B, personal communication, 8 July 2006).

From BCL's perspective, helping the PNGDF to secure the mine area and apprehend the BRA leadership, was the only option available to them in light of the company's long-held strategic position, that concessions could not be given ahead of a definitive solution to the insurgency. Unsurprisingly, PNG's defence force was granted generous use of BCL assets:

> The reality was, 'we can't do our thing because we haven't got vehicles'. So we'd give them vehicles. 'Ah, we haven't got radios so we can't communicate'. So we'd give them two way radios. 'Ah, we can't support our men over here, we haven't got enough provisions'. So we'd put them in the mess, we'd feed them in the mess, we'd provide them with accommodation. We did everything they asked of us to make their life more comfortable, and better able to manage through, with transport, communications, provisions, whatever, fuel. You know we gave them everything, because as a far as we saw it we were hoping that they were going to solve the situation, so we could start operating again. So we supported them every way we could. (BCL official E, personal communication, 26 October 2006)

Brigadier-General (retired) Singirok,[14] who was involved in the 1989 operations, concurs:

> In addition to demanding PNGDF involvement, BCL actively participated in the combat efforts to quell the uprising and reopen the mine. For example, BCL provided the infrastructure and bases for the operations, including the command post, battalion headquarters, essential high-speed and mobile communications, and troop barracks. BCL also provided the logistical support to store and issue combat supplies including ammunition and gear. BCL provided food and rations. BCL quartered the troops. BCL provided medical facilities. BCL provided troop transport vehicles for the patrol and combat operations. BCL provided the fuel (petrol and diesel) for the operations. BCL also provided one helicopter which was used as a gunship, the heli-pad and a few helicopter pilots to assist in the combat operations, field reconnaissance, casualty evacuation, troop insertion and extraction, and supply of critical supplies (e.g. ammunition) to troops in the fields around Panguna. (2001)

Full details of BCL's contributions are outlined in Table 5.1

Table 5.1 The Organisational Integration of BCL and the PNGDF (Source: Yauka Aluambo Liria 2001).

BCL Asset	PNGDF Usage
Administration Block No.4, Top Floor.	Battalion Headquarters, 20 to 30 personnel.
Kusito Camp	Troop accommodation.
Camp 10	Storage space for ammunition, combat clothing and equipment, rations, medical kits, tents and other combat supplies.
BCL Mess Halls (three in total)	The provision of food for troops.
BCL Telephones, Facsimiles, Photocopiers, and Walkie-Talkie Radios	PNGDF communication.
BCL Motor Vehicles.	Troop transport for both defensive and offensive operations. One vehicle per rifle company was supplied.
BCL Pump Stations (Petrol and Diesel) at Loloho and Panguna.	Refuelling of PNGDF/BCL vehicles.
BCL Hospital (Panguna)	Treatment of wounded troops.
BCL Helicopters (including BCL pilots)	Field reconnaissance, casualty evacuation, troop insertion into combat zones, troop extraction from the field, and the supply of combat critical supplies to troops in the field.[15]
Secretarial Services	Typing up etc. of PNGDF reports/internal documents.

As the PNGDF and BCL became increasingly entwined, the company's management met regularly with senior government and PNGDF officials to discuss operational matters (BCL official A, personal communication, 31 May 2006). While mine security was a priority, these meetings also afforded BCL an opportunity to voice its opinion on offensive strategy. For instance, on 13 July 1989, BCL's Managing Director 'told PM that Security Forces Offensive activities OK and should continue', though Cornelius adds: 'Our other main area of concern is the fact that there are some ex-Army people involved with the militants. These people have to be apprehended to make a real breakthrough . . . It is most important that the ex-Army people and Damien Damen, the charismatic Cult Leader must be apprehended' (BCL 1989e).

It would appear that as BCL began to act as the PNGDF's de facto logistic wing, the company's management became more engrossed in the finer points of the offensive operations.

Of course, BCL was not the only external actor engaged in the military operations. The recent support package negotiated with Australia, was also beginning to take effect during this period. For example, four Australian Iroquois helicopters arrived in PNG during mid-July 1989. The Hawke government formally stipulated that these helicopters were not to be employed as gunships. Nevertheless, as Rogers (2002: 233) observes:

> The four aircraft were quickly improvised as gunships. Indeed, offensive fire was regularly directed from the helicopters at suspected targets, including villages. Soldiers fired machine guns [GPMG M60] attached by rope, and grenades from grenade launchers (M203/M79) or simply dropped grenades into villages. The conditions were violated and the Australian government was shown evidence of such instances, but little was done to enforce the prohibitions – something which the PNGDF quickly realised.

With the added air mobility of the four Iroquois helicopters, supplementing the substantial 'built-in facilities' provided by BCL (Liria 1993: 68), the PNGDF now had the capacity to plan and enact more aggressive assaults during operations *Bull Dog* and *Kisim Dog*.

Operation Bull Dog

The PNGDF initiated operation *Bull Dog* on 12 July 1989. While the operation aimed to 'clear' villages in the mine area, the PNGDF hoped an element of surprise might catch BRA troops off guard (Rogers 2002: 229). Accordingly, village clearances now, in effect, became village assaults.

Irenaeus Ivomei of Peumpe village provides an eyewitness account of one such raid:

> On Tuesday 18 July 1989, at about 11am, soldiers came to Peumpe and hid on top of the ridge about half a kilometre away watching us. A helicopter

also flew over our village. We were in their full view, our total population of 40 children and 18 adults. What was to happen in the next few minutes took us by total surprise. At one o'clock they suddenly opened fire on us with automatic weapons, destroying our houses. We had scrambled to the end of the village for safety and cover. While I was getting the children to run for cover, bullets ripped my laplap between my legs, and another man was injured across his belly by a bullet. This fire went on for about 15 minutes then they stopped . . . At this moment a helicopter appeared which also rained automatic fire down onto the village . . . We slept in the jungle on Wednesday 19th July . . . On Friday 20th me and our aid post orderly left our people in the bush and came and reported this incident to the authorities in Arawa . . . When I surveyed the village, all food gardens had been destroyed, and the air was foul with the smell of dead pigs, dogs, cats and chickens. I stayed there for two days waiting for my people to return, but they were nowhere to be seen. It seemed they had walked further into the jungle where it was safe for them. I had personally lost a house which had cost me K27,000 to build [around US$32,000].[16] (cited in Havini 1990: 35–7; see also Liria 1993: 108)

Amplifying the destruction caused by village assaults, was the tactical addition of the 'Defence Force's heaviest firepower, the 81 mm calibre mortar bombs' (Liria 1993: 115). Technically speaking the operational use of mortars had in fact begun on the final day of operation *Nakmai Maimai*, when Guava village was shelled in preparation for a morning assault. Liria (1993: 115) recalls:

I was . . . informed by an elderly man, who was both blind and too weak to walk that with the frightening noise and tremors [of the mortars], the whole village [Guava] rushed out of their houses with mere essentials if anything at all, running in the opposite direction from Panguna, where they knew the bombs were being 'thrown' from. He himself was carried like a child, on his son's back, sleeping in the open that night. Many families, including children, separated that night in the frightened rush, some never to meet again, others to wonder if family members were still alive.

During operation *Bull Dog* the PNGDF's use of mortars became widespread. Indeed, Liria (1993: 113-14) observes, 'mortar rounds searched their targets along the Pakia and Guava ridgelines. Homes disappeared in flames while the guardian spirits of Guava and Panguna haunted our troops in the surrounding jungles'. The military's use of mortars in this respect was strongly condemned by Rogers (2002: 228–9), who had been serving with the PNGDF at the time:

> The use of the mortar platoon on 10 July at night on Guava village was irresponsible and indefensible . . . The mortars would be used again, often deployed as sections (two mortar tubes), over coming years. Mortar rounds often fell indiscriminately, wounding civilians and terrorising the local population. Soldiers confirmed later that the mortars were fired regularly, especially at night, without adequate controls. The PNGDF even fired the mortars from its ships [Australian supplied Pacific Class Patrol boats] – a notoriously unstable platform and dangerous for the troops involved. The PNGDF's use of white phosphorous rounds (WP) attracts particular condemnation. WP burns the skin and can drift well beyond target areas.

In addition to the bombardment of villages, numerous extra-judicial killings were documented by Amnesty International. One example involved Ambrose Leo who was said by Rogers (2002: 220) to be the youngest brother of Francis Ona:

> The body of Ambrose Leo of Guava village arrived at Arawa General Hospital on 18 July 1989 with a note attached to it which read: 'This is the first billion of your ten billion'. This was an evident reference to the BRA's demand for Kina 10 billion in compensation for land and environmental damage. A post mortem report, which was forwarded to the Coroner on 8 August 1989, concluded that Ambrose Leo had been beaten, kicked and stabbed in the ear before being shot at close range. (Amnesty International 1990a: 23)

Such ritualised executions were common. Another example cited by Amnesty International involved Peter Tarupiu:

> Peter Tarupiu, a university student, died on or about 16 August 1989, after being beaten by members of the security forces. His parents, who witnessed the scene, said soldiers beat Peter Tarupiu repeatedly with their rifle butts and a length of wood. An autopsy performed at the Arawa General Hospital showed that he had multiple bruises to his face, neck

and chest and was bleeding from both ears. He had a puncture wound on the right side of his neck. One of his cervical vertebrae was crushed and his spinal column was completely severed. According to the autopsy report, the cause of death was damage to the vertebrae of the neck and spinal column 'which is consistent with heavy blows to the posterior aspect of the neck'. (1990a: 23–4)

The Deputy Matron at Arawa Hospital, Rose Seriotase, corroborated Amnesty International's accounts in a 1991 television interview. She claimed, during 1989–90 bodies marked by torture were regularly left by the military outside the hospital:

They would normally come with a really huge face, round face, and all swollen, and some chain mark. They would whip them with a big chain. And we had all this and sometimes a big blow of something heavy. They blow it on their neck, and the veins on their neck is ruptured, and then sort of swollen . . . They [the security forces] usually just drop the dead body down on the grass, and we usually go and just pick them up. They are wrapped in plastic and, either just a sheet. (Seriotase 1991)

The very public manner in which corpses were dumped, would suggest that the PNGDF intended to send a message to the community, and in particular, those providing support to the BRA.

Indeed, given the destructive and indiscriminate methods employed by the security forces during this period, serious doubts must be raised over the PNGDF's stated priorities of 'evacuation' and 'neutralisation' (of the BRA). The rebels were well trained, familiar with the physical environment, and informed of PNGDF movements. Consequently, village raids had a low likelihood of killing or capturing militants. Indeed, *not one* BRA leader was captured or killed during these operations. Furthermore, the military arsenal employed during village raids made the goal of evacuation difficult to achieve, as terrified villagers fled into the jungle.

Therefore, it may be reasonably concluded that village raids employing a combination of 81mm mortars, helicopter gunships (rigged with M60/M203/M79(s)), and M16s, in combination with graphic extra-judicial killings, had goals less defensible than 'evacuation' and 'neutralisation'. This was a systematic campaign of violence designed to demonstrate the sort of indiscriminate damage the state could inflict, if pushed. Indeed, during a meeting with BCL's management in late July, Premier Kabui complained that the BRA and their supporters had an inflated impression of their ability to resist the national government (BCL 1989f). Consequently, he argued, deployment of the PNGDF's full arsenal, reminded the rebels that 'their bows, arrows and shotguns are nothing compared to automatic weapons' (BCL 1989f). Echoing Kabui's statement, the Minister for Defence publicly boasted in early September: 'We have shown the military destruction that can be caused, if ever they [BRA] decided to start again. I am sure that that lesson is being learnt by the Bougainvilleans' (Hansard, 6 September 1989).

The 'Care Centre' Complex

Many of those displaced by the destructive village raids, elected to live in the jungle rather than be evacuated into the poorly regarded 'care centres'. Although data on the number of villagers living under the jungle canopy during 1989 is unavailable, it would certainly appear that hundreds 'chose' to subsist in makeshift huts or caves, gardening where and when they could. PNGDF intelligence officer, Yauka Aluambo Liria, regularly spotted displaced villagers from the air:

> On many occasions, I detected them making gardens. Only the undergrowth would be cleared, leaving the trees with their canopy untouched, for fear of giving themselves away. They were adapting quickly to jungle living. If they cleared the bush completely, they did so under poor weather conditions, when our flights were impossible, or even if we did fly, cloud cover concealed their presence and activities from our detection . . . [On one occasion I witnessed] a recently cleared garden being hastily cultivated by a large group of men and women, number[ing] about twenty-five. We circled three times and I told the soldiers not to shoot. (1993: 115)

While some villagers may have been 'adapting quickly to jungle living', conditions on the run, particularly for the vulnerable, were precarious. A parliamentary committee set up to monitor the SOE (a mandatory requirement under PNG's Constitution), was informed at a public meeting held in south Bougainville on 9 August 1989, that 'many have died because they were sick and could not get medication, have starved to death or

have died of cold in the bush as a result of the [military] operation[s]'
(Permanent Parliamentary Committee on National Emergency 1989b: 6).

Villagers who did not flee into the jungle, were evacuated into one
of the 18 'care centres' in and around Arawa, which were jointly run by
the national government, BCL and the national Red Cross (Amnesty
International 1990a: 34). Unlike the April operations, where 'care centres'
were a spontaneous result of village 'destructions', they were now being
strategically utilised by the PNGDF to concentrate the civilian population
away from the BRA (ADF officer, personal communication, 1 September
2006). Military senior command believed this would prevent the BRA from
organising further attacks in the general mine area. It was also felt that by
cutting the 'supply routes to [BRA] camps', the government could signal to
Francis Ona 'the hopelessness of the situation that he is facing' (Minister
of State, Hansard, 14 July 1989).

Accordingly, camp numbers swelled. Indeed, following the July–August
operations, the PNG government estimated that around 4,000 villagers
were living in these camps (Tohian 1989b: 8). This statistic caused PNG's
Foreign Minister to complain, 'we are now feeding the families of the
militants – virtually looking after them on a golden plate' (cited in Albon
1989: 16). Though just how golden this plate was, is a debatable matter.

We can at the very least obtain a general sense of the difficulties which
villagers faced in these camps from refugee accounts collected by Gillespie
during 1992 and 1993. One particularly powerful description is provided by
Andrew Purai, a Buin Chief from Konigulu village. He was kept in a 'care
centre' during 1992:

I was kept in the care centre for three months. I was never allowed out
of the centre during that time. There was not enough to eat in the care
centre. We were kept under constant surveillance. We were not allowed
visitors. Women in the Tokaino centre were raped by PNG soldiers. For
example, Leo Naisi's daughter was raped while she was being held at
Tokaino. PNG soldiers also subjected women to sexual harassment and
escorted them to the toilet. This is against our custom . . . Civilians
in the care centre were tortured by PNG soldiers and SBIA's [South
Bougainville Interim Authority, a pro-government civilian paramilitary
unit]. For example, Umin Kibau was hit by PNG soldiers who rammed
the butts of their guns against his back, shoulders and body. PNG soldiers
hit other young men with the butts of their guns and the SBIA soldiers

hit them with the back of their axes. These unfortunate young men were then thrown into the gully close by the care centre . . . After I had been kept in the care centre for 3 months, I asked permission to go back to my village to pick up the rest of my family and bring them back to the centre. I was let out, went back to my village, and never returned. I did not want to go back to the Tokaino 'care' centre. When I did not return to the Tokaino centre, SBIA and PNG soldiers came to my village and shot dead my four sons, Rapheal Morikei, Iamu Kabui, John and Bana Kuriai. (cited in Gillespie 1993: 13; see also Amnesty International 1993)

Kara Mege of Laitaro village in Buin paints a similar portrait:

People who are being kept in the care centre are not allowed to take anything out of the care centre, not even a change of clothes. In September 1992, a man called Peter from the Laguai village was seen carrying a packet of rice to his village. He had left Turiboiru at the allotted time to go to his food garden. He was spotted by PNG soldiers as he passed the PNG army base at Buin town. They captured him and put him in the back of a truck . . . [they] took him down the Kangu road until they reached the crossroads near Laguai village. They put him face down on a log and put a packet of rice on his back. They then sprayed his body with bullets. Peter was used as an example, as a warning of what would happen if anyone took anything out of the Turiboiru centre. The PNG soldiers sent out an instruction that this could happen to anyone else carrying anything out of the centre, so everyone in the centre was told about it. (cited in Gillespie 1993: 55)

According to a senior RPNGC commander, the police were aware of serious crimes occurring inside the 'care centres', but practically speaking they had no way of investigating or prosecuting offenders:

I have to tell you there were atrocious things happening [inside the care centres], which I do not condone for one minute as a police officer. I know military officers who killed innocent people, which I was totally against, and I said I will not have a bar of it guys . . . There were [also] reported cases of rape, carnal knowledge of girls under the age. We had no way of dealing with them. (RPNGC officer, personal communication, 10 July 2006)

Rebels on the Run?

The PNGDF considered operations *Nakmai Maimai* and *Bull Dog* a success, or at least that was the impression they gave the national government. While not a single rebel leader had been captured or killed, the SOE Controller announced: 'The BRA is on the run now and we are now cracking their strong holds' (Tohian 1989a: 3). As a result of these representations, the government in Port Moresby soon 'gained the (false) impression that the militants were off balance and receptive to settlement' (Rogers 2002: 228). Indeed, notes compiled during BCL's meeting with the North Solomons Premier on 26 July 1989, confirm this 'impression' was widespread:

> Prior to the offensive there was a false sense of security among the militants. Soldiers were killed at a time when they were under restraint – when they went into attack there has been a lot more people killed in the bush than has been announced . . . Dialogue may be possible now because the militants now realise they can't achieve what they were trying to do . . . Realities are now dawning on them. Francis [Ona] is allegedly talking of surrender but other militant members like James Singko and Damien Damen will not let him. (BCL 1989f)

Believing that the BRA was close to defeat, the security forces wanted to undertake a final assault in order to eliminate the rebels. Liria (1993: 125) explains, 'the planners went on to convince themselves and persuade the opponents of their plan, that Kongara was the last stronghold of the BRA and their destruction at Kongara was inevitable'. As a result, on 4 August 1989, operation *Kisim Dog* was launched. According to Rogers (2002: 233–34), the offensive was premised on an expectation that the BRA would remain in Kongara and fight. However, as Liria explains:

> What we didn't realise at the time was that [Sam] Kauona had organised the hardcore fanatical members of the BRA into small bands. They were to hold up the military patrols in the Kongara area, inflicting as many casualties as possible, and all the time giving the impression that the bulk of the BRA and its leadership was still in the area, preparing to fight the army. Later from captured prisoners, we learnt that Kauona and the rest of the leadership slipped away down the Laluai River and escaped into the high mountains behind Koromira Catholic Mission. Following this position he convinced the priests in the mission station to contact the

government and advise them to stop the offensive and allow the priests to lead a peace dialogue team. (1993: 128–9)

Nevertheless, the hawks in cabinet wanted to continue with operation *Kisim Dog*, and wipe out the BRA once and for all. One of the Ministers involved recalls:

We surrounded the [BRA] headquarters . . . I wanted to do the helicopter assault, they [the BRA] knew their situation was hopeless. Ona then sent his sister to come to Waigani, and cry to the PM, and said believe me in Bougainville it's the women's voice that is more important than the men. 'Believe me PM, and John Momis'. She came and cried in the cabinet room, and said 'no more military war, finish'. And I said, 'look at her PM, you know she is lying to you, she is absolutely lying to you, I can read it on her face'. I said 'the body language is not right'. And ah, I then said to the PM, 'whatever you do [with respect to peace negotiations], it's not going to work, this is your opportunity now to do it'. I was pressing for an assault on the cliff face. We would have destroyed all the command elements of the BRA, and it would have taken them months to reorganise, by then we would have been in a mop up situation, we would have cleaned it up. (PNG Minister B, personal communication, 9 July 2006)

However, the NEC rejected the proposal for a final assault. The Minister for Provincial Affairs and the Prime Minister both felt a humbled BRA could now be convinced to join the peace process (PNG Minister B, personal communication, 9 July 2006). Consequently, on 22 August 1989, the PNGDF was withdrawn from offensive operations, and placed on static guard duty around the mine (Liria 1993: 150–1).

Conclusion

The declaration of a SOE finally delivered the sort of authoritative response long campaigned for by the company. Yet this was not a sign that BCL's management had triumphed over the Minister for Provincial Affairs and his political allies, other decisive forces were at play. In particular, the abrupt re-entry of Ted Diro into cabinet created a powerful foothold for a rival hawk faction at the centre of state power. Carrying the sympathies of PNG's security apparatus, Diro along with the Defence and Police Minister, was able to articulate a coherent military alternative to the Bougainville Package. Though voicing an alternative was not in itself enough, what made this articulation convincing was the particular way international capital flows had come to increasingly intersect with national reproduction strategies in PNG through the nodal point of the natural resource industry. This intersection ensured that BCL's predicament acutely impacted, in a number of ways, on those charged with the state's response. Indeed, the looming threat of a national fiscal crisis, threatened to bring to a halt critical arterial flows essential to social life for those firmly plugged into PNG's capitalist economy. It was in this particular context that the hawks' solution found favour in cabinet. Indeed, state violence held the immediate appeal of freeing mining capital from its existing state of expropriation on Bougainville, and thus reinstating those fiscal flows essential to the health of the national economy. While for those in cabinet with an eye on the future economic landscape of PNG, hooked as it increasingly was to the extractive industries, this counterinsurgency campaign also offered to set a 'brutal' precedent that would decrease the risk of landowners in other parts of the country emulating the BRA's tactics.

However, for a military solution to be operationalised the PNG state required access to the means of violence. While there existed a standing army, nevertheless, it was unprepared for a major challenge like the BRA. Here the contribution of BCL and Australia became especially vital. By acting as the PNGDF's logistic wing and armoury, BCL and the Hawke government enabled the PNG state to launch a series of increasingly more brutal counterinsurgency operations – operations that were designed to demonstrate the sort of destruction that the state could wreak if villagers continued to support the BRA. Australia's support in particular – prompted by an ambitious foreign policy agenda designed to underpin domestic reforms at home – evidences a crucial international dimension to state power, with different asymmetric units of state power (nation states), switching and channelling resources between each other, inspired by a range of geopolitical calculations.

By September 1989, the national government was beginning to think about signing the Bougainville Package, and reopening the mine, believing that the BRA had been brought to heal. The Defence Minister confidently informed parliament: 'I believe we have solved the crisis . . . the mine will be open for good' (Hansard, 6 September 1989). This statement over-estimated the damage that the PNGDF had inflicted upon BRA morale, and underestimated the rebels' capacity to reflect upon, react to, and strategically organise, on an expanded basis. Indeed, as we will see, the BRA emerged from the July–August operations with a renewed sense of confidence, having observed first-hand the PNGDF's limitations.

6

The Making of Civil War on Bougainville

In his classic historical essay on the peasant wars in Germany, Engels remarks:

> The worst thing that can befall a leader of an extreme party is to be compelled to take over a government at a time when society is not yet ripe for the domination of a class he represents and for the measures which that domination implies . . . What he *can* do contradicts all his previous actions and principles, and the immediate interests of his party, and what he *ought* to do cannot be done. (Engels 1969: 115)

In a qualified sense, this captures the BRA's fate as it assumed a position of provincial dominance during late 1989 and early 1990. For all the government's bold pronouncements, the BRA was not an extinguished force. Far from it, the illicit actions of the PNG state were now echoing throughout the province, providing the rebels with an unexpected opportunity to mobilise popular support behind their movement, in areas well outside the BRA's direct sphere of influence.

As we will see, the BRA's growing popularity created the conditions in which they were able to inflict a considerable toll on the government security forces, leading to the latter's retreat in March 1990. Having won control of the island, the BRA declared Bougainville's independence two months later. This, however, was not a preface to the BRA's ultimate triumph. Conversely, it is argued in this chapter that the BRA's sudden and prolific rise seriously outpaced its organisational capacity to effectively influence and govern. As a result, the BRA's leadership was forced to form an alliance with amenable sections of the disbanded provincial government, in an effort to develop a skeletal political apparatus, the Bougainville Interim Government (BIG), which could oversee independence. Cut off from the outside world by a

PNGDF blockade, the BRA and BIG struggled to maintain order, with the former lashing out violently at internal opponents believed to be conspiring with the national government.

Having registered that the BRA's greatest weakness was its premature success, it is argued, the PNG state undertook a significant strategic gamble in an effort to win back the province. Specifically, rather than initiate a protracted campaign of political isolation and negotiation, which would have given the BRA room to operationalise its influence, the PNG government elected to intensify and militarise emerging divisions on Bougainville in a bid to bring about a civil war type situation that pitted pro-government Bougainvillean paramilitaries against the BRA, with the PNGDF and RPNGC falling behind the former. Tellingly this was done in close cooperation with PNG's Australian counterparts who began to assume a stronger role in the counterinsurgency campaign, following the failures of early 1990.

It is suggested that PNG's strategic gamble prompted a qualitative shift in the social terrain, that amplified the depth and breadth of the antagonisms on the island, out of which grew the social foundations for a brutal war that would continue for another six years.

The Reopening of the Panguna Mine and the Signing of the Bougainville Package

During August 1989 – in the midst of operation *Kisim Dog* – BCL agreed to begin repair work on the mine. These repairs proceeded without major incident. This reflected, in part, the positive working relationship between BCL management and Colonel Dotaona. A senior manager recalls:

I think communications were pretty good between us and the government in terms of what they were doing with their security numbers. For example in that period when we were trying to put the power back on for a restart, we actually sat down with them, and they would tell us how many [security force] numbers were in what area, and we'd sit down and say, no we don't think that would be good enough, or what about this area, and what about that area. So there was a lot of liaising going on in that sense. We [also] had our security group, and they all had two way radios and the appropriate communication tools they normally had. So there was a lot of communication available between different types and different levels of the security. (BCL official D, personal communication, 7 June 2006)

With power having been restored in mid-August, the mine's reopening was slated for 5 September 1989. The signing of the Bougainville Package, however, was not moving ahead as seamlessly. Divisions within the PLA proved difficult to mend, only eleven out of the NPLA's 24 executive members were prepared to break with Francis Ona (BCL 1990a). Indeed, Premier Kabui conceded on 22 August 1989, that a formal election would be needed to resolve matters (BCL 1989g). However, with the mine's reopening a fortnight away, the national government wanted the Bougainville Package in place. Consequently, Prime Minister Namaliu declared that the signing would occur on 11 September 1989, with or without the rebels' support (Hriehwazi 1989f: 1).

As planned, production at the mine recommenced with the day shift on 5 September 1989. This brought to an end 113 days of lost production, which was reported to have cost BCL K180 million (US$200 million) in lost revenue (Hriehwazi 1989f: 1). The first morning shift passed without incident. However, as workers were being ferried home along the Port–Mine Access road – 'cleared' during operation *Nakmai Maimai* – they were fired upon near Birempa (Cornelius 1989). BCL stopped production immediately. Early the next morning the attacks continued. Transmission pylon no. 6 was toppled, while transmission pylon no. 7 was damaged. Only 24 hours after the resumption of production, the mine had once again been knocked offline.

The signing of the Bougainville Package was also successfully derailed by rebel attacks. Indeed, the night before it was meant to be signed in Port Moresby, the BRA shot dead one of the provincial government's key representatives, John Bika (Minister for Commerce) at his home near Kieta (Hiambohn 1989h: 1). Bika had been intimately involved in the Bougainville Package's development, he was also Chairman of the Provincial Government Select Committee that had rejected secession (North Solomons Provincial Government 1989). In response to Bika's killing, the Prime Minister deferred the Bougainville Package signing 'indefinitely' (Hiambohn 1989h: 1).

According to Saffu (1998b) the events of early September 1989, swung political momentum back in the hawks' favour. He writes:

In Cabinet, Bika's assassination apparently strengthened the 'hawks' who gained an important temporary recruit in Michael Somare [Minister for Foreign Affairs]. Even he now advised against signing the peace package, declaring: 'What we need is toughness'. Bernard Narokobi, the Justice Minister, deputy leader of Melanesian Alliance, inveterate peace-monger and the scourge of multinationals, declared his disillusionment with the militants . . . The Parliamentary Committee on the State Emergency reportedly urged an 'all out war'. (Saffu 1998b: 472)

With the mine shut, and the Bougainville Package sidelined, the Prime Minister ceded ground to the hawk faction.

Using this political momentum, the Minister of State placed a K200,000 price (US\$ 230,000) on the head of key BRA leaders (Rea 1989c: 1). This move 'was designed to immobilise Ona, so he wouldn't trust his people, so he couldn't organise his command' (PNG Minister B, personal communication, 9 July 2006). The Minister of State also authorised the military to plant 'booby traps' around the mine. In the weeks that followed two soldiers were killed wiring the devices (Nangoi 1989a: 1; Hriehwazi 1989g: 2). However, arguably the most significant change made by the NEC during this period was the 13 October decision to replace Colonel Dotaona as Deputy Controller of the Bougainville operations (Hiambohn 1989i: 1).

Dotaona's replacement was Colonel Nuia. Rogers (2002: 238) notes, he 'enjoyed a tough man image . . . Nuia was a hardliner with little sympathy for the secessionists'. Indeed, during the PNGDF's successful effort to rout a secessionist uprising on Vanuatu during 1980 Nuia reportedly 'mistreated some prisoners', and was 'sacked . . . from Vanuatu' by the then PNGDF Commander, Ted Diro (PNG Minister B, personal communication, 9 July 2006). Despite these past 'blemishes' Colonel Nuia was felt to be the right man for the job. One member of the hawk faction recalls:

I thought he was a good operational commander, I thought he had the right attributes. He was not diplomatic, he was straight forward, and no nonsense. And when dealing with the civilian government there, and with the Bougainvilleans, he had a fairly no nonsense attitude, which upset a lot of people . . . [but] he is a damn good soldier . . . [though] we didn't have too many [officers] to choose from. He was quite effective. (PNG Minister C, personal communication, 8 July 2006)

Nuia's appointment signalled a critical shift in the military's operational strategy. Indeed, Nuia was strongly in favour of building up and consolidating the PNGDF's strike capacity so an all-out assault on BRA forces could be launched (Rogers 2002: 233–4). To that end, following his appointment as Deputy Controller, Colonel Nuia initiated a significant increase in the PNGDF's offensive capacity on Bougainville.

Preparing the Ground for Renewed Hostilities

During November and December 1989, Colonel Nuia's energies were focused on logistically preparing the PNGDF for a major assault on BRA 'strongholds'. 'By January 1990', Rogers (2002: 241) observes, 'Nuia had assembled an impressive array of military muscle. He had five companies, air support and a logistics base to support his operations'. However, while these preparations were being made, the national government involved itself in a number of last-ditch peace talks. For instance, official support was given to an initiative organised by a local priest, Fr Liebert (BCL 1989h; PMD official A, personal communication, 10 July 2006). Acting as a neutral mediator Fr Liebert made direct contact with the BRA leadership during November and December 1989, including Sam Kauona, James Singko, and Oscar Ampoi. Fr Liebert reported that the rebels were indeed prepared to enter into peace negotiations provided that the national government:

1. Withdraw the security forces from Bougainville;
2. Permanently close the Panguna mine; and
3. Agree to a provincial referendum over the question of secession.

Cabinet, however, was still unwilling to cede ground on the latter two fronts. As a result, Fr Liebert's initiative – and others – failed to halt the momentum towards further armed conflict.

Meanwhile, the BRA was making concerted attempts to mobilise popular support for their movement across the province. To that end, Francis Ona delivered a number of addresses over the radio, and released written communiqués. They were etched in the language of class struggle, ethno-nationalism, and his own brand of liberation theology (see also Hermkens 2011, 2013). For example, in a communiqué dated 29 November 1989, Ona argued:

As we took up arms to defend our land and fight for justice, fairness and equality, we realised that the political leaders of this country are not with us in our struggle for justice. Instead the government and the political leaders of this country have seen fit to declare war against us on behalf of the exploiter, the Bougainville Copper Company . . . We are not going to sit by and watch capitalists and their Papua New Guinean political allies exploit us . . . Our demand for ten billion kina compensation for our land and environmental damages still stands . . . Our politicians and government will continue to defend their foreign capitalist allies by declaring war and curfews against their own people, whenever their cordial relations are threatened . . . [Indeed] the state, being an alien construct does not represent the interest of the society as a whole . . . [Consequently] there is no other way of protecting our motherland than to take up arms. It is happening in many Third World countries where the religious people are taking up arms to defend the poor and exploited against their governments and multinational companies . . . Like Moses who led his people from slavery to freedom, we are also fighting for liberation. We are fighting to liberate ourselves from the exploiters and the neo-colonial forces . . . There is no turning back, if we are lured with peanuts and carrots, as the Namaliu government is attempting to do, all we can say is this, it is too late for that. (Ona 1989)

It is impossible to know just how important these statements were in garnering village support. Nevertheless, by December 1989 both government and PNGDF officials were observing, with concern, BRA guerrilla bands operating in Siwai, Buin and Boku (south Bougainville),[1] areas outside the traditional rebel heartland of Panguna, Kieta and Kongara (central Bougainville). Colonel Nuia was mindful that his forces could not afford to be split down multiple fronts. Consequently, during December and early January 1989–90, he attempted to hem the BRA into the Kongara region of central Bougainville.[2]

To this end, it was necessary to shut down the rebel units operating in Siwai, Buin and Boku. Both the national government and the PNGDF were of the opinion that this demanded local collaboration (BCL 1989h, 1989i, 1990b). In an effort to co-opt local leaders, a goods and services embargo was placed on south Bougainville. A senior PNG civil servant, articulated the strategic thinking behind this move, 'when people start to feel the hardships in education and health they may start to turn against the militants' (BCL 1989i). This view was also shared by Colonel Nuia (BCL 1989h, 1990b).

The national government initiated the goods and services blockade on 12 December 1989. According to a *Post-Courier* report published that day:

> All public servants serving at government posts at Buin, Tonu, Boku, Torokina and the Siwai areas are expected to be moved out by today. . . The moving of public servants which include aid post orderlies [medical assistance], policemen, postal workers, teachers and provincial government workers, would now mean a virtual closure of all basic government services to these areas. (Nangoi 1989b: 1)

The day after public servants were withdrawn, the movement of bulk cargo through Koromira, Buin and Boku was prohibited under Emergency Order No. 75.

Less than two weeks into the goods and services blockade, the North Solomons Administrative Secretary noted the embargo was producing positive results: '[In Boku] the leaders there are identifying the hardcore and turning them into the authorities. A similar thing is happening down in Buin' (BCL 1989i). However, in order to deter community leaders from collaborating with the PNGDF, local BRA units began targeting suspected informants. Amnesty International (1990b: 1062) notes, some of those under suspicion were executed by BRA forces during this period. Nevertheless, by 8 January 1990, both the North Solomons Administrative Secretary and Colonel Nuia felt confident enough to claim, 'Boku and Buin is under control with leaders taking an increasingly important role . . . [as a result] services at Buin and Boku are to be re-established today' (BCL 1990b).

While the operating environment in south Bougainville may have been made more challenging for the BRA, in central Bougainville the rebels still enjoyed considerable support. Indeed having suffered most during the military operations of July–August 1989, considerable animosity remained in central Bougainville, as a Red Cross Rehabilitation team discovered during their visit to Oune village on 5 January 1990:

> The next speaker spoke strongly about the retention of people in the care centres and requested their immediate return . . . The next speaker indicated that contrary to Francis Kabana's statement that houses had been burnt by the Defence Forces, militants and rascals [criminal

gangs], he believed the Defence Forces were solely responsible . . . A further speaker supported him by saying that in his observation the Security Forces were the only ones involved in burning the villages . . . In response to continued requests for the return of people from the care centres Wendelinus [Bitanuma] spoke initially in Pidgin and then in ples tok [regional dialect] indicating that it was up to Col Nuia to release people from the care centres but in his perception, they were better off in the care centres than back in the villages at this stage. The response to these statements was quite vocal and the mood of the meeting at this stage was quite ugly with several of the radical group gesticulating with axes and bush knives . . . The next speaker stressed that the Prime Minister must come and see the problems in the care centres and in the bush for himself. On the one occasion that he has visited the island he saw nothing. (BCL 1990a)

Unless the government could develop a convincing strategy for winning over villagers from central Bougainville – and everything had failed thus far – the BRA would be difficult to militarily pin down.

Such a 'hearts and minds' campaign, however, would require time and by early January 1990, developments within BCL were about to force the PNGDF's hand. Indeed, for a number of months the company had been considering its future on the island. Despite the setbacks of September 1989, management had decided to persevere with the situation. Nevertheless, '[a]t year end [BCL's] cash reserves were almost depleted', despite having halted its substantial capital works programme and cutting costs (BCL 1990o: 6). Compounding matters, Colonel Nuia was allocating less resources to mine security – as a result there had been,[3] 'numerous incidents of violence against BCL employees and damage to BCL property . . . throughout the Panguna, Arawa, Loloho, Kieta and Jaba River areas' (Jopling 1989). With the fiscal and security situation deteriorating, BCL's management could no longer justify keeping 2,317 largely idle employees on the books (BCL 1990o: 5). Therefore, on 28 December 1989, BCL's Board of Directors voted to initiate a major retrenchment programme, which in effect placed the mine onto a 'care and maintenance' footing (BCL 1990o: 8).

The company began staff retrenchments on 7 January 1990. Fortuitously, BCL's Managing Director was approached the following day by Colonel Nuia with news. Cabinet, Cornelius was informed, had made the decision to mount another major counterinsurgency offensive (BCL 1990b). This news was received with a degree of scepticism. Nevertheless, one senior manager recalls, '[now that] the government [had] decided that it would mount up a military effort to have a final throw . . . it caused us to wait a little bit' (BCL official D, personal communication, 7 June 2006).

Operation Footloose

On 11 January 1990, the Prime Minister announced before parliament that a new PNGDF offensive had begun:

> We have used every possible means to bring about a return to peace by a peaceful solution . . . There is no real alternative to stronger security force activity given the attitude of the rebel elements . . . We intend to pursue our security force option as the only reasonable alternative left open to us. The force is presently engaged in a stepped-up exercise to end this problem once and for all . . . I ask, and I hope for the last time, for the full support of this Parliament to crush this terrorist element, which is unable to listen to reason, to negotiation, or to common sense. (Hansard, 11 January 1990)

The counterinsurgency operation – which the Prime Minister euphemistically labelled a 'stepped-up exercise' – was codenamed *Footloose*. *Footloose* had a number of tactical objectives that were later outlined by the SOE's Controller. In short, the PNGDF aimed to flood the Kongara region with troops in a coordinated manner, in order to surprise and scatter rebel units, creating the conditions under which disorganised guerrilla bands could be isolated and 'neutralised' (Tohian 1990: 21–2; see also Rogers 2002: 241–2).

At the Deputy Controller's disposal in this respect were 500 PNGDF troops, 300 RPNGC mobile squad officers, and 100 Correctional Service officers (CIS) (Police Minister, Hansard, 14 March 1990) – although the CIS contingent was mainly employed on static guard duty. According to PNG's Foreign Minister, the PNGDF was also assisted by 'the people of Buin and Boku [who] have now decided to support our security forces by allowing 160 of their men to help the security forces flush out the rebels' (Hansard, 11 January 1990). This was the first documented use of loyalist paramilitaries by the PNG state, the practice would intensify over coming years.

Possessing a ground force almost double the size of Dotaona's contingent in 1989, Colonel Nuia employed air support to transport troops into strategic locations around Kongara. Once deployed, the security forces conducted aggressive assaults on BRA areas and villages, employing the full range of military hardware available to them, including 81mm mortars, M16s, M203s, M79s, and four Iroquois helicopters rigged with M60s (Rogers 2002: 242). The Police Minister was to later observe: '[The operation was a] real "traim bun"[4] exercise and in fact bones rattled on the island. A lot of men on either side were lost and innocent people who got in the way of the two opposing forces were innocently affected' (Hansard, 14 March 1990). According to one report cited by Amnesty International (1990a: 35), 'at least 27 villagers, including elderly people and children, were killed between mid-January and mid-February as a result of heavy mortar fire and aerial bombing into areas of suspected rebel activity'.

These aerial attacks were supplemented by heavy-handed village raids. Indeed, on 17 January 1990, Premier Kabui reported that indiscriminate gunfire had already taken the lives of two women, and three children (BCL 1990d). The military also targeted Bougainvillean civilians through extra-judicial killings. Indeed, during operation *Footloose*, around two dozen individuals were reported to have been executed by the security forces (see Amnesty International 1990a; de Gedare 2000; Havini 1995). Amnesty International documents a number of examples, including that of Samson Materiva:

> Samson Materiva, a minibus driver, was shot and killed on 23 January 1990; he was last seen in the custody of military personnel. According to relatives he was arrested at about 2pm while waiting at the Aropa bus stand, and taken to the military camp at Aropa for questioning. Later that day, he was shot in the chest and killed; his body was brought to Arawa hospital in a plastic bag at about 4pm on 24 January . . . The soldiers suspected him of being a militant because of his 'dreadlocks' a hairstyle worn by some BRA members but also popular among young Bougainvillean men . . . Military authorities reportedly claimed that Samson Materiva had been shot while trying to run away from a roadblock at Aropa. (1990a: 26)

The escalated rates of beatings and extrajudicial killings under Colonel Nuia's command so concerned the National Emergency Committee that its

Chairman, Sir Hugo Berghuser, petitioned parliament on 13 March 1990, with evidence of PNGDF war crimes:

> Documentary evidence received from Arawa General Hospital clearly shows, that many of the civilians or militants who died at the hands of the security forces may have been brutally assaulted to death or deliberately murdered in circumstances in which death could have been avoided. We are not referring to the deaths caused by gunshot wounds in self defence or during confrontation with militants. We are referring to deaths where according to medical reports, the security forces were in control of the situation and yet decided to kill. (Hansard, 13 March 1990)

Nevertheless, no significant disciplinary action was taken against those accused. Indeed, writing a decade later, the former National Court judge, Brian Brunton, notes that while PNG:

> [H]as a detailed Bill of Rights and very flexible powers under the Constitution to enforce those rights . . . [nevertheless] a large number of claims alleging repeated serious human rights abuses by government forces in Bougainville . . . lodged before the National Court . . . more than ten years later . . . have not been adjudicated. That fact speaks for itself. (2001)

The BRA Counterattacks

Despite the extra firepower and force employed during operation *Footloose*, the PNGDF failed to kill or capture a single BRA leader. This, of course, has shades of 1989, when BRA leaders proved largely immune to security force assaults. However, unlike 1989, on this occasion the rebel forces staged a 'well-orchestrated' counterattack (Rogers 2002: 241–2). 'While the PNGDF was harassed in the Kongara', observes Rogers (2002: 241–2), 'the rebels targeted other areas of Bougainville'. According to the North Solomons Premier, the BRA had 'wanted a real fight for some time' (BCL 1990d).

The first major BRA assault occurred on 17 January 1990. Around 70 to 100 militants were reported to have besieged the Kuveria Corrective Institution, just outside Arawa (*Kalang FM News* 18 January 1990; *NBC North Solomons News* 17 January 1990). The building was guarded by approximately 20 CIS officers, of which 13 were armed (BCL 1990d). In the ensuing skirmish four CIS officers were killed, while an adult civilian and a 13-year-old girl also died in the attack (BCL 1990d; *Kalang FM News* 18 January 1990). The likely motivation for this offensive was the seizure of weapons and ammunition, to boost the BRA's limited stockpile (BCL 1990c, 1990d). The PNGDF responded by raiding villages thought to be harbouring those involved in the Kuveria attack.

Another significant BRA offensive occurred on 12 February 1990. At around midday, a security force detachment stationed on Buka – consisting of PNGDF and mobile squad officers – was ambushed. According to Rogers: 'Bougainvillean rebels crossed Buka Passage undetected and attacked. Panic gripped the platoon. Amid the confusion soldiers leapt into Buka Passage to escape. Four soldiers were killed – Privates Mark Barin (Madang), Allan Miria (Central), Maino Lakasisi (Central) and Mano Taguna (Southern Highlands)' (2002: 243–4). Strategically speaking, this was a revealing confrontation. It demonstrated that the BRA now had the organisational capacity to conduct coordinated assaults across the entire province.

In response to the Buka ambush, the PNGDF undertook reprisal attacks on villages in north Bougainville. For example, United Church Pastor, Raumo Benito, and six members of his congregation, were arrested by the military on 14 February 1990, and taken south to Aropa. They were then beaten, stripped naked and all but one was executed (Amnesty International 1990a: 27). The corpses were loaded onto an Iroquois helicopter (flown by Australian pilots) and dropped into the ocean. Colonel Nuia was to later acknowledge this atrocity on the Australian Broadcasting Commission's (ABC) *Four Corners* program (ABC Television, 24 June 1991). His political masters were unimpressed by the unsanctioned admission:

> It embarrassed me, it embarrassed the government, it embarrassed the Australian government. I got dirty phone calls from the Australian government. I don't know why he had to tell the ABC, he didn't have to tell them. I mean I thought it was a good media relations exercise, I approved them to go. I guess I didn't pull aside Nuia and say listen these are the things you don't say. You know, maybe on my part I should have done it. (PNG Minister C, personal communication, 8 July 2006)

Nevertheless, PNGDF reprisals against civilians had become commonplace as the BRA inflicted greater losses on the military. Indeed, these reprisals were even casually recorded in meeting minutes between Colonel Nuia and BCL's Managing Director. For example, at a meeting on

18 February 1990, BCL minutes note: 'Nuia indicated Defence Forces and Army had moved out after one policeman killed in the morning and two policemen killed in the afternoon after attacks at Pakia. Moroni Village had been burnt in retaliation' (BCL 1990j).

As the BRA stepped up its counter-offensive, attacks on the mine site escalated. For instance, on 16 January 1990, two static guards were ambushed and injured near the mine's waste spreader. The following day a company vehicle was hit by a single shotgun blast when travelling north of Birempa (BCL 1990f).

During this period, BCL continued to hold regular meetings with Colonel Nuia. However, now that security force energies were being monopolised by the counterinsurgency offensive, the company was advised that little manpower was left over for mine security. As a result, BCL's Managing Director phoned the Police Commissioner directly on 17 January 1990, and requested he deploy further mobile squad units (BCL 1990d). The Police Commissioner agreed to immediately dispatch 117 mobile squad officers (BCL 1990d). When they failed to arrive, BCL's frustrated Managing Director petitioned the Prime Minister:

I presume you have been kept well informed of the serious deterioration in personnel safety on Bougainville . . . I have been asking for some time now for increased *armed* protection for personnel and property around the operation, but without any result . . . Because of the low level of armed cover, many of our unarmed static security guards have withdrawn, leaving us even more vulnerable in respect of personnel and equipment safety . . . I would appreciate your involvement in facilitating the despatch of additional security personnel. (BCL 1990g)

Fortuitously, on the day this letter was written a senior expatriate manager, Cameron McRae, was shot and seriously wounded while driving home. One of BCL's General Managers recalls the change in mood this attack inspired:

In January when Cameron McRae got shot, and then there was a Goodyear Tyre manager who got shot and killed up at the waste dump in Panguna, those two things said to everybody well that is it, they [security forces] are not getting control of the situation, it's getting worse, so we have no option but to get people out in an orderly fashion, which is what we did. (BCL official E, personal communication, 26 October 2006)

Indeed, with security conditions deteriorating rapidly BCL opted to accelerate the withdrawal of its employees from Bougainville (BCL official D, personal communication, 7 June 2006).

The company's decision, which was widely reported in the media during early February, belied the more confident accounts of the military's achievements being trumpeted by the SOE's Controller (see, for example, *Sydney Morning Herald*, 13 January 1990, p. 21). The decision also surprised Prime Minister Namaliu, who had not been consulted by BCL before the embarrassing news broke. In a letter to BCL's Chairman, Namaliu complained:

> I am particularly disappointed that such an important decision was taken without apparent consultation with my Government, and was subsequently made known to staff, and the media without my Office or Department being informed . . . Given the public significance of this action, I would have expected the Company to advise the Government in advance, and to have consulted with the Government, which remains a shareholder in BCL, prior to the actual decision being made. (PNG National Government 1990)

This, of course, was just one of a number of heated exchanges that had punctuated the relationship between BCL's Chairman and PNG's Prime Minister during 1988–90. Relations between BCL and the PNG government deteriorated further when a cash-strapped BCL began to issue the PNGDF with invoices for use of company messing facilities (BCL 1990e, 1990f). According to one senior manager, no payment was ever received (BCL official A, personal communication, 31 May 2006). To make matters worse, in mid-February 1990, BCL publicly denounced PNGDF soldiers for allegedly looting homes left vacant by company staff (BCL official E, personal communication, 26 October 2006). According to a senior BCL manager, PNG government officials were unimpressed:

> We had to go and get permission for the company aircraft to come in. They [PNGDF] would give us blanket approval for a month, it was coming near the end of the current licence, I went in to get it renewed, and I think Ted Diro [Minister of State] was there, I think Paul Tohian [Police Commissioner] was there, along with [Major] Singirok. I knocked on the door, I went in, they were having a meeting: 'Sorry to barge in, but the current approval for the aircraft expires on Monday'. I got all these dirty

looks, 'you have been telling the Australian press all about our soldiers stealing from company houses'. I said, 'well the fact is they are stealing from company houses . . . It is of concern to the company, but that's not why I am here, I am here because I want to get the aircraft sorted out so we can move people in and out as we need'. 'Oooohhh I don't think we can protect your aircraft from our men' . . . They were saying basically their men were so incensed about these reports about stealing from company houses that they might take pot shots at the company aircraft themselves. I went back to get Bob Cornelius to come over to hear the same story. That was the day we decided that if that was the case we had no option but to leave [immediately] if we were at the stage where they were threatening us, despite *all the assistance* we were giving . . . [i]t was a Saturday, the guys that were left were having a game of golf or tennis. And we just rounded everybody up and said it was time to go. We took another 10 days to get the last out, but that was it. [Italics added] (BCL official E, personal communication, 26 October 2006)

BCL's occupancy on Bougainville thus ended unceremoniously, under a volley of threats delivered by a military outfit they had supported throughout operations *Nakmai Maimai, Bull Dog, Kisim Dog* and *Footloose*. Ironically the public criticism that precipitated this final dispute was the only occasion BCL openly condemned the PNG state for its crimes on Bougainville during 1988–90.

The BRA's Ascendancy

As the company's fortunes declined, the BRA's fortunes rose. Indeed, in late January Rowan Callick (1990a: 8) writing in the *Australian Financial Review* observed that the red rebel flag was being raised in areas all over Bougainville (see also BCL 1990h). A month later, it was noted in the *Post-Courier* that civil servants were being hastily evacuated by the national government (Rea 1990a: 2), while most major business houses had suspended their operations on Bougainville (Darius 1990a: 2; Hiambohn 1990a: 2). Even the security forces were beginning to withdraw from strategic locations around the mine, after they had lost three RPNGC officers along the Port–Mine Access Road, in two separate incidents on the same day (BCL 1990i, 1990j).

In tandem with the BRA's expanding military reach, brutal revenge attacks orchestrated by the security forces began to cement the rebels growing influence outside of central and south Bougainville. An archaeologist, Matthew Spriggs – who was visiting family in the Tinputz district of north Bougainville during December and January of 1989–90 – explains:

> When I went up to the village on 22 December the situation was calm and the people neutral over a conflict seen as being the concern only of people around the Panguna mine. When I left, almost exactly one month later, there was generally support for the BRA against the government and army. The situation had changed dramatically only one week prior to my leaving. Increasing rumours of army brutality; the fantasy-like pronouncements of Police Commissioner Tohian on the radio about the situation being under control; the mobility, courage and military prowess of the small number of BRA operating in the area; the total abandonment of the area by the government and police in the face of operations by four to six active militants, and the promise of the BRA cracking down on the raskols [criminal gangs] in a situation of deteriorating law and order, all contributed to this dramatic change of opinion in North Bougainville. Later army atrocities in the area would have firmed up support for the BRA and changed passive support into active participation. (1990: 30)

With the BRA's support base widening, and the PNGDF on the back foot, cabinet was forced to broker a ceasefire from a position of considerable weakness. The Minister for Provincial Affairs and the Minister for Foreign Affairs, were given responsibility for commencing dialogue with the BRA's Supreme Command (BCL 1990k; O'Callaghan 1990a: 9). To their good fortune, the Ministers were able to tap into a peace initiative that was being developed at the time by the academic Graeme Kemelfield (see Kemelfield 1990, 1992). Kemelfield's objective was to create a neutral security framework, which might allow the political question over Bougainville's independence to be decided free from violence. However, in the interim, the rapport which Kemelfield had established with BRA leaders, secured rebel consent for a formal ceasefire, on the condition that villagers were released from 'care centres', the goods and services blockade was removed, and the security forces vacated the island.[5]

Given the national government's weak negotiating position, one Minister recalls, 'it was my . . . thinking that, well, if this is going to be the last attempt at a peaceful solution, why not' (PNG Minister A, personal communication,

5 July 2006). Accordingly, a ceasefire agreement was signed on 28 February 1990, by Colonel Nuia and Sam Kauona (Hriehwazi 1990a: 1; O'Callaghan 1990b: 1). Not everybody, however, was happy with this decision. According to a senior official from the Prime Minister's Department: 'We civil servants were dead against that political decision. "We are going to lose the prime location in central Bougainville, to come back to regain it will cost us much"' (PMD official A, personal communication, 10 July 2006). Similar concerns, he suggests, were also raised by PNGDF senior command. Indeed, the civil servant concerned was one of Colonel Nuia's confidants and was thus sent by the Prime Minister to break the news of the ceasefire initiative, 'he [Nuia] was more calm with me, if they had sent another fella he would have put a pistol to their head and blown them away' (PMD official A, personal communication, 10 July 2006). Nevertheless, with the defence force demoralised by BRA ambushes, which in turn was leading to revenge attacks on civilians, neither the conciliators nor the hawks were happy to prolong the situation, even if there was vocal dissent.

The NEC, of course, did its best to characterise the ceasefire as a major government victory. For example, Prime Minister Namaliu announced to parliament on 13 March 1990:

> There is no doubt that the increased security force operations in January, and part of February, made an impact and helped create the situation we now have in which there is a ceasefire, a program for negotiations, and at the very least reasonable prospects for lasting peace and harmony. (Hansard, 13 March 1990)

In reality the PNG government was defeated and disillusioned. One of Namaliu's Ministers recalls:

> I think we had to face the reality that the situation was getting out of our control, we could not control it anymore. We didn't want to say it publicly, we didn't want to admit it publicly, it's like admitting defeat, which means morally you are giving the BRA the upper hand. We felt we couldn't publicly admit the situation. People could see for themselves on the ground . . . Once the BRA started to come closer into Kieta, Arawa, starting to build up their support, we just couldn't handle it.[6] (PNG Minister C, personal communication, 8 July 2006)

The national government kept, in part, to the ceasefire terms. For instance, the 4000 civilians held in government 'care centres' were released. Additionally, the security forces vacated the island, though with more haste than had been expected. Indeed, the agreed date for the military's exit was 16 March 1990. The SOE's Controller, however, made a unilateral decision to accelerate the withdrawal of the security forces. Thus, they in fact left the island on 9 March 1990. Rather importantly the withdrawal included all regular RPNGC officers, a decision that went against NEC wishes (Hansard, 16 March 1990).

As a result, when an international observer team arrived on Bougainville during mid-March as part of the Kemelfield peace initiative, they found 'somewhat to their astonishment', that they were to be looked after by 'young BRA soldiers' (Kemelfield 1990: 69). Kemelfield (1992: 142–3) notes, the international observers were there to support an environment of neutrality which they hoped might facilitate dialogue on Bougainville's future political status. Peter Wallensteen from the University of Uppsala was employed as a mediator. However, according to Kemelfield (1992: 152), Wallensteen's 'intended lengthy visit was undermined and shortened by bureaucratic delays, and was marred by suspicions' (Kemelfield 1992: 152). He adds, 'the government opted for direct negotiations at the end of the ceasefire period. This was not properly planned within the terms of the ceasefire, and the departure of the international observer team removed the neutral presence vital to facilitating talks' (Kemelfield 1992: 152–3). Consequently, the political framework which Kemelfield had been developing since September 1989, was abruptly set aside by the national government during March–April 1990. Given that government intelligence sources believed Kemelfield was a BRA agent, the official abandonment of the peace initiative was perhaps not surprising (Defence Intelligence Branch 1990: 10).

The Formulation of a New Counterinsurgency Strategy

Facing international political pressure from key allies, growing indebtedness, major budget cuts, and a significant loss of investor confidence, the national government needed, in lieu of an acceptable peace agreement, to develop a coherent plan for retaking Bougainville. Ted Diro was made Deputy Prime Minister on 29 April 1990, reflecting the urgency of the situation. A Minister recalls:

There was a feeling we had lost Bougainville completely, so we had to restore it . . . It wasn't because of a desire to protect property or anything [like that], at the time it had already been damaged. It was simply a desire to reinstate control. After they understood the significance of Bougainville in Papua New Guinea's environment, the cabinet said to themselves, well we have to fight. (PNG Minister B, personal communication, 9 July 2006)

However, some of those pushing for renewed military pressure in cabinet were rather less clear about how to proceed. For example, the Minister for Minerals and Energy argued that the government could 'get some more money and arm the choppers to the teeth and blast the militants' (BCL 1990m). Fortunately for Prime Minister Namaliu, a more complex strategy was being engineered by the Department of Defence, in consultation with the NEC, and senior Australian Defence Force (ADF) officers stationed in PNG (ADF officer, personal communication, 1 September 2006). This emerging plan was publicly acknowledged by the Prime Minister in late March 1990. Namaliu informed parliament that were peace negotiations to fail, 'we have a fallback position' (cited in *Post-Courier* 23 March 1990, p.2).

The government agency responsible for designing this 'fallback position', was the Defence Intelligence Branch (DIB), which formed part of PNG's Department of Defence. The DIB was a relatively new addition to Defence. According to May:

In 1987–88 growing antipathy between defence intelligence and the NIO [National Intelligence Organisation] provided the occasion for a 'rationalisation' of intelligence capability under a Defence Intelligence Branch (DIB). The DIB is located within the Defence Department, headed by a civilian, and is responsible to the Defence Council; within the DIB are a civilian Directorate of Strategic Defence intelligence, responsible for providing strategic assessments, and a Directorate of Military Intelligence which directly supports PNGDF operations. (1993: 31–2)

The 'rationalisation' of PNG's intelligence agencies, Rogers (2002: 129) argues, 'proved timely. On Bougainville the following year, the PNGDF found it was poorly served by the National Intelligence Organisation (NIO). The DIB assumed a greater role, well beyond that of military intelligence, in an attempt to make up for NIO deficiencies' (see also Liria 1993: 2).

Thus, during March and April 1990, the DIB in effect became the main conduit through which a contingency plan was formulated. The DIB's strategic recommendations, in this respect, were formally outlined in an April 1990 document entitled, *An Intelligence Résumé for Contingency Planning for North Solomons Province*. The résumé advocated a multi-pronged approach for reinstating government control on Bougainville, which included a full military blockade, the amplification and militarisation of local anti-BRA sentiment, and the redeployment of PNGDF troops, aided by pro-government paramilitaries. With the Kemelfield peace initiative side-lined by suspicion, and direct peace negotiations at a standstill, this multi-layered approach came to the fore in May 1990, as the basic blueprint for the national government's Bougainville strategy. It is to the plan's operationalisation that we will now turn.

Blockading the North Solomons Province

Following the withdrawal of the security forces from Bougainville in March 1990, the DIB believed that a general state of anxiety had gripped the North Solomons province. They claimed:

The[re is] general uncertainty about what will happen next in NSP [North Solomons Province], the next government action, the next BRA action, the redeployment of the PNGDF issue, and concern over whether services or normality will return to the island continues. This is detrimental for the NSP population's well being and good for the government in that these hardships may have a profound effect on the largely peace loving NSP population. (DIB 1990: 1–2)

As a result, the DIB argued:

The government should continually push for peace talks outside of NSP, at the same time cut off further shipping, *deliberately to worsen the hardships* people are already facing. Simultaneously, a psychological warfare effort must go into action to exploit the situation. [italics added] (1990: 14)

In fact, despite public denials by the Prime Minister, a de facto blockade had already been placed around the island following the departure of the security forces in March 1990 (BCL 1990n), a move which contravened the ceasefire agreement. The blockade, however, became official government policy following the failed peace talks. It was implemented through Emergency Order No. 31 – the order stated that from 6 May 1990, a 12 nautical mile exclusion zone would be placed around the islands of Bougainville and Buka (Hriehwazi 1990b: 2, 1990c: 2). The order warned, 'all unauthorised vessels within the exclusion zone will be fired upon without prior warning' (cited in Hriehwazi 1990b: 2). Policing the 'exclusion zone', was the PNGDF's naval and air contingent.[7]

PNG's key allies were supportive of the tactic. Indeed, the Hawke government backed the blockade both in principle and practice (HC official A, personal communication, 25 August 2006). A senior DFAT official explains:

> Every effort was being made to make it plain to Ona and co that they were not viable, that they needed the rest of Papua New Guinea as their support . . . With secession, looking practically at it, Ona would have had to have thought, 'where will I get my supplies from, my guns and bullets, who is going to help me', and the answer is 'nobody, you will be totally on your own', and Australia was using its diplomatic leverage to ensure that nobody would come in there to do it. (DFAT official B, personal communication, 21 September 2006)

That the blockade would have a specifically punitive effect on civilians was viewed positively by some Australian diplomats:

> The government was in spite of itself on the right course, which was to deny goodies. They [Bougainville] were well off, comparatively speaking. And the way to bring them to heel, was frankly to cut off the tap, to ensure that they would pay for not having the mine to operate, that they would pay for their defiance if you will . . . But of course they got all the human rights people up there, saying kids were dying and so and so or whatever. And I don't how true that was, but I suspect there was enormous hyperbole in the claims. (HC official B, personal communication, 6 September 2006)

BCL also supported the blockade, indeed when briefed on the proposed embargo the company's Chairman is alleged by PNG's then Foreign Minister to have quipped, '[let's] starve the bastards out' (Somare 2001). A senior manager from BCL remembers some of the company's main concerns at the time:

> There were two things we were worried about. One was the ability of the militants to get more weapons to increase the level of their militancy. And the second was that there was always these threats that they were going to sell off the mine equipment.[8] (BCL official D, personal communication, 7 June 2006)

Once the blockade was formally implemented with Australian and BCL support, it began to inflict the humanitarian effects anticipated by the DIB. MP for north Bougainville, Michael Ogio, reported to parliament in May 1991 the suffering he had witnessed first-hand:

> The first three months of the embargo was hell and the people faced the most brutal kind of hardship that can only be equated to a war situation . . . Because the fighting between the Security Forces and the BRA during 1989 and the early part of 1990 had prevented the people from making good gardens, during the first three months of the embargo food shortages was very acute, trade store goods ran out and everybody had to survive on Tapioka and coconuts. Malnutrition claimed the lives of infants and it was now survival of the fittest. We all had to revert back to the bush for food and within these three months of hardship everybody made good gardens to serve themselves. At the same time medical supplies ran out forcing the closure of Arawa Hospital, all health centres and the aid posts. Malaria and other communicable diseases increased claiming the lives of many, while malnutrition and the lack of immunisation programmes affected infants. The lack of medicine was probably the biggest threat to the population. Many pregnant mothers experiencing problems during child birth due to the closure of health centres, aid posts and the Arawa General Hospital, died. I witnessed many such sad situations. It was either the life of the mother or the new born baby or both. It was indeed a terrible situation . . . It is estimated that up to 8,000 babies have been born and are in need of immunisation. These must be attended to. (Hansard, 10 May 1991)

Lissa Evans, who visited the island to document the blockade's health impacts, supports Ogio's general assessment:

> After two years experience working for Community Aid Abroad's Disaster Response Desk, with a focus on the Asia-Pacific region, it is my firm opinion that the total lack of medical supplies to Bougainville between May 1990 and February 1991 has created an emergency situation. Bougainvillean doctors who have remained on Bougainville throughout the conflict estimate that over 3,000 people have died as a direct consequence of the blockade and that many thousands more are suffering unnecessarily because of a lack of medicines, soaps, detergents and dressings. The island's 300 bed hospital was shut down in June 1990 and there has been no surgery performed since last September. Those in need of surgical care must go to the Solomon Islands (putting serious pressure on the health system there) or rely on traditional practices. An estimated 3,000 children remain unvaccinated against easily preventable diseases. The incidence of malaria has increased markedly. Since January 1990 malaria has killed 200 people, representing a 189 per cent increase over 1989. Many of these are children and pregnant women . . . The incidence of tuberculosis and leprosy has also increased particularly amongst the 10 to 20 years age group. Because of the protracted course of supervised therapy required (a maximum of six months for TB and two years for leprosy), these diseases are being virtually unchecked. Yaws and tropical ulcers are increasingly in evidence because of a lack of penicillin, soaps and detergent. In the past year 70–80 per cent of outpatients have been children under five years of whom 50 per cent are suffering from gastroenteritis, while over 70 per cent of deaths are due to respiratory-related diseases. In addition those people with drug dependencies for illnesses such as diabetes and asthma are dying from lack of medication.[9] (1992: 45–6)

Of course, for the PNG state these effects were neither unexpected nor unwelcomed. To the contrary, the Namaliu government readily acknowledged the strategic role which the humanitarian crisis played in its campaign to win back the island. For example, in a September 1990 press conference, the Prime Minister observed:

> If for instance you look at the situation as it has existed now since March – the level of services in the province has collapsed totally – in which

case those that were in some position of decision-making over there [i.e. the BRA] would not have been in a position to satisfy the vast majority of the people in the province, with increasing pressures for access to services . . . So in that sense it is difficult to entrench your position if you don't have the goods to deliver to the people. Eventually the people themselves would get frustrated and will start applying, as they are in fact doing, pressure on you to either resume the services or something else might develop. (Namaliu 1990)

This strategic belief is not surprising, after all, the Namaliu government had registered the effect a goods and services blockade had in invigorating opposition to the BRA in south Bougainville during late 1989. Now they hoped to generalise this strategy across the province, in an effort to stimulate overt resistance to the rebels, particularly in those regions where the BRA's influence was less potent. It is to this latter issue we will now turn.

Igniting Internal Divisions on Bougainville

With the mass exodus of civil servants, businesses and migrant workers from the North Solomons province during early 1990, the BRA faced the considerable challenge of establishing administrative control over a war-torn island, without the relatively substantial resources that the PNG state could command. While Bougainville's once thriving rural economy could be reinvigorated, the BRA nevertheless would need to restore order, and construct a skeletal political apparatus, as a condition precedent to renewed economic activity. The blockade represented a major barrier to the resumption of normality in this respect. However, the BRA also faced challenges from within, in particular, maintaining discipline among its fighters, many of whom were young unemployed or underemployed men, who had just successfully resisted their economic and social marginalisation. Forster observes:

They won the battle against authority. The fruits of this victory were manifold: they were in charge; they could drive any car that took their fancy – executive air-conditioned dream machines that were never going to be available to them in the normal courses of their lives and four-wheel drives that their fathers had had to work twenty years for. They carried weapons and strolled the streets like cowboys in Dodge City. The moral code of the young Bougainville Revolutionary Army was entirely at their section, the old code had been swept away by the conflict. (1992: 371–2)

Regulating the appetites of these young men proved a considerable challenge for the BRA's Supreme Command. Initially, the rebels set up a squad to combat those 'hooligans' who were 'grabbing vehicles and goods at will' (*Post-Courier* 12 March 1990, p.2). The squad was reported to have executed a number of criminals in early 1990 (*Post-Courier* 12 March 1990, p.2; see also Havini 1995: 12). Additionally, Francis Ona made a personal plea for calm. He claimed that if *raskols* (crime gangs) did not cease their lawless activities, then he would surrender to the national government (Hiambohn 1990b: 1). Nevertheless, with a state of anomie setting in, a much more substantive initiative was required if order was to be restored in the province.

Thus, in May 1990, the rebels set about constructing a decentralised political apparatus. After having consulted with Premier Kabui – who illustrated a willingness to work with the rebels – the BRA's Supreme Command opted to develop a clearly delineated political arm, the Bougainville Interim Government (BIG) (Regan 1996: 11). The BIG's formal inception coincided with the declaration of Bougainville's independence on 17 May 1990 (see Ona 1990b). In parallel with BIG, the BRA Supreme Command also authorised the construction of a multi-layered Council of Chiefs. The latter organ was created to assist customary authorities regulate social activity at a village level. Chiefs were to be endowed with considerable judicial and administrative authority (Regan 1996: 11; Sagir 2005). Indeed, they would even be expected to elect BIG representatives, once the situation on the island was normalised.

This was, in effect, an ambitious attempt to win a wider swathe of the peasantry over to the BRA's side, drawing on the authority of local Chiefs. Indeed, while Francis Ona may have articulated a radical vision for Bougainville's independence during 1989, now that his province-wide leadership was rapidly actualising, he would need to moderate rebel aspirations to mobilise a broader social base behind secession.

However, due to the extreme circumstances in which this political project was initiated, it was beset with problems. Most fundamentally, local BRA factions, it would seem, were unwilling to subordinate themselves either to the authority of Chiefs, or BIG representatives (Sagir 2005; Tanis 2002). The revolt had, in a sense, ignited social forces that were growing beyond the Supreme Command's control. Furthermore, with limited financial resources – a situation which was seriously exacerbated by the blockade – a politically isolated BIG lacked the inputs to establish a semblance of government. Regan (1996: 11) reports:

> Ministers in the BIG were appointed to a wide range of portfolios, some of them people who had not long before been Ministers in the North Solomons Provincial Government. But with no staff or resources, and little direction from Kabui or Ona, many melted away. Efforts were made to appoint government officials – even district coordinators and kiaps – but they quickly found they could do very little in practice without resources.

Given the substantive barriers which stood in the way of the BIG and Council of Chiefs, an alternative political framework for governing Bougainville, failed to blossom. Meanwhile, theft, rioting, and sporadic violence plagued the province, especially outside central Bougainville, where the Supreme Command's authority was weaker.

The BIG's impotence in the face of growing disorder, in conjunction with the province's economic stagnation and isolation, encouraged prominent politicians and business leaders in the north and south to actively oppose secession. According to Regan (1996), the BRA began countering emerging opposition through arrests, interrogation, torture and in some cases, execution. He argues, 'there were numerous instances of brutal behaviour – torture and murder – by BRA elements against individuals and groups alleged to have supported the national government. There was never even a pretence of a trial – suspicion was sufficient basis for action' (Regan 1996: 10). Indeed, the north Bougainville MP, Michael Ogio, informed parliament in 1991 that the:

> Supporters of the BRA were identified and left alone, while those of us who were suspected to be Pro-National Government were rounded up and interrogated in the three main command posts. I went through two such interrogations in Panguna where I was taken to. Many people who could not prove beyond any doubt to the BRA that they were neutral were placed under house arrest, today they are still under house arrest. Others simply went missing and are still missing. (Hansard, 10 May 1991; see also Onsa 1992)

Facing an emboldened but overwhelmed rebel force, the BRA's opponents on Bougainville approached the national government soon after the March 1990 ceasefire. Their aim was to garner covert support for a local initiative to counteract rebel influence. The details of this initiative were enumerated in a report attached to the DIB's intelligence résumé:

> [The] BRA's strength really lies in the fact that there is no systematic pressure exerted against it by the people, as [is the case with] all dictatorships, and that there is [also] a general realization that its members are mobile and have weapons. In our view as time goes by we think that the BRA will learn to deal with internal and external threats more effectively and thus tighten its grip over Bougainville if no pressure is exerted quickly both internally and externally to counter its activities and influence over Bougainville. (DIB 1990)

Given this assessment, the report argues that groups loyal to the government must be empowered to exert 'systematic pressure' both on the civilian population, and on those sections of the BRA less committed to secession (DIB 1990). Indeed, it claims, a loyalist militia consisting of several hundred men had already been organised. If these men were to be trained and armed by the PNG state,[10] the report argues, they could provide security for local political leaders as they travelled the province, 'to create awareness on the benefits for a negotiated settlement' (DIB 1990).

The report suggests that villagers in the north and south of Bougainville, would be more receptive to a negotiated solution. These communities, 'do not know what is happening . . . they do not know what [the] BRA's plans are. They do not know what the government's plans are' (DIB 1990). Thus, it is explained, 'we will continue to target this group of people in our campaign, with the view of securing their total commitment to the process of peaceful negotiations' (DIB 1990). The report also highlights the importance of instrumentalising tensions within the BRA:

> You will note that there is the supreme advisory council. This is made up of mainly central Bougainville people . . . Central Bougainville members of the BRA do patrols around the island to see that the councils and Kauona's commands are adhered to. When one analyses this practice we have in effect a situation where central Bougainville is dictating its intentions to the rest of Bougainville. This has been highlighted to both Northern and Southern [BRA] Command and it appears that there is

already a degree of resentment for [the central] organization developing within the Province. (DIB 1990)

The report concludes:

> Our recommendation for a practical course of action to counter BRA activities within the BRA itself is to channel information to BRA North and South which would discredit the organization especially the supreme advisory council which is made of central Bougainvilleans. We believe that the most effective manner of doing this is to hold direct meetings with the members of BRA north and south within their respective areas, away from Central BRA. Members of both BRA north and south have been encouraged in our brief meetings with them to redirect their energies . . . [to] safeguarding the people and leaders of North Bougainville and South Bougainville who opt for a negotiated settlement and already there have been a positive result and as such we are here . . . In our future talks with them we would tend to be more forceful. All of us should contribute towards achieving total isolation of central command. (DIB 1990: Attachment)

This frequent reference here to the tensions, or the potential for tension, between north, south and central Bougainville, registered the fractured social terrain on which the BRA's uprising was built. Indeed, the gradual immersion within global capitalism had not eroded localised allegiances on Bougainville, it had, in fact, entrenched forms of clan and regional differentiation, for reasons that were pointed to in chapter two. In this sense the rebellion was a nascent attempt to develop a higher unity that could supersede these groupings through a broad appeal to class interest, ethno-nationalism, and a respect for 'traditional' Melanesian ideals. But to develop the sort of sophisticated organisational technologies and cultural esteem needed to bring this project to fruition would take years, and the reality was by March 1990, the BRA had abruptly and unexpectedly assumed a position of pan-Bougainville authority. Exposing the fragility and weakness of this adolescent movement was what their loyalist opponent appeared to have had in mind.

PNG's security forces were generally sympathetic to this strategy. Indeed, drawing on local intelligence, the DIB (1990: 13–14) résumé optimistically notes that there was an opportunity to split the province into three, isolating the BRA 'hardcore' in central Bougainville. In this context, the blockade's strategic role was especially vital. According to the DIB (1990: 14), 'the split in the province . . . will grow and can become explosive if services are completely out and Kauona continues to delay peace talks by being stubborn on using Panguna as the venue' (DIB 1990: 14). Indeed, the DIB (1990: 13) claimed that were tensions on the island to be carefully amplified by government and pro-government forces, '[a] civil war could eventuate in the province, the central [BRA] command against the north and the south'. Collectively, these conditions would create a favourable environment for the PNGDF to be redeployed on Bougainville (DIB 1990: 11). This, the DIB anticipated, would pressure the more moderate BRA factions to agree to a resolution short of secession (DIB 1990: 14). We thus see here a strategic coming together of the blockade, PNGDF redeployment and the militarisation of local opposition to the BRA.

The NEC was persuaded. Consequently, amplifying and militarising the divisions on Bougainville, became an essential part of the national government's blueprint for retaking the island. A Minister recalls:

> Well it is better to have Bougainvilleans fighting Bougainvilleans. They knew the terrain better, they understood the customs better, [thus] it was better for us to organise them. So those [on Bougainville] who believed in the nation's unity, provided the resistance to the BRA. It started as a village protection system, and they then were developed and taken over by the [PNG] military, and trained and equipped. It became an effective organisation. (PNG Minister B, personal communication, 9 July 2006)

The first region in the North Solomons province to see pro-government leaders successfully convert local tensions into armed opposition, was on Buka, the densely populated island just off Bougainville's northern tip. Here it is claimed Thomas Anis, a former commerce Minister in the North Solomons provincial government, and Sam Akoitai, a prominent Bougainvillean businessman, had managed to organise local men into an anti-BRA paramilitary group, which they named the Buka Liberation Front (BLF) – it later became part of what was known as the resistance forces (PMD official B, personal communication, 4 July 2006; PNG Department of Foreign Affairs official, personal communication, 11 July 2006). Following the breakdown of a short-lived peace accord signed in early August 1990, the BLF's leaders approached the national government for assistance. The senior official from the Prime Minister's Department recalls:

We had one of our warships sitting outside [Bougainville] in the middle of the ocean near Buka. The Buka Liberation Front organised themselves, they went in a small dinghy, they went out there, and this defence vessel saw the small boat coming. They were ready to knock them out, because they were not sure if they were genuine or not. So anyway, they came right up to the boat, and they saw their leaders, Sam Akoitai, and Thomas Anis. They came on board . . . [and] invite[ed] the national government to come back. (PMD official B, personal communication, 4 July 2006)

A senior official from PNG's Department of Foreign Affairs (DFA) also remembers this important meeting:

The present [2006] Minister for Mining [Sam Akoitai] . . . he came in as the leader of the resistance forces . . . He was drained, he was all gone, just bones. We had to deal with him, we had to encourage him, and give him money. In the end he became the best thing, to have the resistance forces . . . It was quite a seductive thing. I gave out lots of money. (DFA official, personal communication, 11 July 2006)

According to media reports, the BLF did not come empty handed; indeed, they had successfully organised a petition signed by 125 'individuals' requesting the reinstallation of national government control on Buka (Spriggs 1992a: 10–1; see also Rea 1990b: 1). Thus, the national government now had an attractive opportunity to get a toehold in the region, as a result of internal tensions which they had helped to exacerbate. Fortunately for Prime Minister Namaliu, the military was ready to seize this opportunity, owing in part to greater input from the ADF.

Retaking Buka

Early 1990 was arguably one of the bleakest periods in the PNGDF's history. They had, relatively speaking, suffered serious losses on Bougainville. Making matters worse, the military had been forced to make a tactical retreat from the island, under humiliating circumstances. For those ADF soldiers present on the island, the PNGDF's performance was a matter of serious concern. As one officer recalls: 'We drove up to what they called the pink palace [BCL administration block] and then watched this crisis team try and manage what was going on, and it was not being done very well' (ADF officer, personal communication, 1 September 2006). Given that the use of ADF troops in combat positions was off the cards, Australian officers stationed in the High Commission, and on exchange in the PNGDF, attempted to improve matters by shaping the PNGDF's redeployment strategy:

> I don't think it is stretching the point too much to say that XXXX [ADF officer on loan to the PNGDF] and a few others, and we were included in this [ADF staff at the Australian High Commission], started to devise an operation to win back Bougainville. Which was to start by getting back Buka, getting Buka, and then working to expand your bases, thereby winning it [Bougainville] back in a military sense, when it was in total darkness, the case was totally hopeless. (ADF officer, personal communication, 1 September 2006)

When asked how ADF officers managed to become so active in a military operation ostensibly under PNGDF command, it was explained:

> Well that is always the difficult part, but look with any idea it's an ownership thing, they have got to feel ownership, they have to be comfortable with it. So we realised, we stepped back from the fact it was our idea, you have to organise the whole thing so it's like the PNGDF have thought it, otherwise it is not going to work. If people don't have ownership of an approach they are not going to do it. You can see it in everyday life, if you say to your children you know I want you to do it this way, they're not going to do it. It is only when they have ownership of it that they'll do it. (ADF officer, personal communication, 1 September 2006)

The ADF steered re-entry strategy that emerged from this process was buoyed considerably by extra logistic support that had been pledged by Australia in January 1990. In particular, the Hawke government had promised to assist PNG train and arm an additional 450 troops, at a cost of AUS$13 million (around US$10 million) (Australian Department of Defence 1990: S757–8). These new recruits would allow PNG to 'bring the existing three companies in each of the two PNGDF infantry battalions to full strength, and to add a fourth company to each battalion' (Australian Department of Defence 1990: S757; PNG Minister C, personal communication, 8 July 2006). According to a senior official from Australia's Department of Defence (ADoD):

> What we did was to persuade them to raise a new battalion, because they were running short of battalions to rotate through Bougainville. And when they were in Bougainville, if they had a clash with the rebels, and took causalities, morale dropped . . . and they didn't have enough battalions to rotate through. So we persuaded them to raise another battalion. (ADoD official A, personal communication, 23 August 2006)

Buoyed by extra troops, ADF strategic assistance, BLF ground support, and a concrete redeployment strategy, the PNGDF made its Buka landing on 19 September 1990 (Saffu 1998c: 484). According to one Minister from the Namaliu government:

> We had the resources, not in leaps and bounds, but we did have sufficient resources to go in there . . . Buka was successful. On the day we arrived we shot up 14 or 15 Bougainvilleans, I mean the message got out loud and clear. When they came on board there, the boys really got stuck into them, there was a big battle there. To go back to Bougainville, we had better preparation. (PNG Minister C, personal communication, 8 July 2006)

Indeed, the *Post-Courier* reported that 20 BRA soldiers were killed by the PNGDF/BLF following redeployment (Hiambohn 1990d: 1). Additionally, dozens of BRA suspects had been arrested (Hiambohn 1990d: 1). These prisoners were alleged to have been seriously mistreated by the security forces. In a report aired on *Four Corners* (ABC Television 24 June 1991), a former Bougainvillean Red Cross worker testified to seeing the security forces line up five prisoners near the shores of Buka passage, they were then told to swim across to Bougainville. When they entered the water, PNGDF soldiers picked them off one by one.

By October 1990, the BLF boasted that only 50 insurgents remained on Buka, 'they are in the jungles there somewhere and it will not be long before we track them down and terminate them' (Darius 1990b: 2). To that end, over the final months of 1990, the PNGDF, BLF and BRA were pitched in fierce skirmishes across Buka. With tensions at a high, and popular allegiances divided by kin and class loyalties, villages were subjected to punitive raids by both sides. A *Post-Courier* report from December 1990 relayed refugee accounts:

> [H]omes had been destroyed at random in some of the strong BLF villages, especially in and around Haku and Halia . . . [However] another person [refugee] told the Post-Courier that many families feared the Buka Liberation Front more than the Bougainville Revolutionary Army and Defence Force soldiers. Homes, gardens and valuable property had been destroyed 'for no good reason' and old people and others and children had been frightened by BLF members armed with guns and other dangerous weapons. (19 December 1990, p.3)

It was becoming apparent that the militarisation of internal divisions on Bougainville-Buka had sparked an intense episode of retributive violence. The gravity of this struggle was captured by the BLF leader, Thomas Anis, who claimed, 'we are fighting a civil war which involves arms, violence and psychological struggle for power – a warfare in which only the fittest will survive' (*Post-Courier* 7 January 1991).

By December 1990, it was the BLF and its supporters who had obtained the upper hand on Buka, assisted by the PNGDF. According to Spriggs, the human cost of their ascendancy was large: 'A document recently acquired lists 49 people said to have been killed on Buka by the BLF and/or security forces. Some allegations are gruesome in the extreme, describing people cut to pieces, buried or burned alive, disembowelled or dismembered before death' (1992b: 188). Amnesty International (1993) paints a similarly disturbing image:

> On Buka Island the most serious and extensive human rights abuse was reported to have occurred after the military landing of September 1990 and throughout 1991, during which time the military-armed and backed Buka Liberation Front (BLF) was at its most active. Both PNGDF soldiers and BLF members are alleged to have perpetrated serious human rights violations, including extrajudicial execution. Other violations, such as torture and sexual abuse were said to have been common on Buka during this period. Women were frequently reported to have been humiliated and raped by soldiers and young girls forced to cook and work for the PNGDF.

As a result of the escalating violence on Buka, thousands of civilians fled to Rabaul in PNG's East New Britain province. Additionally, government 'care centres' were also constructed to house the displaced. Approximately, 7,000 villagers were living in the Buka 'care centres' by January 1991 (Spriggs 1992a: 11–3).

Conditions inside these refugee camps appear to have been particularly bleak. According to Amnesty International (1993):

> Residents are said to be under constant surveillance and to be subjected to various forms of intimidation and persecution by government security forces, including death threats and beatings. Residents in Buka care centres have reported many cases of civilians being taken away by PNGDF soldiers and beaten with the butts of guns or kicked with army boots. Residents have also alleged that during late 1990 and 1991 PNGDF soldiers killed people living in the care centres as 'payback' or revenge for the deaths of PNG soldiers during combat with BRA forces. Others have reported rape and other forms of sexual abuse of women in care centres during this period.

Having cleared away large sections of the civilian population, by mid-1991 pro-government forces were reported to have gained complete control over Buka (Dorney 1998: 49). This was an important victory for those that backed the DIB blueprint, it vindicated the strategy of selective deprivation, militarisation, and reengagement. Accordingly, the tactics employed on Buka, were replicated during 1991 and 1992 as the PNGDF attempted to obtain footholds in the north and south of Bougainville. Dorney writes:

> The PNGDF, with the help of the Buka Liberation Front, effectively returned Buka to PNG control by the middle of 1991. The Buka Liberation Front set a pattern for other communities in north-west and north-east Bougainville in 1991 and for those in the Siwai district of south-west Bougainville wanting to split from the Nasioi-led [central Bougainville] revolution in 1992. They established their own local forces to fight the BRA. (1998: 49)

Thus, by 1992 the PNG government had successfully harnessed the internal schisms on Bougainville – many of which were exacerbated by the BRA's own atrocities and inability to control criminal elements – to cultivate the civil war situation that had been envisaged by the DIB in April 1990.

Conclusion – The Making of Civil War on Bougainville

The fighting on Bougainville would persist for another five years. Following a 1997 military revolt, triggered by the national government's attempt to contract private military company, Sandline International, a permanent ceasefire was signed, while in 2001 the *Bougainville Peace Agreement* was endorsed by the warring factions. Under the peace agreement the North Solomons would remain part of PNG, in return for greater autonomy, and an option for a referendum to be held over independence within ten to 15 years, conditions that echoed the agreement secured by Bishop Gregory Singkai twelve years earlier, but which had been rejected by the Namaliu government. This mediated outcome put an end to the hostilities which by this stage had taken between 10,000–20,000 lives, in addition to causing immeasurable damage to the island's infrastructure and industry (Alley 2003: 231).

Yet, back in 1988, there was little hint that a local landowner dispute, *seemingly* over mine benefits, would eventually culminate in the worst humanitarian crisis the region had witnessed since the Second World War. Indeed, there were good reasons to think that the NPLA's demands could be contained and managed within the mine lease area, where their support base was centred. However, the chances of co-opting moderate factions of the NPLA, and isolating its more radical elements, were limited by BCL's enduring focus on the legal arrangements governing the mine, which married them to a conservative interpretation of custom. In contrast, PNG's Prime Minister was more sympathetic to the NPLA's aspiration, at least during 1988. That said, the political terrain within the PNG state proved complex, a fact which was powerfully demonstrated by the RPNGC's unsanctioned attack on landowner villages just hours after the government achieved a political breakthrough in December 1988. Soon after, the BRA was formed.

As we observed, several months of low-level security disturbances followed, however, this abruptly escalated into rioting and ethnic bloodshed following Deborah Dovonu's murder. With the security situation rapidly deteriorating on Bougainville, the PNG government fell back on paramilitary force. This type of punitive reaction had become a default setting of sorts for the PNG state when responding to significant disturbances, such as tribal fighting and gang-crime. However, in the case of Bougainville the disturbance was of a different character and intensity, to what the government had faced in the past. As a result, the rebels were able to co-opt RPNGC attacks to boost local support. Yet even by the end of April 1989, with dozens of villages reduced to ashes, the BRA's ascendancy was far from assured. While they had successfully recruited beyond ethnic lines, village sympathies remained hooked to clan and custom, which for reasons pointed to in chapter 2, continue to be vital conduits for organising life on Bougainville.

Over the course of 1989, the national government attempted to emphasise the priority of these local networks by championing the Bougainville Package through a unified PLA. The BRA used secession, alongside further mine attacks, to short-circuit the national government's political program. For a range of reasons, the BRA's tactics worked, as a result a powerful hawk faction came to the fore in cabinet, led by former PNGDF Commander Ted Diro. This created the political conditions in which a military solution to the crisis could be implemented, while the material conditions were secured through Australian and BCL support; this helped fill gaps in arms, equipment and logistics. With a steady supply of equipment and arms the PNGDF attempted to clear the mine area, and rout the BRA. As we observed, they failed in both respects. Instead, it was civilians who ended up becoming the chief target for a military force eager to demonstrate their firepower.

As the BRA counter-attacked across the North Solomons province, they emulated NPLA campaigning tactics. Accordingly, more immediate interests centring around race and security, were grafted to a long-term vision for Bougainville's independence. In this light, the government's increasingly brutal attacks on civilians, and civilian infrastructure during 1989–90, only served to accelerate the rebels' ascendancy. When this ascendancy reached its peak in May 1990, the Namaliu government realised they seriously risked losing a significant geopolitical asset. This led to the PNG state's most significant gamble during the war's formative years. Sensing that the rebels were experiencing overreach, the Namaliu government blockaded the island, militarised local opposition and reoccupied Buka, with the intent of inciting civil war.

In this respect, they achieved some success as the province split down complex fault lines during 1990. Indeed, by the end of 1990 the tables had turned on Bougainville. It was now the BRA, and its political arm, which were in the position of having to re-establish order – albeit of a different nature to the one that the NPLA had risen in defiance of – while, the PNG government, using local paramilitaries and a military blockade, were focused upon its disruption. As the latter tactics matured, the hostilities escalated; acts of revenge on both sides increasingly embroiled civilians. In the end, this amplification of the conflict and the extreme bitterness it provoked, successfully impeded BRA plans to secede, creating the conditions in which a more prolonged battle for Bougainville could be waged. However, it came at great human cost, which to this day remains barely acknowledged.

7

State Crime and Really Existing Capitalism: The Lessons of Bougainville

Internment camps, the mortaring of homes, aerial bombardment, extra-judicial killings, the torture and humiliation of prisoners, rape, and the denial of humanitarian aid; these are just some of the criminal state practices endured by Bougainville residents during 1988 and 1997. Even on the margins of Empire, retribution was cruelly and indifferently applied to those who challenged 'pax capital'.

This book offers the first criminological account of the state-corporate actions which lay behind the criminal events on Bougainville. Indeed, we have observed, not through factual deductions but through the words of the perpetrators themselves, that a highly coordinated, international campaign of state violence was organised by the PNG state, in collaboration with their Australian counterparts and BCL. This campaign of state violence, moreover, consciously and actively targeted civilians in a number of illicit ways, in a bid to suppress a social uprising in a vital strategic region of PNG.

However, the articulation of truth without an attempt to also make meaning diminishes truth. In this respect, we cannot afford to remain neutral on the scholarly framework employed – not all approaches are equally well poised to valorise truth through enriched meaning. To that end, it has been argued that classical Marxism offers one of the most fertile scholarly soils for understanding how the contradictory rhythms of Empire systematically produce the social conditions in which the crimes of the powerful become possible and probable.

In this final chapter we consider in more detail the rather different complexion a classical Marxist approach can give to our understanding of state crime, by reflecting on the example of Bougainville. In particular, this chapter highlights the way in which Marxist theory can help to illuminate layers of empirical complexity not apparent from an empiricist vantage point, which in turn critically affects how we go about mobilising against state crime. The chapter will conclude with six generalisable lessons that can be employed when framing future state crime interventions from a classical Marxist stand point.

Illuminating the Fault-Lines of State Crime on Bougainville

At first glance, the origins of the Bougainville crisis would appear to lie in the neglect of landowner grievances, an issue which came to the fore when the NPLA issued a demand for K10 billion in compensation. When this demand was forcefully operationalised through protest, civil disobedience, and industrial sabotage, the mine operator BCL was prevented from extracting minerals, realising revenue, and achieving their overriding objective of profit – accordingly, they demanded an authoritative response from the Namaliu government. This demand reverberated through the PNG state owing to its dependency on the resource sector. Facing fiscal ruin, a series of progressively more violent counterinsurgency operations were launched by the Namaliu government, with material support from BCL and their Australian counterparts. Facing an elusive, well trained opponent, PNG's security forces attacked civilian targets, with minimal oversight.

From an empiricist perspective, this summary *concretely* relates essential determinates – goals, opportunity structure and operationality of controls – underpinning state crime on Bougainville, and were I working in this tradition, I would now apply one of the relevant theoretical schemas to bring these determinates into a cause and effect relationship. On the other hand, from a classical Marxist perspective, this summary remains fundamentally *abstract* in the absence of theoretical mediation.

For example, the category landowner conflict, which is a common reference employed by scholars when discussing Bougainville, is an abstraction, if we leave out the critical changes in rural social relations, precipitated by the generalisation of petty commodity production and patrimonial politics. These changes, as we observed in chapter two, altered the way Bougainvillean households related to land, labour and kin. As a result, the social mediations of clan, custom and tradition assumed new meanings, as families struggled to avoid the simple reproductive squeeze. Out of this struggle emerged the possibility of rupture. That said, the possibility of rupture has been significantly reduced in PNG by the unifying force of patrimonial politics and the hegemonic blocs it prompts. Nevertheless, in the mine lease area of Bougainville, where the contradictions of rural development were condensed in time and space, an articulate group of young leaders were able to harness heightened tensions to build an anti-capitalist movement. Indeed, unlike their predecessors (OPLA), the NPLA's movement was not for a little more – if so, it would have been suppressed more easily – rather, they aimed to radically rearticulate how Bougainville functioned within Empire. Yet, in the absence of careful theoretical scrutiny, the richness of the reality emerging during 1988 is significantly diminished by abstractions such as 'landowner conflict'.

The same lesson can be applied when it comes to understanding the company's role in the conflict. Although, in the first instance, BCL's criminogenic reaction to the NPLA would appear to have been a result of profit-seeking and heightened competition, these categories are impoverished if we are not familiar with the social composition of competition and profit. Marx's theory of value, and surplus value, as we observed (see chapter 3), are critical tools in this respect. In brief, Marx argues that socially necessary labour time is the source of value, and consequently surplus value, however, it is extracted by capital in multiple ways, and then enters upon a mediated journey. The sum consequence of this journey, for our purposes, is that individual capitals invested in productive industries can realise an above average rate of profit – assuming their class as a whole is successfully extracting surplus value from the working class – by applying the variable *and* constant component of their capital more efficiently than rivals. Rivals who wish to avoid expropriation must innovate in response to these competitive pressures. We observe this critical dynamic come into play during 1988, a period when BCL's relative position in the copper industry was going into decline. In a bid to restore BCL's global position, company management embarked upon a program of efficiency savings. Yet this was not the only force conditioning BCL's strategic response to the NPLA, the company's value composition also proved important in this respect. Indeed, as a mining concern, BCL's operation was constructed through a particularly high ratio of constant to variable capital, which saw the company bonded to a specific geopolitical region for a substantive period of time, while it extracted the copper and gold.

These two relationally-bounded processes – the coercive effect of competition and the spatio-temporal demands of valorisation – engendered a corporate culture at BCL intensely focused on the enforceability of contractual arrangements and the reduction of costs. This, in turn, married the company to a static definition of tradition, and a cautious, verging on rigid, approach to landowner negotiations; a posture made more likely by the generational shift in senior managers. As a result, when the NPLA initiated a campaign of industrial sabotage, BCL's senior managers in effect asked the government to forcefully restore the OPLA, under the auspices of tradition, an approach which made BCL a willing accomplice when the PNG government finally implemented a military 'solution'. However, like with the example of 'landowner crisis', the character and meaning of BCL's strategic response only becomes apparent in richer degrees, through the selective application of certain concepts that help tease out the social content of the different currents which the company was immersed within, and reacting to.

Of course, when it comes to understanding the criminogenic posture gradually assumed by the PNG state, we need to branch out beyond those general tendencies articulated by Marx in *Capital*. That said, Marx remains a critical starting point. His pioneering theoretical contribution orients us to the relationships that permit surplus value to be extracted from the immediate producer, without the *direct need for* application of sovereign power. This critical change in social dynamic, as we observed (chapter 1), deprives the latter of its previous social content, creating the impulse for a reorganisation of the power relations that mediate rule. The new modality of power to emerge from this process of historical change, is usefully articulated by Foucault, through the concept of governmentality. A state which has been governmentalised, Foucault argues, takes the economic and social rhythms of civil society as its 'natural' object, and in a bid to achieve desirable outcomes conceptualised at the level of population – attempts to stimulate, calibrate and in certain cases, suppress these rhythms through the tactical deployment of different political technologies. Yet, Foucault is less clear when it comes to the mediated relationship that develops between specific political articulations of governmental power, and the broader process of class struggle. In this respect, as I noted in chapter 4, the political theory of Poulantzas, offers helpful guidance. In a social whole fractured by complex class divisions, it may be argued that governmental regimes emerge through a war of positions (see Gramsci 1971), which takes place across the earthworks of the state and civil society, viewed not as 'things', but as strategic fields. Championed by particular power networks, if a governing project is to assume a position of hegemony it must first seize critical positions within the state – the military, a specific ministry, cabinet, a political party etc. – which exude their own selectivity, and second, the project must be capable of unifying the dominant classes, while disorganising the exploited masses (see also Jessop 2007).

In PNG, a decade of economic stagnation in conjunction with diplomatic and donor pressure, had allowed a variant of neoliberal governance to seize key positions within the state during the late 1980s, under the patronage of coalition power-brokers. This engendered a concerted push towards deregulation (for capital), tax breaks, privatisation, wage restraints, removal of import duties, an expanded security apparatus, etc., in an effort to stimulate foreign investment into PNG's sluggish national economy. However, successive PNG governments recognised their reliance on indirect rule was a persisting concern for international investors, particularly in the resource industry on which hopes were increasingly pinned. To that end, the Namaliu government engineered a range of technologies for stabilising and managing their relationship with customary authorities in resource development areas.

However, when the Bougainville crisis erupted disagreements emerged over the role violence should play in this arrangement. Certain leaders, such as the Prime Minister, viewed it as a final measure for channelling landowner groups back into acceptable forums. Others, like the Police Commissioner and the PNGDF's senior command felt a zero-tolerance approach needed to be adopted when rent-seeking behaviour exceeded set legal boundaries. This latter view resonated with national and international capital, both of which were growing tired of the 'Melanesian compensation mentality'. Nevertheless, this strategic perspective did not have a strong enough foothold within cabinet, until a major reshuffle during May 1989, brought Ted Diro and Ben Sabumei to the fore. Yet even with strong coalition power-brokers championing a military option in cabinet, the hawks' temporal ascendancy was not assured. Rather, it was mediated to a large extent by PNG's resource dependency, which through a range of nodal points – specifically, state revenues, patrimonial politics, and national bourgeoisie accumulation strategies – transmitted capital's concerns into cabinet politics. This was enough to sway the balance of power in the hawks favour on successive occasions during 1989–90, owing to the fact they offered a strategy that had the immediate appeal of restoring financial flows essential to the national economy's arterial systems.

Nevertheless, the latter shift may not have led to such an unmitigated episode in state violence, were it not for the significant diplomatic and military support lent by the Australian state. Upon first examination, this support seemingly reflected an instrumental desire on the part of the Hawke government to protect Australian capital, which at the time was facing expropriation (remembering, BCL was majority owned by CRA). However, such an assessment adopts an overly narrow understanding of the relationships that influence how state power is projected abroad. A degree of clarity, in this respect, has been brought by Harvey (2003) and Callinicos (2009) who argue that the international projection of state power must be understood as taking place within a framework of geopolitical competition between states. Furthering this approach, I argued in the opening chapter that this is a historical modality of geopolitical competition specific to capitalism, where states look to accumulate sovereign power and strategically project it more effectively than rivals (imperialism) – be it in bilateral or multilateral forums – because this puts them in a position of having a greater impact on the regional and global milieus through which the circulation of capital takes place. Mediating, and informing this process, is the uneven way capital spatially distributes itself, in the search for surplus value. According to Ashman (2006: 101), 'capitalism is . . . clumpy and territorialized, but dynamically so and in complex ways, clustered around certain capitalist cores and states'. So while capitalism indeed operates through economic centres, it is important to keep in mind, as Ashman notes, these regionalised configurations of accumulation are subject to significant change and recalibration. State managers must strategically manoeuvre on this basis, using a range of foreign policy technologies to shape the international environment through which capitalised flows of wealth move, in an effort to engender – to the best of their nationally mediated abilities – international conditions sympathetic to domestic governmental strategies.

   With this dynamic in mind – during the 1980s, the Hawke government was facing a dilemma, as new, more competitive regional articulations of capital accumulation in Asia, were accelerating Australia's economic decline. In response, the Hawke government attempted to reconfigure Australia's fit within the world economy. At home this involved the championing, and operationalisation, of a particular modality of neoliberalism, while abroad, the Hawke government was focused on amplifying Australia's middle power status through strategic coalitions, bulwarked by US support. In this particular context, Australia's self-anointed role as 'regional sheriff', had a number of dimensions that stretched beyond national security, and indeed the security of its capital and citizens embedded in the South Pacific. Specifically, failure to maintain a regional space somewhat sympathetic to the international liberal order, risked complicating Australia's important relationship with the US, and undermining its international credibility, at a time when the Hawke government was attempting to flex its foreign policy muscle, through a number of key fora, in aid of major domestic reforms. In this light, those in charge of amplifying Australia's punch as a middle-weight power, wanted to see the Bougainville uprising brought to a relatively quick, well-handled end, which communicated to allies that Australia was 'on the job' (ADoD official A, personal communication, 23 August 2006). Believing the BRA to be ill-prepared, and sitting on the fringes of Bougainvillean society, the Hawke government felt the rebel movement could be rapidly brought to heal through a decisive show of military force on the part of the Namaliu government. As a result, the Australian state lobbied PNG to get their 'people [PNGDF] over there', and actively aided the security forces when the Namaliu government indeed chose to do so (HC official A, personal communication, 25 August 2006).

What each of the examples enumerated above suggest is, that the reality of state crime is much richer and more complex than what first appearances suggest. Accordingly, the development of more precise understandings of state crime cannot be achieved by placing theoretically unmediated abstractions into causal relationships. Rather, a very different style of science and theory must be employed if we are to replace first appearances with a series of more concrete approximations that are capable of illuminating the mediated way in which the relations constitutive of Empire develop in particular spatialised configurations, to produce social balances that favour criminal state practices.

Indeed, if effective resistance is to be mounted against state crime, social movements must be guided by theories that can approximate in greater clarity, the weight of forces being opposed, their social context and the opportunities that exist for mobilising coalitions capable of ending impunity and effecting change. In the absence of such theory resistance will be forced to pragmatically navigate a partially seen social terrain.

General Lessons for State Crime Studies

Over the previous five chapters it has been argued that state crime on Bougainville emerged from PNG's *particular* path of immersion into Empire, which engendered certain contradictory social currents that brought a range of organisations into collision. It follows from this point, that we should exhibit serious caution when attempting to extrapolate from this case study generalisations about the relationship between capitalism's laws of motion and state crime. That said, a number of general lessons can be identified, which might usefully inform future Marxist interventions in the area.

First, when conducting analyses of state crime – which always take place within certain regional contexts – it is important to recognise that the relationships constitutive of global capitalism can be operationalised through a diverse range of socio-cultural arrangements, exploitative forms and political systems. Accordingly, it would be a mistake to assume that because a particular state crime event takes place within contexts which fail to conform to classical models of capitalism and liberal democracy – PNG is an obvious example – that the relations constitutive of capitalism do not operate. The challenge is to understand how these relations can function through diverse ensembles of institutions and political forms, and the conjunctural intricacies, tendencies and contradictions, that arise from these particular articulations of capitalist development.

Second, at its most abstract, capital is a particular sum of value that when successfully invested, returns to the owner in expanded form, owing to a class-organised process of exploitation. In order for this exploitative transaction to take place, however, the invested capital must assume particular forms. Each form, in this respect, will have its own set of criminogenic potentialities. In the case of Bougainville, we dealt with an example of mining capital. As an articulation of mining capital, BCL's reaction to social rupture was critically shaped by the nature of the mineral extraction process in which it was engaged, and the value composition this process necessitated (high ratio of constant to variable capital). This engendered managers who were acutely sensitive to contractual arrangements, and minimising the long-term impact of political change. Out of this dynamic emerged a definite set of criminogenic potentialities as Bougainville became increasingly volatile during 1988–89. However, presumably finance capital, for example, functioning through the conduit of the securities markets, would have different concrete characteristics, engendering in turn a different set of criminogenic potentialities. An important task then is to define more specifically the criminogenic potentialities associated with different articulations of capital, and to understand the role states play in mediating their actualisation.

Third, in the previous chapters it was observed that the relationship between state and capital can be a tumultuous one, owing to the different range of pressures their respective positions presuppose. Yet, for Empire to have endured for so long, it may be deduced that tendencies exist which syncronise to a degree, the actions of state and capital. Indeed, in the case of Bougainville, we observed how a trajectory of capitalist development specific to PNG, generated certain nodal points which forcefully transmitted capital's concerns to PNG state managers. Specifically, resource dependency and its subsequent effects on national bourgeois accumulation strategies, patrimonial politics and political reproduction, created critical points of transmission which allowed capital to discipline power networks operating within the state. However, presumably in other regions of Empire, different nodal points will exist. It is important, therefore, particularly when examining crimes jointly organised by state and capital that we identify the mediating processes which permit capital to discipline the state, and vice versa.

Fourth, although this book has emphasised the importance of approximating state crime with greater conceptual clarity, it does not necessarily follow that criminogenesis exhibits lawful qualities, which can be deciphered in a style akin to the natural sciences. Certainly, regional articulations of Empire featured discernible social tendencies, out of which emerge probable historical trajectories. However, that said, within these trajectories the probable can be negated, and the improbable (though not impossible) actualised, owing to explainable but not necessarily predictable mediations.

For example, in the case of Bougainville, it was improbable that a small group of young activists located in the interior of central Bougainville, would in the space of two years, lead a province wide secessionist campaign that the PNG state would attempt to suppress through heightening forms of criminal violence. Intervening, in this respect, was a mix of probable and improbable strategic actions. For instance, BCL assumed an unsurprisingly rigid posture when faced with the demands of the NPLA, yet the company's failure to convert economic power into enduring institutional influence within the PNG state, was an unpredictable result of managerial failures which were compounded by a rapid change-over of senior executives, all of which placed BCL on a more intense collision course with the NPLA. Similarly, it was also fairly predictable that the conciliatory posture first assumed by the Namaliu government, was not a universally accepted position within the PNG state. However, the abrupt unsanctioned attack on landowner communities by the Police Commissioner during December 1988, which unravelled an infant peace, was an improbable result of heightened inter-institutional tensions, and individual temperament. With these examples in mind, it may be argued Bougainville's historical motion during 1988–90 was informed by a mixture of predictable tendencies, and unexpected fractures, which took place within a context defined by broader historical motions engendered by the relations of Empire. Out of this reality emerged an unprecedented campaign of state violence that created the conditions in which an improbable occurrence, a province-wide secessionist campaign, was rapidly actualised.

Accordingly, if we can generalise from this example, it may be argued that the broad historical motions of Empire, and the uneven trajectories it engenders, can be identified with a degree of predictive clarity. Nevertheless, within these broad motions, and regional configurations, exist a range of possible historical paths; which is actualised, depends on discernible, but not always predictable mediations. Understanding then the relationship between lawful motion, the potentialities it engenders, and the mediations affecting actualisation of potential, is critical if we are to develop an approach capable of situating state crime within the logic of structure and history.

Fifth, although in its infancy, a coherent Marxist research agenda is beginning to emerge within state crime studies. While I have defended the study of state crime from a Marxist vantage point, there are dangers associated within framing interventions through a criminological lens. In particular, there is a strong tendency within criminology to treat crime as a pathological result of deviations in environment, circumstances or individuals. Were we to transplant this problematic frame to a Marxist study of state crime, our inquiry would in effect become a search for criminogenic deviations within Empire. The problematic consequences of such an approach are pointed to by Bensaïd:

> Treating Nazism and Stalinism as pathological forms, rather than seeing them as entirely original historical phenomena, results in simultaneously valorizing the normal societies from which they deviate, and minimizing the specific import of their temporary 'deviancy'. Stalinism and Nazism are neither monsters nor exceptions, they reveal 'other possible norms of life'. (2002: 33)

The same point could be made with respect to the Bougainville war. That is, it would be a mistake to frame the conflict as a pathological product of a national context which deviated from the normal workings of Empire, owing to the historical weight of Melanesian social forms, and capital's 'weak' penetration. PNG is rather, another form of existence of Empire, of which there are many. Accordingly, while the starting point of state crime studies may be acts that deviate from the contested norms governing the behaviour of states, the broader social currents and mediations which inform these deviant practices, are not exceptional determinations, but rather different possible social arrangements through which Empire functions. Our inquiry then is not into the exceptional, but the many 'others' of Empire.

The last critical point which I wish to extract from this study relates to resistance. Resistance, as we observed in chapter 1, is an enduring feature of Empire's landscape. Yet these movements of opposition that fuel resistance to state crime, have not attracted the same degree of scholarly attention from criminologists as the illicit practices constitutive of state crime.[1] In the first edited book to address this lacuna, Stanley and McCulloch (2012a: 1) note, 'criminologists have generally failed to consciously consider a number of key questions related to resistance, such as: how are state crimes contested, prevented, challenged or stopped'. By resistance, Stanley and McCulloch mean intentional acts, ranging from the hidden and discrete through to the overt and organised, which oppose state crime, communicate wrong and attempt to transform, however subtly, the criminogenic terrain upon which these illicit acts take place (Stanley and McCulloch 2012a: 4–6; see also Friedrichs 2009: 7–8; Rothe 2009: 1).

Yet, as Stanley and McCulloch's edited volume proves, a research agenda is emerging. This agenda offers criminology an opportunity to not only build data-sets on poorly understood communities of resistance, but also rather importantly, to improve existing understandings of resistance through a theoretically mediated process of analytical enrichment. That said, there is a danger, given the strong empiricist tendencies within criminology, that the emerging scholarship on resistance will increasingly focus on developing empirical registers of successful and unsuccessful tactics, drawn from case studies, which are given general forms through a violent mode of abstraction that strips reality of its 'luxuriant plumage' (Bukharin 2005: 83). With an emerging range of general concepts, that are not 'biased' towards particular social contexts, theoretical schemas are then developed, and subsequently applied to comprehend new scenarios, without a *concrete* – i.e. more complete or enriched – understanding of either the contexts which these tactics have been extracted from, or of the new contingency being faced. In such a situation we risk engaging in 'practical politics' (Lukács 1974: 153), a process where strategies and tactics trialled in one situation, are seen as having an immediate practical allure in another scenario – for whatever pragmatic reason – and are thus applied, without a correct appreciation of either the concrete social conditions in which these strategies and tactics had laudable effects, or whether these conditions indeed exist in the conjuncture under consideration.

To avoid this problematic tendency, theory and theory development has a double role to play. First, it can be used retrospectively in order to unpack the precise social arrangements that condensed in moments of state criminality, and to gauge the particular way in which different networks of resistance emerged from these social arrangements, looking specifically at the mediated effect their strategies and associated tactics had on how certain historical potentialities were actualised. Second, it can be applied prospectively in an effort to develop enriched understandings of contemporary struggles that pinpoint the limits and possibilities for resistance contained in the present concrete. Of course, these two applications are not mutually exclusive. Retrospective analysis provides the terrain on which we can learn from the past, adopt what is generalisable, and abandon what was mistaken or merely conjunctural in application. Prospective analysis alerts us to the concrete characteristics of the here and now; in particular, the social potential for resistance can be teased out, while the precise applicability of strategic technologies handed down from previous struggles may be gauged.

Conclusion

Currently, state crime studies stands at an important juncture. Two decades of pioneering interventions have provided a sophisticated conceptual and empirical foundation for studying and thinking about illicit state crime practices. However, the growing sophistication of state crime research also means we can no longer justify our inquiry on the grounds of novelty alone; that is, by pointing to criminology's silence on state crime. This omission is – courtesy of quite vocal scholarly efforts – increasingly well known. Now is the time then to think in more detail about how we do state crime research, the frameworks we employ, and the conditions under which scholars engage with civil society.

In this book I have attempted to articulate the scientific fault-lines on which current disagreements in state crime studies hinge, while also championing, through example, a fertile way forward. To this end, it has been suggested that the fault-lines go to the very ontological, epistemological and methodological roots of science. Consequently, the scholarly stakes resting on this debate's resolution could not be more important; indeed it will determine whether state crime studies can establish the sort of popular research agenda that will make it of overt relevance to movements of resistance in years to come.

Afterword: Impunity, Civil Society and the Struggle Ahead in Melanesia

Even a snake has friends
—Nasioi proverb

The war on Bougainville formally ended with the signing of the 2001 peace agreement. Yet, in its wake a new struggle over state-corporate impunity has emerged. Indeed, while many Bougainvillean combatants have participated in a process of truth telling and reconciliation (see Braithwaite et al. 2010), those at the most senior levels of state-corporate power have yet to acknowledge the wholesale crimes they helped author. Nor has any form of atonement been forthcoming. Arguably, there is no greater demonstration of the impunity enjoyed by those implicated in state crime on Bougainville, than BCL's recent campaign to reopen the mine, which has gained considerable pace over recent years.

At the company's 2008 annual general meeting BCL's current Chairman, Peter Taylor, informed shareholders that 'the company is better positioned now than at any time in the past nineteen years to make a return to profitable mining on Bougainville, for the benefit of all stakeholders' (cited in BCL 2008). The 'confluence of factors' supporting BCL's return, the Chairman argued, include Bougainville's need 'for economic development to underpin its economy and support service delivery and social advancement', in addition to the island's preparedness to look 'forward rather than dwelling on the past' (Taylor cited in BCL 2008). In a subsequent speech to the Australia PNG Business Council, the Chairman elaborated further:

> There is a very wide consensus on Bougainville today that peace and continuing good order will be best achieved by economic means. That the normal aspirations of the people for a good life and a fulfilling future for their children will be delivered by employment, training, regular income, infrastructure and business activity. After a few false starts the

consensus is now firmly in favour of BCL being the preferred operator of the mine at Panguna if it restarts, and that the mine and its associated activities will be the engine driving all those benefits. (Taylor 2011)

He continues: 'Economic self-sufficiency is an important goal for Bougainville, particularly when its people are endeavouring to become highly autonomous within PNG, and also to address the question of independence, which requires revenue developed by major projects such as a re-opened Panguna' (Taylor 2011).

Having been deeply enmeshed in a military campaign which led to the mass-destruction of Bougainvillean communities, the decimation of the island's population, and the suppression of a BRA led independence movement, BCL is now looking to achieve something of a miraculous public relations coup by reconstructing itself as the solution to Bougainville's current political and economic challenges, which it had no small part in creating.

However, given that the 2001 peace agreement has seen considerable political power devolve to the rebranded Autonomous Bougainville Government (ABG) – with a referendum over independence on the immediate horizon – BCL's return presupposes strong ABG support. Under the Presidency of former rebel leader Joseph Kabui (2005–08), this seemed an unlikely prospect, especially with Francis Ona still enjoying informal political sway in central Bougainville. However, Ona's death in 2005, purportedly from malaria, and Kabui's demise in 2008 from a heart-attack, created a political vacuum which has subsequently been filled by Bougainville's elder statesman, John Momis, who became ABG President in 2010.

For a great part of his political career, Momis had been a strong critic of BCL. Prophetically in 1987 he likened BCL to an 'invader' with the 'ideology of a cancer cell' (Momis 1987a). In the war's immediate aftermath, Momis also lent his support to the US Alien Tort class action against Rio Tinto (see chapter 1). In a signed affidavit composed for the action, Momis alleges that BCL had been the principal architect of the conflict (Momis 2001). He thus concludes, 'it is important to Bougainvilleans and the long-term reconciliation process that Rio Tinto's responsibility be addressed in an impartial forum by an impartial judge' (Momis 2001).

Despite these provocative remarks Momis has always been broadly supportive of an economic model powered by the extractive industries. Indeed, he has consistently maintained that Bougainville's 'ancient entrepreneurial spirit' can be best ignited by large-scale foreign investment in the island's natural resources, and has visions in this respect that extend well beyond Panguna, including multiple mines (Autonomous Bougainville Government 2014; Momis 1987a, 1987b, 2011). In line with this belief, and despite past rhetoric, Momis has marshalled the ABG's resources in support of the company's return. In a meeting with landowner leaders from the mine area on 10 November 2011, Momis declared '[the] Panguna mine . . . must be opened and there is an important need for a unified stand by ABG and Panguna Landowners' (Panguna Management Consultative Committee 2011). The considerations underpinning his position were outlined earlier to the PNG Australia Business Council. 'The ABG supports re-opening Panguna', he argued, because 'we see that as the most realistic way of contributing to broad-based economic growth, and generating the ABG revenues required to meet the needs of our people' (Momis 2011). This, of course, was a general position that Francis Ona, in particular, opposed.

Nevertheless, Momis has suggested his position extends, rather than challenges, Ona's political programme. 'Francis was not trying to end the mine for ever', Momis told parliament in 2013, 'no – his complaint was about the unfair treatment of Bougainville. He wanted the rights of Bougainvilleans recognised. He wanted fair distribution of the revenue . . . We have continued that same struggle throughout the peace process' (Momis 2013).

Of course, given the near unanimous condemnation of BCL's past conduct on Bougainville, the ABG's choice of BCL as the preferred operator has raised eyebrows. In defence of his government's position, the ABG's Vice President argues, 'it's maybe better to work with the devil [BCL] you know than the devil you don't know' (Nisira 2014).

Accompanying the above shifts in the national and provincial political terrain has been important changes to the power structure within the mine area. Although influential Chiefs remain loyal to the original vision that guided the 1988–89 uprising, the last five years has been marked by the resurrection of the PLA leadership ousted by Francis Ona and Perpetua Serero in August 1987. Lawrence Daveona and Michael Pariu,[1] in particular, have led efforts to re-establish a landowners' representative association, with support from the ABG, BCL and the European Shareholders of Bougainville Copper. According to the *Post-Courier*, in a January 2014 visit by PNG Prime Minister, Peter O'Neill, Daveona claimed that the 'landowners of Panguna mine and the surrounding leases were united for the re-opening of the mine' (cited in Masiu 2014: 4). This follows a prolonged programme of reconciliation within the different mine lease areas, designed to unite communities into an overarching umbrella organisation that can negotiate a new, more favourable mining agreement (Umbrella Panguna Landowners Association, no date).[2] For example, the remodelled PLA has argued that were mine royalties to go to the landowning community, this would give households, 'K49,920 [$US18,470] per annum or K 4,160 gross per adult landowner per month' (Umbrella Panguna Landowners Association 2010) – in essence creating a rentier class in the mine area. Moreover, the association has also argued that the mine will 'create thousand [sic] of jobs for us and provide a freepass to every Bougainvillean for free education, free healthcare and good income opportunities' (Umbrella Panguna Landowners Association 2007).

Nevertheless, while quite triumphant overtures are being made with respect to the mine's reopening, simmering in the background, is enduring discontent over injustices and grievances associated with the war. These are explicitly articulated by community members across the mine area, who continue to take questions of state-corporate liability very seriously, but also, in addition to this, demonstrate a strong desire to pursue an alternative model of development, which gives communities a greater sense of self-reliance, stability, security, and sustainability.[3]

There is also evidence that many of the harms caused by the war still await proper remedy. This is signalled at a Bougainville-wide level by widespread, but largely undiagnosed, mental illness, elevated levels of inter-personal violence, and the abuse of alcohol and drugs.[4] Indeed, many communities have never been afforded the opportunity to formally register their experiences, or memorialise the abuse they suffered at the hands of the PNG and rebel forces. Some have begun to write their stories down, others are seeking to articulate their memories through art – nevertheless, *prima facie* evidence suggests that the depth and breadth of suffering endured during the conflict has only been faintly recognised, and with growing state-corporate pressure to 'look forward', a climate has emerged that implicitly shuns those reflecting on the past and its meaning.

And, perhaps not surprisingly, given this climate, there has been no evidenced inclination particularly on the part of BCL or Australia, to publicly acknowledge their role in the conflict,[5] engage in a truth-telling process, or develop pathways of justice at the more senior levels, whether grounded in restorative, or retributive principles.[6] Instead, with the ABG firmly committed to the mine's reopening under BCL auspices, the momentum is in favour of reconstructing the past, to suit contemporary agendas. Increasingly this has taken the form of a revisionist narrative that simplifies considerably the conflict's complex fault-lines. Put simply, the war's origins are being located in the mine's colonial foundations and a distributional crisis over the apportionment of benefits, problems that can be resolved today through largely technocratic means (Momis 2011; Taylor 2011; Umbrella Panguna Landowners Association 2007). On the other hand, the conflict itself is increasingly treated as a discrete civil war, primarily involving domestic actors. We see this narrative evoked not just by BCL, and the relevant state bodies, but journalists and scholars too.

One critical effect of this emerging discourse is that it obscures significant criminal dimensions of the war, and the responsibility attributable to key international actors, such as Rio Tinto (via BCL) and the Australian government. Yet arguably this absolving narrative would be unable to take root today were it not for skewed discourses that were constructed during the war by a small number of civil society actors in Australia, who were among the more authoritative and influential voices commentating on the Bougainville conflict internationally.

In this respect, it is worth remembering a certain contradictory characteristic of civil society highlighted by Green and Ward (2012). Civil society, they argue, 'is both a complement to state power, educating and disciplining responsible citizens within a hegemonic order, and a potential source of opposition, capable of educating and disciplining the state itself' (Green and Ward 2012: 28). With respect to the Bougainville conflict in particular, and its representation within *international spheres*, civil society actors with the access and expertise to relay and interpret the events, have, with honourable exceptions, constructed a narrative that is on the one hand forgiving of state-corporate criminality, and on the other, overtly hostile to those who expropriated BCL and then campaigned for Bougainville's independence.

Indeed, during the 1990s the BRA and its founding members were frequently portrayed as bitter extremists whose primary ambition was to cleanse Bougainville of modernity's corrupting influence, and bring about a form of 'primitive' socialism. One of the more strident voices advancing this position was Rowan Callick, a prolific international commentator who was writing in the *Australian Financial Review* (and later *The Australian*). For Callick the BRA was a 'cargo cult movement' (Callick 1989b: 1), motivated by 'zealotry', and led by what he termed 'Bougainvillean terrorists' (Callick 1989e: 13). 'These are not Castros or Kenyattas or even Begins in the making (God help PNG if so), as Australian sympathisers have suggested', Callick wrote in 1990, 'they are terrorists seeking to corner for themselves, material wealth that in justice should be distributed by an elected government' (Callick 1990b: 16). This foreboding image of the BRA can also be found in the work of James Griffin, a celebrated historian and impassioned public intellectual who prior to the Bougainville war had worked both at the Australian National University (ANU) and the University of PNG. Griffin (1997: 11) claimed, 'there has never been any legitimacy in Francis Ona's rebellion'. The BRA, he argued, are 'inchoate and terrorist', and consumed by 'fanatical cultism' (Griffin 1996: 24).

During the conflict, it was not uncommon for international observers to draw parallels between the BRA and the Khmer Rouge, in order to press home the threat posed by the BRA. For example, as the BRA rose to prominence during early 1990, Callick (1990c: 16) emotively claimed, 'it is year zero on Bougainville'. In a similar vein, the ANU scholar Anthony Regan – who is one of the most cited and respected Bougainville authorities – suggested that the rebels were seeking power in order to cleanse Bougainville of modern influences. Writing in 1996, Regan argued: '[T]here are cultist elements [in the BRA], including not only Damen Damien, but possibly also Francis Ona. They may see little chance of achieving the kind of anti-development and anti-education "kastom" based society which they want for Bougainville except in a Bougainville which they and like-minded people control' (1996: 29). He adds, 'Ona and those closest to him had limited education and experience, and had little understanding of the complex practical issues and problems involved in establishing an independent nation' (Regan 1996: 7).

As both the BRA figurehead, and one of the NPLA's founding members, Francis Ona, was, as the latter remark suggests, a popular focal point for condemnation. Some linked his political actions to petty personal intrigues. For instance, the anthropologist, Eugene Ogan (1990: 47), a noted authority on the Nasioi people of Bougainville, claimed 'Ona represents, in the first instance, a younger man dissatisfied with older Nasioi leadership and, in more crass terms, his own share of the compensation pie'. In the Australian media an even more unflattering portrait was painted. Callick (1989b: 1) labelled Ona a 'Melanesian cult figure', and 'a man of dramatically alternating moods'. The Australian Broadcasting Commission's (ABC) Pacific correspondent,[7] Sean Dorney, who is arguably Australia's most respected PNG journalistic authority, claimed Ona 'never deviated from what he saw as his destiny – leading Bougainville back to a pre-contact, self-reliant, subsistence independence free from the contamination of outside influences, no matter what the cost' (Dorney 1998: 38).

These deeply critical accounts of the BRA, and its leadership, had the important effect of positioning the PNG state as a moderate force, responding to an unpopular, extremist element in Bougainville society, which seriously threatened to leave in its wake, mass property destruction and significant loss of life. This stance, for example, was overtly assumed by Rowan Callick. He claimed in May 1989 that the rebel forces' obstinacy had made necessary 'a substantial and messy military operation' (Callick 1989b: 1). Writing two years later, following a period of bloodletting between BRA and PNGDF/BLF forces, Callick (1991b: 15) continued the argument, stating 'no responsible government would legitimise such a rule as theirs [BIG]'. In a similar vein, James Griffin suggested, 'it would have been anomalous if the Prime Minister had not called out his security forces, however incompetent, to deal with saboteurs of his nation's primary industrial base' (Griffin 1998: 6).

Indeed, in contrast to Francis Ona's treatment, PNG's Prime Minister was often applauded by key international commentators for his stance against the BRA. Writing in 1990 Griffin (1990b: 76), for that instance, claimed the Prime Minister 'was generous and inventive in his efforts to effect a compromise'. Dorney (no date) goes further still, labelling Namaliu a 'humanitarian'.

That said, some of this praise was tempered with qualified criticism, as evidence of PNGDF atrocities came to light. However, while BRA violence was often portrayed by key Australian scholars and media authorities as consciously brutal in its very design, PNGDF violence was frequently treated as an unfortunate and officially deplored by-product of breakdowns in discipline and command structure. For example, Callick (1989c: 8) scolded what he called 'discipline failure' within the PNGDF, while Griffin (1990b: 76) lamented, 'a disturbing degree of indiscipline and even lack of co-ordination at higher levels'. That individual commanders were brought in by the PNG government, specifically because of their 'tough man image' (Rogers 2002: 238), or that many of the most formidable tactics deployed by the military forces – such as the blockade, and village burnings – were both sanctioned and welcomed at senior levels, is glossed away in such characterisations.

The very different standards used to judge the BRA and PNGDF respectively can be seen in the following remark by Anthony Regan, which came at a time when dissident elements in Australian civil society were placing a spotlight on the Bougainville counterinsurgency operation. Under the heading 'BRA/BIG propaganda and international popular opinion (especially in Australia)' Regan argued:

> The BRA has been very effective in portraying itself as fighting for a just and attractive cause. They are seen as similar to FRETLIN, in East Timor – brave fighters against powerful odds. There is a considerable 'liberal' constituency in Australia, sympathetic to 'romantic' causes. The profound ignorance of Australians about the situation in Bougainville plays into the BRA hands. The brutality and intransigence of the BRA and their lack of popular support are not understood or are ignored by the international media. Such alleged actions by PNGDF or Resistance Groups as executions of former BRA member, clearing out of civilians from Central Bougainville, the use of mortars on villages, incursions into Solomon Islands territory combine to create an impression of unreasonable use of force (especially – but not only – in Australia).[8] (Regan 1996: 12)

Some went further, and overtly denied the malicious character of key PNGDF tactics. Writing in 1997 with Melchior Togolo – a PNG civil servant closely involved in the conflict during 1989–90 – Griffin, for instance, labels PNG camps commonly used to concentrate civilians away from rebel forces, 'protective custody' (Griffin and Togolo 1997: 381). While some camps may have indeed provided safe-haven for civilians – the 'care centre' complex was far from homogenous – nevertheless by 1997 it had been authoritatively established that many were sites of systemic and egregious human rights abuses (Amnesty International 1993, 1997; Gillespie 1992, 1993).

The military blockade employed to exacerbate the humanitarian crisis on Bougainville, was also defended. For example, writing shortly after the announcement of an ill-fated peace agreement in 1991, Rowan Callick applauded the blockade's strategic effects. While acknowledging that it had killed 'women and children' through the denial of 'medications', Callick (1991a: 15) nonetheless argued, 'who said sanctions don't work . . . peace has been declared – chiefly as a result of the pressures applied by PNG through its blockade of Bougainville'. In a more recent paper, submitted to an Australian parliamentary inquiry into the Bougainville peace process, Anthony Regan goes one step further, and suggests the military blockade may have even produced an alive toll (although a caveat, is added, further research is necessary). While noting that there has 'yet to be a rigorous attempt to assess numbers of deaths' associated with the war, he nonetheless forwards the following hypothesis:

> [T]here is some evidence that deaths from untreated illness or injury may well have been offset to a significant degree – *or even outweighed* – by the improved general health of the population in areas under blockade. There are numerous reports from people who lived in such areas to the effect that improved general health standards were related to two main factors. The first was a diet far more healthy than before the conflict. It was free from most processed foods, fats, high salt and sugar contents, and without alcohol. The second was much increased physical exercise than prior to the conflict. This was due to such things as the need for subsistence gardening and increased walking due to lack of motor vehicles. [Italics added] (Regan 1999; see also Ogan 2005: 396)

Needless to say, it is unorthodox, near unheard of, to cancel out civilian deaths by offsetting them against people hypothetically kept alive as an unforeseen and unintended consequence of the blockade. Nevertheless, Regan's (2000b) revisionist position was uncritically aired on the ABC's *The World Today*.

Once we broaden our lens to include those international actors involved in the conflict, we see a similar apologetic stance assumed by key regional commentators narrating events on Bougainville. Indeed, both BCL and its managers have been frequently praised. For example, in his celebrated book on PNG's post-independence history, Sean Dorney (2000: 105) wrote: 'By any third-world criteria, Bougainville Copper Limited was an exemplary corporate citizen of PNG from the day the Bougainville Copper agreement was renegotiated in 1974, the year before Independence, till the mine was knocked out of action by sabotage attack fifteen years later'. In a congruent fashion, Rowan Callick (1990d: 15) stated ten years earlier, 'CRA pioneered what has become PNG's only reliable source of revenue, [and] gained a unique reputation for its training programme'. During the same period, Callick also described Don Carruthers as 'the long-suffering and humane Chairman of Bougainville Copper Ltd', in a foreword for a book written by former BCL Managing Director (1982–87), Paul Quodling (see Quodling 1991: VII). While Douglas Oliver, the 'doyen of Pacific anthropologists' (Griffin 2005: 199), went so far as to dedicate his book, which featured extensive coverage of the Bougainville conflict, to BCL's first Chairman, Frank Espie, such was the belief in the company's innocence.

Complimenting these accolades for BCL and its management, are accounts which raise doubts over allegations that implicate BCL in PNGDF military operations. For example, writing in 2003, Anthony Regan (2003: 159) argued, 'despite some claims to the contrary, there is as yet no credible evidence that BCL took any direct part in the operations against the BRA'. He adds in a footnote, 'for example, in the claims made in a class action launched in 2000 in a U.S. court by some Bougainvilleans against BCL' (Regan 2003: 166). As we shall see, these defences of the company have become increasingly shrill as the evidence against BCL grows.

In a similar fashion to BCL, the Australian government has also largely escaped criticism (for honourable exceptions see Gillespie 1992, 1993; Sharp 1997; Snow 1991). Australia's official position that the Bougainville conflict was an 'internal matter' for PNG to handle independently, has been largely accepted in orthodox accounts of the conflict (see, for example, Bullock 1991; Jennings and Claxton 2013; Regan 2010). Indeed, it is rather, Australia's contribution to the Bougainville peace process that has cultivated the most detailed scholarship (see Adams 2001; Braithwaite et al. 2010; Regan 2010; Wehner and Denoon 2001).

Nevertheless, that said, the above international narratives, which dilute and distort criminogenic components of the conflict, have not gone entirely unchallenged. On the margins of the news media, in the alternative press, pieces frequently appeared during the 1990s offering counterhegemonic views on the Bougainville conflict. These interventions were complemented by several feature length documentary films.[9] Additionally, a range of human rights (Amnesty International), humanitarian (Community Aid Abroad, Médecins Sans Frontières), and activist (Bougainville Freedom Movement, Aid/Watch) civil society organisations (CSOs), also made substantive attempts to record the atrocities being perpetrated on the island (by all sides), and draw attention to the increasingly desperate humanitarian situation brought about by the military blockade. These efforts prompted powerful public interventions and protests, which kept these important issues on the international agenda, even when the most 'authoritative' mainstream voices on Bougainville were often pointing international audiences in other directions.

Not surprisingly, these critical interventions were resented by the commentators cited above. For instance, Rowan Callick argued in 1991, that Australia's 'human rights lobbyists and aid agencies are effectively the BRA's chief foreign supporters' (Callick 1991c: 15). Casting principled criticism as BRA propaganda, was a common neutralising technique. For instance, when renowned US public intellectual Noam Chomsky condemned the Bougainville military operations, an incensed James Griffin wrote 'someone eventually told Noam Chomsky, prince of political *idiots savants*, about the secessionist strife in Bougainville; so he had to become a supporter of the Bougainville rebels' (Griffin 1995: 11). Other scholars were equally damning. For example, having already accused Australia's 'liberal constituency' of 'profound ignorance' in 1996 (Regan 1996: 12), Anthony Regan informed an Australian parliamentary inquiry several years later:

> May I first of all make the point that a heck of a lot of the people from outside who have been involved in Bougainville since the beginning of the conflict have had major involvements often dictated by their own agendas rather than Bougainvillean agendas. I will not name names, but I would love one day to send out an invitation to a list of about 20 people to make contributions to a book called 'My role as a white person in solving the Bougainville conflict'. I suspect that most of them would make their contributions without any sense of the irony that would be involved. (Joint Standing Committee on Foreign Affairs, Defence and Trade 1999)

As the above remarks suggest, two of the key academic authorities on Bougainville, Griffin and Regan, preferred to cast themselves as the true bipartisan voices in Australian civil society, unlike other impressionable and naïve critics. Reality proved more complex. For example, while Griffin was frequently referred to as 'Professor Emeritus of History' in the press, he was in fact part of Australia's intelligence apparatus. In a series of obituaries published after Griffin's death in 2010, authored by close friends, it was revealed that he had been recruited in 1990 as a senior analyst for the 'top secret Office of National Assessment', with specific responsibility for guiding the Australian government on the Bougainville situation (Callick 2010; see also Howie-Willis 2010). Regan has also worked closely with Australian government departments/organisations, serving as an adviser to the Australian Joint Standing Committee on Foreign Affairs, Defence and Trade, DFAT, and Australia's aid agency, AusAID – though unlike the example of Griffin, these roles are publicly acknowledged in ANU annual reports (see ANU 1999, 2000, 2001). More recently, Regan has been appointed legal advisor to the ABG, a role that is funded by AusAID. As part of his duties, Regan has controversially overseen the drafting of mining legislation that will potentially facilitate BCL's return to Panguna, a move that has attracted particular condemnation from those in the mine area.

Challenging Impunity: Melanesian Independence and Predatory Capitalism

During the fog of war orthodox narratives constructed within the mainstream hubs of Australian civil society could to an extent be maintained, without significant dissonance. With the blockade now lifted, and organisational gatekeepers less guarded, there is emerging a powerful body of evidence that makes these narratives unsustainable. The first cutting incision in this respect came when the Bougainvillean class action against Rio Tinto uncovered a large body of internal BCL documentation. These records evidence, in rich detail, the substantial pressure company management put on PNG during 1988–90, and the multiple forms of collusion that took place between the PNGDF and BCL. Additionally there is now a large body of elite-actor testimony, complemented by further BCL/PNG documentation, which has been presented both in this volume, and in earlier publications, including an online repository of primary sources set up by the International State Crime Initiative (Lasslett 2010c, 2012b, 2012c). While these materials challenge certain received wisdom on the war, and evidence criminal actions jointly organised by state-corporate actors, they have prompted little interest from the news-media in Australia or PNG.

Though one notable exception to the rule in this respect, involves a 2011 report aired on *Dateline*, a news programme that is broadcast on Australia's Special Broadcasting Service (SBS). In a story that would go on to win a United Nations Association of Australia Peace Award, *Dateline* correspondent Brian Thomson revealed an affidavit composed by the former PNG Prime Minister Michael Somare, for the US court action (Somare was Foreign Minister during 1988–92). In the affidavit Somare accuses Rio Tinto – through its subsidiary BCL – of being both the principal architect of the military solution on Bougainville, and the PNGDF's defacto logistic apparatus (Thomson 2011). The *Dateline* report prompted an angry response from those respected regional authorities who had defended BCL.

Rowan Callick countered the story from the pages of *The Australian*. He begins by condemning the growing rancour surrounding the Bougainville mine's reopening, which Callick (2011: 6) portrayed as largely instigated by Australian 'trade unions', 'non-government organisations', and the 'Socialist Alternative'. When turning to the allegations aired on *Dateline*, his principal authority is Sir Rabbie Namaliu, who had been appointed a BCL Director in early 2011 (a provocative move which failed to raise a single eyebrow in the media). Relying on Namaliu's account, Callick (2011: 6) remarks, 'by the time the government deployed troops, BCL's staff had left Bougainville leaving vehicles behind, some of which were commandeered'. Had Callick returned to *his own* reporting from 1989–90, he would have known that troops arrived on the island well before BCL made the decision to abandon their investment, let alone evacuate staff. Callick nevertheless apparently defers to Namaliu's flawed memory.

Other news-outlets simply provided BCL with uncritical space to deny the allegations. For example, the day after the *Dateline* allegations aired, Radio Australia reporter, Jemima Garrett, asked BCL's Chairman, Peter Taylor: 'It is common for mining companies to help the police in Papua New Guinea, just what sort of help did Rio Tinto, or Bougainville Copper, provide to the police or the PNGDF during the war on Bougainville?' (Garrett 2011). In reply, he argued: 'Bougainville Copper only did what it had to do. There was a state of emergency declared and like any state of emergency you had to comply with the requirements' (Taylor cited in Garrett 2011). No attempt was made by Garrett to probe into this somewhat curious statement that appears to concede assistance, while at the same time obfuscating responsibility.

In a more recent interview published in June 2013, News Corporation reporter, Paul Toohey, dilutes the fact of logistic support down to tenuous allegation. BCL's Chairman is asked by Toohey: 'Are you satisfied that allegations that Rio/BCL provided equipment to the PNG forces during the war have been put to rest?' (Toohey 2013). To which the Chairman replied: 'This is the allegation in a US court case that BCL provided helicopter gunships? It's not true. BCL never owned a helicopter. We chartered them, we never had them' (cited in Toohey 2013). Of course, the US court case is premised on more than one allegation, a fact which Toohey declined to point out.

Academic authorities have also come to BCL's aid. For example, Anthony Regan (2013: 132) argued that the *Datelines* allegations, 'are of dubious veracity'. Then when asked by this author whether he would reconsider his 2003 position (see above), in light of new evidence (see Lasslett 2010c, 2012c), Regan replied, 'credible evidence is yet to emerge. Perhaps such evidence will emerge one day, but I'm yet to see it' (cited in PNG Mine Watch 2013) – a confounding response given that internal BCL records, corroborated by senior management testimony, is now freely available both online and in readily locatable scholarly sources.

That said, while the landscape of international civil society is seared to a significant degree by the obstinacy of mainstream media and academic authorities, there is emerging new pockets of resistance on both Bougainville and in Australia, which are producing narratives and interventions that overtly challenge state-corporate impunity. In Australia, where so many of the war's criminogenic decisions were made, this resistance is led by the NGO, Jubilee Australia, who has, in collaboration with victim campaigners on Bougainville, established the 'Not on My Watch campaign'.[10] The campaign aims both to seek redress for past state-corporate wrongs on Bougainville, and to establish a collaborative dialogue on issues of development, self-determination, transparency and corporate accountability – themes, of course, that are of wider regional relevance. To date, the campaign has bulwarked extensive fieldwork in the mine area on Bougainville in a bid to obtain representative data on questions of justice, mining and development, with plans underway for a speaking tour of Australia, and a scholarly workshop during 2014.

These efforts compliment sentiments being articulated at a village level in the mine area, where impunity remains a powerful issue. For instance, one Bougainvillean university student from the mine area told Jubilee Australia in 2013:

> Up to this date I still question why civilians were killed? It is a question which [the] PNG government, Australia and Rio-Tinto will have to answer before they talk about anything else . . . There is no way . . . [that] mining will pay [for] the lives of those killed. I became an orphan as a result of the bloody crisis too. I am totally against the re-opening of mine. (Theonila cited in Jubilee Australia 2013)

Another young Bougainvillean victim of the conflict argues:

> Many of us lost the lives of our loved ones during the Bougainville crisis and it is a very big issue which is still lingering in the minds of . . . Bougainvilleans. I as a Bougainvillean . . . strong[ly] believe that it would be best if Rio Tinto and the Australian Government . . . compensate Bougainville for life [lost]. (Zilpha cited in Jubilee Australia 2013)

We have also seen ex-combatants from both sides of the conflict – that is the BRA, and the resistance forces loyal to the PNG government – come out in condemnation of BCL. Speaking at an ex-combatant workshop held in August 2013, former BRA leader, Sam Kauona, remarked, 'what BCL did on the island was injustice, *was injustice* . . . our government should consult with the Panguna people . . . actual landowners, go down to the village'.[11]

That said, while communities in the mine area are, it seems, strongly opposed to BCL's return, and in favour of challenging impunity, they face organised opposition from the ABG and the umbrella landowners' association, set up to facilitate the mine's reopening. Complicating matters further, Australia through its aid apparatus is employing soft-power somewhat more adeptly than it used hard-power. And to this end, the Australian government is shepherding momentum away from issues such as impunity, justice, and community-led development, and instead is supporting a new hegemonic narrative that centres on delivering 'stability' to Bougainville through a model of development that relies on the extractive industries, and the commodification of resources.

Whatever path is eventually pursued, the case of Bougainville palpably demonstrates the way capital can withstand prolonged periods of resistance, and then in the aftermath fluidly adapt itself to new circumstances, keeping regions of even marginal importance within its orbit. It also alerts us to the complex, and sometimes inchoate, range of organisational actors who are critical to this process.

And while, in this respect, Bougainville has unique characteristics, it nonetheless shares certain core features with the rest of Melanesia. Indeed, this diverse region of the world is earmarked by capital not because of its rich cultures and proud people, but because it holds within its unique ecology, a bounty of mineral, oil, gas, timber, and marine and land resources. To that end, capital has proven quite adept at fashioning complex intersections of formal and informal authority, of varying configurations, into a structure capable of mediating its entry and valorisation. This has often left in its wake people dispossessed, and lunar-like landscapes, while at its most extreme it has prompted prolonged conflict punctuated with gross human rights abuses.

In order to end this cycle of conflict and predation, communities in Melanesia are faced with a stark choice. They must find concrete ways of organising that forge new bonds of solidarity between communities at a provincial, national and regional level, out of which can emerge organisational structures capable of concentrating common interests and championing the rights of working people both in the countryside and the city.[12] Only inventive and honed attempts to bridge cultural and geographical divides can create the sort of mass-movements capable of refashioning the state apparatus, and breaking the stranglehold a class of predatory capitalists have obtained in countries like PNG. Breaking this stranglehold is an essential condition if resource rich nations lying on the margins of Empire are to steer a more independent and peaceful path in the future.

Notes

Chapter 1

1. That is, state actions conducted for organisational purposes, which deviate from those fundamental norms on which the state's legitimacy is grounded (Green and Ward 2000; Ward and Green 2000).
2. By classical Marxism, I refer to a tradition of scholarship which professes a strong commitment to the scientific method (dialectics), and theoretical framework, developed, articulated and applied, by classical Marxism's founders including, for example, Marx, Engels, Lenin, Trotsky, Bukharin and Gramsci.
3. My usage of Empire here departs from the way it is applied by other state crime authors such as Michalowski (2009), Iadicola (2011) and Boggs (2010). In short, they associate Empire with the network of state vassalages that operate under US hegemony.
4. Such transactions, of course, are often buttressed by a range of coercive political and legal instruments which favour and protect capital.
5. Marx (1976: 300) explains, 'the value of labour power, and the value which that labour power valorizes in the labour process, are two entirely different magnitudes; and this difference was what the capitalist had in mind when he was purchasing the labour-power'.
6. Of course, capitalism is also compatible with directly coerced labour. In such cases, Marx observes, 'the civilized horrors of over-work are grafted onto the barbaric horrors of slavery, serfdom etc.' (1976: 345).
7. Looking at recent US military incursions abroad, Kiely (2010: 204) remarks: 'Military intervention could be regarded as the most extreme manifestation of neo-liberalism, a kind of military structural adjustment, linked to older processes of pro-market reform and institutional shock therapy.'
8. Marx observes:

   > My dialectical method is, in its foundations, not only different from the Hegelian, but exactly opposite to it . . . The mystification which the dialectic suffers in Hegel's hands by no means prevents him from being the first to present its general forms of motion in a comprehensive and conscious manner. With him it is standing on its head. It must be inverted, in order to discover the rational kernel within the mystical shell. (1976: 102–3)

9. Under the *Bougainville Peace Agreement* (2001) the North Solomons province has been renamed the Autonomous Region of Bougainville.
10. This empirical focus – state-corporate crime – has become an emerging and significant theme within the criminological cannon, owing to the ground-

breaking efforts of Kramer, Michalowski and Kauzlarich (see Kauzlarich and Kramer 1998; Kramer and Michalowski 1991; Kramer et al. 2002).

11. Marx (1995) observes in this respect: 'It is . . . paradox that the earth moves round the sun, and that water consists of two highly inflammable gases. Scientific truth is always paradox, if judged by every-day experience, which catches only the delusive appearance of things' (see also Marx 1976: 433).

12. Lebowitz remarks in this respect:

> The problem with the laws that we develop upon the basis of observation is that even repeated observations do not go beyond appearances: I see the sun rise every day in the East and move to the West where it sets, and can even predict successfully the sun's route round the Earth in the future without knowing anything about the real processes involved. The ability to predict (under controlled conditions) and true knowledge, however, are quite different things. (2009: 72)

13. The formal name given to cabinet in PNG.

Chapter 2

1. Speaking more generally on the framework he engineered with Marx, Engels remarks: 'Our conception of history is above all a guide to study, not a lever for construction after the manner of the Hegelian. All history must be studied afresh, the conditions of existence of the different formations of society must be examined in detail' (Marx and Engels 1982: 393–4).

2. Put simply, clans are extended kinship units that trace their origins to a common ancestor. Clans are usually subdivided into lineages, which may be organised on a matrilineal or patrilineal basis. On Bougainville, matrilineal clans are the norm, on the PNG mainland the reverse is the case.

3. Given that in 1939 Papua and New Guinea had annual revenues of £150,000 and £500,000 respectively, this paltry spending on government services was not surprising (Griffin et al. 1979: 71).

4. Hawksley notes the vigour with which colonial officers enacted the administration's goals: 'Under colonial rule, Papuans and New Guineans had to adapt their lives as administrators drew parameters around those parts of premodern society they deemed incompatible with the new order: magic, sorcery, violence, and cannibalism were prohibited while peace, Christianity, discipline, and industry were encouraged' (2007: 198).

5. The national currency of PNG is the Kina. In 1989, K1 was equivalent to USD1.2.

6. Petty commodity production is defined by Gibbon and Neocosmos as:

> A phenomenal category of commodity producers who possess the means of production necessary to produce commodities and who engage in

production [for exchange] on the basis of unpaid household labour alone. It is assumed that such producers are capable of reproducing themselves as private producers of commodities without employing wage-labor and without selling (part of) their labour power. (1985: 170)

7. The Nasioi are an ethnic grouping from central/south Bougainville.

8. This analysis is grounded in interviews I conducted during 2010–12 with senior officials from PNG's anti-corruption agencies, including the Ombudsman Commission, the Auditor General's Office, Taskforce Sweep, the Royal Papua New Guinea Constabulary, the PNG Australia Law and Justice Partnership, and the Judiciary.

9. Paul Quodling served as BCL's Managing Director from 1982 until 1987.

10. The *Bougainville Copper Agreement* defined the company's 'leasehold entitlements', as well as their 'ongoing obligations' in terms of taxation, royalties, and the provision of benefits to PNG (for example, localisation of employment, road construction, the development of port facilities, power generation, water supply, hospital construction and the provision of equity to the administration) (Denoon 2000: 90–6; Quodling 1991: 23).

11. It was envisaged that the board of BCL would report to CRA in Melbourne, who in turn would be accountable to Rio Tinto in London (Denoon 2000: 80).

12. Don Vernon served as BCL's Managing Director (1975–77), and Chairman (1979–86).

13. According to Quodling (1991: 5) this was a product of BCL's strategy of 'continued investment in technology and economies of scale'.

14. Perhaps not surprisingly, given the anti-capitalist sentiments which inspired the rebellion on Bougainville, 'key members of the Board of Directors [of BDC] were known to be on a [BRA] "hit list" due to perceptions that they had been seeking to benefit at the expense of ordinary Bougainvilleans' (Regan 1996: 18).

Chapter 3

1. Although as this colleague opines, 'the very things we could condemn Carruthers for, are almost the virtues for rising in a corporate career' (BCL official C, Personal Communication, 9 September 2006).

2. Dorney (2000: 112) explains, 'any Bougainvillean who had done really well with the company and had risen to a senior management job was referred to, by the landowning village people, as a coconut – dark on the outside, but white inside'.

3. Harvey observes in this respect:

> Why do capitalists reinvest in expansion rather than consume away their profits in pleasures? This is where 'the coercive laws of competition' play a decisive role. If I, as a capitalist, do not reinvest in expansion and a rival

does, then after a while I am likely to be driven out of business. I need to protect and expand my market share. I have to reinvest to stay a capitalist. (2010: 43)

4. Thompson and MacWilliam observe:

> In 1979, the Panguna Landowners' Association (PLA) was formed. All customary landowners in the three lease zones (Special Mining Lease, the Tailings Lease and the Port-Mine Access Road) automatically became members of the group and at their first meeting they drew up and issued a set of grievances to the Company. When BCL refused to take note of the demands there was a demonstration and the Panguna supermarket (run by BCL) was looted and damaged. (1992: 24)

5. The *Bougainville Copper Compensation Agreement* was initially signed in 1980 and renewed in 1986. According to Applied Geology Associates the agreement,

> Incorporated all previous agreements in respect of: (a) occupation fees; (b) physical disturbance compensation (new); (c) social inconvenience compensation (new); (d) resettlement; (e) bush compensation; (f) rivers and fish compensation; (g) crops and economic trees . . . The Agreement also introduced the new concepts of consumer price indexing and the Road Mining Tailings Lease (RMTL) Trust Fund into which compensation payments for social inconvenience would be paid. The Agreement attempted to achieve a more equitable distribution of compensation, through a wider recognition of the extent of damage and disturbance and the recognition that social inconvenience also applied to villages outside the boundaries of the lease areas. (1989: 4.25–26)

6. Geoffrey Ewing was BCL's Company Secretary during the crisis period.

7. For instance the Road Mining Tailings Leases Trust Fund (RMTLTF or RMTLF), which was set up to administer and invest certain forms of landowner compensation, was viewed as a vehicle for the personal aggrandisement of the PLA's executive, whose personnel overlapped with RMTLTF's executive. Connell explains:

> The basic assumption underlying the establishment of the RMTLF was that it would act as a form of 'business arm' for the landowners . . . It was also intended to provide assistance for . . . basic services . . . Over time concern grew that the directors of the fund were 'eating the money' of the fund themselves, mismanaging it and not using it directly or indirectly for the benefits of the members . . . Broadly the RMTLF was increasingly seen as very closely associated with the . . . Panguna Landowners Association. (1992: 41–2)

Okole, who interviewed villagers in the mine lease area, adds:

There were allegations that the whole operation of the RMTLTF, like that of the PLA itself, had come to be geared to the personal gain of the board members. For instance, sponsorship of students to higher education institutions was said to have been monopolized by the board members. There were also rumours that the fund had begun to operate as an integral part of the Bougainville Development Corporation – a move described by some of our informants as 'greedy' and 'self-benefitting'. (1990: 20)

8. For mining capital in particular, securing stability and predictability in fluid social environments is fundamental, given that the enormous sums of money invested/reinvested in infrastructure and machinery is often valorised over a period of *decades*.

9. The North Solomons Premier was the elected head of the North Solomons provincial government.

10. BCL's Secretary characterises the dilemma in the following terms:

The New Panguna Land Owners argued they had been elected and were now the office bearers of the official association. However, this claim was of limited value bearing in mind there was nothing really to an office bearer as the Panguna Land Owners' Association was simply a name. So there were obviously two camps at that stage and BCL did meet in early 1988 with the new group and the old group. (Ewing 1989)

11. There are a number of common variations of Damien Dameng's name in the literature, including Damien Damen and Damien Damien.

12. With good reason, many Papua New Guineans treat the term 'development' with scepticism. It is viewed as an ideologically loaded category that implicitly celebrates wealth in its capitalist form, while ignoring the cultural and socio-economic riches accumulated by village communities in PNG over many generations.

13. Tanis (2005: 450–1) writes, '[i]n Nasioi one meaning would be the parliament of clans in Kieta District to protect our autonomy over our land and culture that we have possessed from time immemorial to enhance wholeness, unity, peace and holiness in the society' (Tanis 2005: 450–1).

14. The North Solomons Administrative Secretary, Peter Tsiamalili, was 'the most senior public servant in the province' (Dorney 2000: 128).

15. The Pangu Party was one of PNG's largest political parties.

16. Chief Minister was the title given to PNG's Prime Minister during the period of self-government (1972–75), that preceded independence.

17. Ostensibly the Bougainville Copper Foundation was an independent charitable organisation set up at BCL's initiative. AGA explain:

Bougainville Copper Foundation (BCF), formerly the Panguna Development Foundation, was established in 1971 as a charitable body, with the broad aim of improving the welfare and development of the people of Papua

New Guinea. As a charitable body at least 80% of income, after operating expenses, must be used for charitable purposes. Although it is technically not a subsidiary of BCL, being a company limited by guarantee, BCL provides management and financial support and it is widely viewed as being a BCL enterprise. (1989: 7.20; see also Quodling 1991: 43–5)

18. Wolfers suggests AGA's method of presentation was unnecessary provocative: 'Few of the experts involved in assessing the environmental impact of the mining project at Panguna displayed the humility before local experience which many scientists have learnt – sometimes at the cost of unnecessary injury to people whose understanding of the local environment they had initially discounted' (1992: 42).

Chapter 4

1. Momis told parliament in July the following year, 'I strongly believe that in the end the only way to resolve the crisis is by the use of the Melanesian way of talking' (Hansard, 12 July 1989).

2. Indeed, the Minister for Provincial Affairs explained to parliament in 1989:

   The way the landowners are going about taking up arms to show their dissatisfaction is not good. We have a Mining Forum where landowners have their right to express their views . . . The Government in fact approved a Mining Policy which will accommodate the needs and the aspirations of the landowners, not only in Panguna but in other provinces as well and it is unfortunate that Mr Francis Ona has decided to take up arms against the very Government which is sympathetic and which is also determined to take necessary steps to correct the injustices that were committed in the past against the people. (Hansard, 6 September 1989)

3. This included the Minister for Provincial Affairs, the Lands Minister, the Minister for Minerals and Energy and the Minister of Police.

4. This included the Secretary of the Prime Minister's Department, the Justice Department, Minerals and Energy Department, and the Department of Provincial Affairs.

5. By April 1989, 200 people were reported to have been arrested for breaching curfew, of which nine were imprisoned (*Post-Courier* 13 April 1989, p.2).

6. Arawa Enterprises Limited was 75 per cent owned by Bougainville Copper Foundation, BCL's benevolent arm. The supermarket chain was perceived to be directly undercutting indigenous retailers.

7. The formal call-out was actually made on 23 December 1988, but the troops were not deployed until March 1989 (Kaputin 1992: Appendix XII).

8. De Gedare (2000) argues that rape, due to its sensitive nature, was an 'invisible' but common weapon used by the security forces to terrorise the civilian population. He observes:

> There are very few documented instances of rape . . . Havini records 32 cases of rapes between 1989-1995: but the figure I believe is still very low . . . Whatever the exact figures may be, it is certainly true that a lot of sexual abuses did occur. Various women leaders of Bougainville have also cited to me cases of sexual abuse, which resulted in the birth of children. (de Gedare 2000: 202)

Evidence suggests that these sexual assaults were not a spontaneous result of the pressures placed on the security forces in Bougainville. They were, in fact, engrained into the security forces' culture. Standish (1994: 76) notes:

> Never acceptable, and perhaps the most damaging politically to the PNG state, are reports of rape by police, documented in the case of Enga Province, and mentioned in an AIDAB review of the police project. There are also stories from the Tari area of police 'parties' in which mobile squads from other Highlands provinces are invited in by the locally-based squads to feast and have their way with local women, events which are later reciprocated by the visitors. (1994: 76)

9. By 1990, the Australian Government was estimated to have provided around AU\$4 billion in financial aid to PNG (approximately US\$3 billion) (Joint Committee on Foreign Affairs, Defence & Trade 1990: 968).

10. Writing in 2002 Rogers (2002: 144) observes that since independence (1975) the Australian government provided PNG with around AU\$500 million in defence aid (approximately US\$355 million), which included an extensive training and personnel loan/exchange program. Furthermore, apart 'from two landing craft . . . and three Avara transport aircraft' Australia had 'provided the PNGDF with all its major items of equipment' (Bullock 1991: 3).

11. All Australian High Commission officials interviewed were stationed in Port Moresby during 1988–90.

12. During the 1980s, the Hawke government was facing a dilemma of sorts, as new, more competitive regional articulations of capital accumulation in Asia, accelerated Australia's economic decline (Beeson and Hadiz 1998: 295). Conley explains:

> As Australia entered the 1970s policy-makers were confronted with both a cyclical and structural crisis. In addition to the problems that afflicted other advanced capitalist economies to varying degrees in the 1970s and 1980s – low growth, high inflation and unemployment, declining productivity and profit levels, and the growing power of global financial markets – policy-makers began to realise that Australia had 'the wrong type of economy

for the late twentieth century'... By the 1980s, it was increasingly obvious that the Australian economy was in need of major structural change. The OPEC oil shocks of the 1970s accelerated the shift to less intensive use of energy and raw materials. Technological advances led to the substitution of synthetic products for primary products. High levels of agricultural protectionism throughout the developed world and increased dumping of subsidised agricultural exports continued to restrict trade opportunities for Australia's rural sector. Many manufacturing industries in Australia were struggling to compete with imports even with high levels of protection. (2001: 200 & 209)

In response, the Hawke government embarked upon a series of radical neoliberal reforms. These reforms were typified by de-regulation, privatisation, new public management techniques, wage restraints, large tariff/quota reductions, subsidies for big business and a relaxation of foreign ownership rules. Calibrating Australia's international environment to these domestic reforms became a major priority. For example, one of the government's most trumpeted achievements in this respect was the creation of the Asia Pacific Economic Cooperation (APEC) process in 1989. The Foreign Minister argued that APEC would facilitate:

> Very practical issues like common technical standards, mutual recognition of qualifications, customs harmonisation, removal of non-tariff barriers to trade, and achievement of significant commonality in investment rules, all within the framework of intellectual commitment to 'open regionalism' (that is, regionally based economic cooperation, trade facilitation and liberalisation – but pursued in the context of a larger commitment to a free and open global trade and investment environment). (Evans 1993)

13. Australia's diplomatic presence in PNG at the time was large. Evans and Grant (1991: 69) observe, 'Port Moresby is one of Australia's biggest missions, about the size of our embassy in Beijing and only slightly smaller than the Tokyo and Jakarta missions'.

Chapter 5

1. The national government promised to make available 10 per cent of its equity in BCL available for purchase, both by the North Solomons provincial government and the landowners, with special loan arrangements.
2. BCL's benevolent arm, BCF, owned the North Solomons Agricultural Foundation, and had a 75 per cent stake in Arawa Enterprise Limited. The latter was the island's leading supermarket and retail chain, while the former was involved in commercial agriculture (AGA 1989: 7.20; Connell 1991: 69–70; Quodling 1991: 43–5).

3. NEC is a name given to Cabinet in PNG.

4. Government participants included, Rabbie Namaliu (Prime Minister), Akoka Doi (Deputy Prime Minister), Kala Swokin (Minister for Lands and Physical Planning), John Momis (Minister for Provincial Affairs), Galeva Kwarara (Minister for Trade and Industry), Paterson Lowa (Minister for Minerals and Energy), Michael Somare (Minister for Foreign Affairs), Peter Garong (Minister for Labour and Employment), Jim yer Waim (Minister for Environment and Conservation), Bill Searson (Secretary, Minerals and Energy), Paul Bengo (Secretary, Prime Minister's Department and NEC), Mel Togolo (Acting Provincial Secretary), and Joe Kabui (Premier).

5. Landowner participants included, Lawrence Daveona and Francis Kinima for the OPLA and Wendelinus Bitanuma and Philip Miriori for the NPLA.

6. Ted Diro was also a particular favourite among the expatriate business community. One BCL manager recalls:

   I thought he was one of the most impressive men in the whole country. You walked into his office there was not a thing out of place. And if you wanted something done, he snapped his bloody fingers and some people went and did it. If he had been PM [during the Bougainville crisis], it would have been a pretty good situation. The fact he took bribes didn't worry me, as the others did too, it was just that he got caught . . . But if Ted had led the thing, and ran it, it may well have worked. The pressure Rabbie was under, he went half way. (BCL official B, personal communication, 13 September 2006)

7. Namaliu's Pangu Party had won 35 seats at the 1987 elections, making it the largest party in PNG's national parliament, followed by the People's Democratic Movement which held 20 seats (Saffu 1998a: 437).

8. The precedent effect of the Bougainville situation also alarmed a special Ministerial committee set up to investigate the Bougainville crisis:

   [A]s a body formed by traditional landowners discontented with returns received from use and damage of traditionally-owned lands, the BRA has obviously aroused the sympathy of people who have been seen themselves as being in similar situations in other parts of the North Solomons Province and elsewhere in the country. A victory by the BRA might, so some people hope, pave the way for them. (Kaputin 1992: 4.51)

9. These arguments were also being echoed in the media: 'Landowners are watching events very closely. They have already observed the K400 million five-year boost in grants [Bougainville Package] to Bougainville offered by the national government, and have seen how it is violence or the threat of it, that appears to bring such a response' (Callick 1989d: 29; see also May 2004: 84).

10. A BCL executive who went on to steer other companies in the industry observes:

I would never send any of my own people, or invest anything in PNG, it is too difficult . . . It comes back to when is a nation a nation? That is something that the Chinese have done right, and the Russians have done wrong. The Chinese have said lets develop economically first, and then develop politically. Democracy like the environment is a luxury. Whereas Russia changed on both counts at once, in the same time frame, and it is a right royal bloody mess. Look at China it is powering the world. (BCL official G, personal communication, 22 August 2006)

11. Australian capital was primary invested in PNG's minerals industry.
12. The DCP facilitates 'cooperative activities between the Australian Defence Force and regional security forces' (Australian Department of Defence 1995: ch.2 p.2). Between 1975 and 1990 defence cooperation with PNG consumed around half the DCP budget.
13. This operation was named after the dog breed which certain PNGDF officers felt a senior BRA commander, bared a likeness to (Rogers 2002: 229).
14. In 1989 Brigadier-General (retired) Singirok was a Major in the PNGDF.
15. It is unclear whether these helicopters were provided by a contractor, Heli Bougainville, who services were also employed by BCL. Nevertheless, an internal BCL facsimile from March 1990, addressed to the Managing Director, explicitly mentions helicopters: 'By tonight 2/3, all choppers should have left Bougainville. I understand the *military* may require one of their's and may hold it back for a couple of days longer. Will follow up' (BCL 1990l).
16. Villagers were not always fortunate enough to escape the PNGDF's indiscriminate fire. For example, during a similar raid on a village near Panguna in late August, 'Maria Miringori Bangi, a mother of nine, and her daughter, Joyce Bangi Manenu 15, were shot and killed by security forces' (Amnesty International 1990a: 34).

Chapter 6

1. BRA's growing presence in south Bougainville was discussed in meetings between BCL and the North Solomons Provincial Government, and in meetings between BCL and the SOE's Deputy Controller (BCL 1989h, 1989i).
2. Colonel Nuia argued, 'the strategy is to localise and isolate the centre where there is support for the militants. When this occurs then military action may be possible' (BCL 1990b).
3. Security force resources, at this stage, were being concentrated in preparation for a major offensive.
4. *Traim bun*, means to 'try bones' or simply put 'to test one's strength in a fight'.
5. There was confusion over whether this included regular RPNGC officers. On its part, the national government believed they were exempt from this demand.

6. Kemelfield paints a similar picture of the military conditions on Bougainville during February 1990: 'At the time of the ceasefire there appeared to be a real danger of the security force camps being overrun by the BRA, the security forces being heavily outnumbered by rebel forces motivated by a strong sense of anger and of holding the moral high ground' (1990: 68–9).

7. The PNGDF's naval contingent included five pacific-class naval vessels, two landing craft vessels, a combat support boat, and 12 Avon boats (Papua New Guinean Department of Defence 1989, 1990). The PNGDF's air wing consisted of four DC-3 aircraft, four Nomads, four Iroquois helicopters, and three Arava aircraft, all of which suffered from maintenance problems (Papua New Guinean Department of Defence 1989, 1990).

8. The argument over weapons trafficking through the Solomon Islands was commonly used to justify the blockade. However, according to a senior PNGDF officer, the BRA was not acquiring weapons from the Solomon Islands in any significant quantity (PNGDF officer A, personal communication, 3 July 2006). Moreover, weapons trafficking was not listed as a concern by the DIB when discussing the blockade in their April 1990 contingency plan.

9. Mercy rides to the Solomon Islands were not exempted from the blockade, thus the seriously ill and wounded risked being killed along with their travel companions, during the sea journey to medical aid.

10. The loyalist leaders argued:

> Under the present situation, so tense and sensitive, no leader or anyone for that matter is willing to take risks without some sort of guarantee to their lives and families. It is for this reason our group has proposed to you that your assistance in supplying us with limited arms is going to enable us to have access to areas during our mobilisation for an awareness campaign to bring about negotiations. (DIB 1990)

Chapter 7

1. That said, the London-based International State Crime Initiative is currently conducting a major cross-comparative study of resistance that includes Tunisia, Kenya, Burma, Colombia and PNG. This study has been funded by the UK's Economic and Social Research Council to the tune of £830,000, a powerful demonstration that spaces of resistance still exist within the academia to undertake research that does not conform to neoliberal orthodoxy.

Afterword

1. Both men sat on the OPLA executive and were Directors of the controversial RMTLTF (see chapter 3).

2. Umbrella Panguna Landowners Association is used to differentiate this landowner association from the OPLA and NPLA.

3. This is based on a sample of 86 in-depth interviews conducted with communities in the mine area by Jubilee Australia during 2013–14.

4. These issues were flagged by a psychologist, who has done diagnostic work on the island (personal communication, 4 July 2013). It is also reflected in a recent study by Fulu et al. (2013) on gendered violence.

5. In contrast, during a visit to Bougainville in January 2014 PNG's Prime Minister apologised for the national government's role in the conflict.

6. It is not clear how amnesty provisions included in the *Bougainville Peace Agreement* would affect such a process, were it to occur.

7. The ABC is Australia's national broadcaster.

8. Regan's criticism of the international media is somewhat perplexing, given that his particular take on the BRA was frequently echoed in the *Australian Financial Review*, *The Australian*, *Islands Business*, and the ABC (see Cass 1992). Indeed, two of the most prolific journalistic voices, Rowan Callick and Sean Dorney, overtly shared Regan's position on the BRA.

9. Examples include The Coconut Revolution, An Evergreen Island, and Bougainville – Our Island Our Fight.

10. At the invitation of Jubilee Australia, I have acted as an academic advisor on this campaign.

11. This quote is transcribed from footage of the event shared by Bougainvillean filmmaker, Clive Porabou.

12. Without, of course, deflating the importance of ethnic heritage.

Bibliography

Adams, R. (ed.) (2001) *Peace on Bougainville: Truce Monitoring Group Gudpela Nius Bilong Peace*, Wellington: Victoria University Press.

AGA – Applied Geology Associates Limited (1989) *Environmental, Socio-Economic and Public Health Review of Bougainville Copper Mine, Panguna*, Wellington: Author.

Albon, C. (1989) 'Back to the Battle', *Islands Business*, October, pp.12–18.

Allen, B., Bourke, M. and Gibson, J. (2005) 'Poor Rural Places in Papua New Guinea', *Asia Pacific Viewpoint*, 46(2), 201–217.

Alley, R. (2003) 'Ethnosecession in Papua New Guinea: The Bougainville Case', in Ganguly, R. and Macduff, I. (eds) *Ethnic Conflict and Secessionism in South and Southeast Asia: Causes, Dynamics, Solutions*, London: Sage Publications.

Amnesty International (1990a) *Papua New Guinea: Human Rights Violations on Bougainville 1989–1990*, London: Amnesty International Secretariat.

—— (1990b) *Submission*, submission to the Joint Committee on Foreign Affairs, Defence and Trade, Foreign Affairs Sub-Committee on Australia's Relations with Papua New Guinea, Canberra: Australian Government Publishing Service.

—— (1993) *'Under the Barrel of a Gun': Bougainville 1991–1993*, <www.amnesty.org/en/library/info/ASA34/005/1993/en>.

—— (1997) *Bougainville: The Forgotten Human Rights Tragedy*, <www.amnesty.org/en/library/info/ASA34/001/1997>.

Anderson, K. (2010) *Marx at the Margins: On Nationalism, Ethnicity, and Non-Western Societies*, Chicago: University of Chicago Press.

Anis, T. (1977a) 'The Wakunai Local Government Council', in Connell, J. (ed.) *Local Government Councils in Bougainville*, Christchurch: Bougainville Special Publications.

—— (1977b) 'Buka Local Government Council', in Connell, J. (ed.) *Local Government Councils in Bougainville*, Christchurch: Bougainville Special Publications.

Ashman, S. (2006) 'From World Market to World Economy', in Dunn, B. and Radice, H. (eds) *One Hundred Years of Permanent Revolution*, London: Pluto Press.

Auditor General's Office (2001) *Report of the Auditor General on the Department of Works and Implementation*, Waigani: Author.

—— (2006) *Report of the Auditor General on the Sepik Highway, Roads and Bridges Maintenance and Other Infrastructure Trust Account*, Waigani: Author.

—— (2007) *Report of the Auditor General to the National Parliament on the Department of Lands and Physical Planning*, Waigani: Author.

Auna, J. (1989) 'Proof of Evidence', *Bougainville Copper Limited v. Metals and Minerals Insurance Pte Limited, GRE Pacific Insurance Pty. Ltd., Taisho Marine &*

Fire Insurance Co. Ltd. and American Home Assurance Company, Supreme Court of Victoria, No.CL220.

Australia, Senate (1990) Hansard, Canberra: Australian Government Publishing Service.

Australian Department of Defence (1976) *Australia's Defence*, Canberra: Australian Government Publishing Service.

—— (1987) *The Defence of Australia, 1987*, Canberra: Australian Government Publishing Services.

—— (1990) 'The Australia Papua New Guinea Defence Relationship', supplementary submission to the Joint Committee on Foreign Affairs, Defence and Trade, Foreign Affairs Sub-Committee on Australia's Relations with Papua New Guinea, Canberra: Australian Government Publishing Service.

—— (1995) *Defence Cooperation*, Canberra: Directorate of Publishing.

Australian National University (1999) *Annual Report: 1998*, Canberra: Public Affairs Division, the Australian National University.

—— (2000) *Annual Report: 1999*, Canberra: Public Affairs Division, the Australian National University.

—— (2001) *Annual Report: 2000*, Canberra: Public Affairs Division, the Australian National University.

Autonomous Bougainville Government (2014) 'Media Release', 12 February.

Bainton, N. (2008) 'Men of *Kastom* and the Customs of Men: Status, Legitimacy and Persistent Values in Lihir, Papua New Guinea', *The Australian Journal of Anthropology*, 19(2), 194–212.

Banks, G. (2001) 'Papua New Guinea Baseline Study', *Report No. 180*, International Institute for Environment and Development, <www.iied.org/pubs/pdfs/G01003. pdf>.

Barnes, C. E. (1969) 'Business and Investment Opportunities in New Guinea', *Current Notes on International Affairs*, 40(6), 333–334.

BCL – Bougainville Copper Limited (1987) Correspondence from R.J. Cornelius, Managing Director Bougainville Copper Limited, to Perpetua Serero, Chairlady Panguna Landowners Association, P. O. Box 1108, Panguna, North Solomons Province, 16 November.

—— (1988a) Correspondence from J. L. Auna, General Manager Personnel Services Bougainville Copper Limited, to the Panguna Landowners Association, P.O. Box 1108, Panguna, North Solomons Province, 24 March.

—— (1988b) Correspondence from R. J. Cornelius, Managing Director Bougainville Copper Limited, to the Panguna Landowners Association, P.O. Box 1108, Panguna, North Solomons Province, 21 April.

—— (1988c) Meeting Minutes, Panguna, 28 April.

—— (1988d) Correspondence from D. S. Carruthers, Chairman Bougainville Copper Limited, to Rt. Hon. Paias Wingti, Prime Minister of PNG, Office of the Prime Minister, National Parliament, Waigani, National Capital District, 18 May.

—— (1988e) Meeting Minutes, Panguna, 31 July.

—— (1988f) Meeting Minutes, Provincial Government Assembly Room, 18 November.

—— (1988g) Memorandum from R. J. Cornelius, Managing Director Bougainville Copper Limited, to D. S. Carruthers, Chairman Bougainville Copper Limited, 22 November.

—— (1988h) Meeting Minutes, Port Moresby, 25 November.

—— (1988i) Meeting Minutes, Port Moresby, 26 November.

—— (1988j) Correspondence from R. J. Cornelius, Managing Director Bougainville Copper Limited, to Rt Hon. Rabbie L. Namaliu CMG MP, Prime Minister of PNG, P. O. Box 6605, Boroko, National Capital District, 2 December.

—— (1988k) Fax Transmission to Sedgwick, 9 December.

—— (1988l) Meeting Minutes, 8 December.

—— (1988m) Security Incident Report, 20 December.

—— (1988n) Meeting Minutes, Siromba Hotel, 12 December.

—— (1989a) Correspondence from R. J. Cornelius, Managing Director Bougainville Copper Limited, to the Hon. P. Lowa, MP, Minister for Minerals and Energy, P. O. Wards Strip, Waigani, N.C.D., 10 May.

—— (1989b) Correspondence from R. J. Cornelius, Managing Director Bougainville Copper Limited, to Rt. Hon. Rabbie Namaliu, MP, Prime Minister of PNG, Office of the Prime Minister, P. O. Wards Strip, Waigani, National Capital District, 18 May.

—— (1989c) Meeting Minutes, North Solomons Government Office, 8 June.

—— (1989d) Memorandum from R. J. Cornelius to D. S. Carruthers, 26 June.

—— (1989e) Meeting Minutes, 13 July.

—— (1989f) Meeting Minutes, 26 July.

—— (1989g) Meeting Minutes, 22 August.

—— (1989h) Meeting Minutes, Colonel Nuia's office, 20 December.

—— (1989i) Meeting Minutes, 22 December.

—— (1989j), *Annual Report 1988*, Papua New Guinea: Author.

—— (1990a) Meeting Minutes, Oune village, 5 January.

—— (1990b) Meeting Minutes, Defence Headquarters, 8 January.

—— (1990c) Notes on Telephone Discussion 08:45 between Douglas Fishburn and Bill Daniels, 16 January.

—— (1990d) Meeting Minutes, 17 January.

—— (1990e) Correspondence from R. J. Cornelius, Managing Director Bougainville Copper Limited, to Colonel Nuia, Deputy Controller, Bougainville State of Emergency, Arawa, Bougainville, North Solomons Province, 17 January 1990.

—— (1990f) BCL Employee Communications Update, 18 January.

—— (1990g) Correspondence from R. J. Cornelius, Managing Director Bougainville Copper Limited, to Rt. Hon. Rabbie Namaliu CMG MP, Prime Minister of Papua New Guinea, Office of the Prime Minister, Waigani, National Capital District, 19 January.

—— (1990h) Correspondence from D. S. Carruthers, Chairman of Bougainville Copper Limited, to Rt Hon. Rabbie L. Namaliu CMG MP, Prime Minister of PNG, Morauta Haus, Waigani, PNG, 6 February.

—— (1990i) Meeting Minutes, 17 February.

—— (1990j) Meeting Minutes, 18 February.

—— (1990k) Meeting Minutes, 20 February.

—— (1990l) Facsimile Transmission from John Whitehouse to Robert Cornelius, 2 March.

—— (1990m) Meeting Minutes, 13 March.

—— (1990n) Meeting Minutes, 26 April.

—— (1990o) *Annual Report 1989*, Papua New Guinea: Author.

—— (2008) 'Bougainville Copper Limited AGM', Press Release, 8 May.

Beazley, K. (2003) 'The Hawke Years: Foreign Affairs and Defence', in Ryan, S. and Bramston, T. (eds) *The Hawke Government: A Retrospective*, Melbourne: Pluto Press.

Beeson, M. and Hadiz, V. (1998) 'Labour and the Politics of Structural Adjustment in Australia and Indonesia', *Journal of Contemporary Asia*, 28(3), 291–309.

Bensaïd, D. (2002) *Marx for Our Time: Adventures and Misadventures of a Critique*, London: Verso.

Bernstein, H. (1988) 'Capitalism and Petty-Bourgeois Production: Class Relations and Divisions of Labour', *Journal of Peasant Studies*, 15(2), 258–271.

—— (1994) 'Agrarian Classes in Capitalist Development', in Sklair, L. (ed.) *Capitalism and Development*, London: Routledge.

—— (2001) '"The Peasantry" in Global Capitalism: Who, Where and Why?', in Panitch, L. and Leys, C. (eds) *Socialist Register 2001: Working Classes, Global Realities*, London: Merlin.

—— (2010) *Class Dynamics of Agrarian Change*, Black Point: Fernwood Publishing.

Blackwell, E. (2012) 'PNG People Lose Billions to Corruption', *Australian Associated Press*, 8 October.

Block, F. (1977) 'The Ruling Class Does Not Rule: Notes on the Marxist Theory of the State', *Socialist Revolution*, 33, 6–28.

Böge, V. (1995) 'Mining and Conflict on Bougainville', in *Development as a Cause of Conflict. The Bougainville Issue in Papua New Guinea*. Proceedings of a Conference held in the Evangelische Akademie Bad Boll/Germany from 10 to 12 March 1995 (= Protokolldienst 22/95), Bad Boll.

Boggs, C. (2010) *Crimes of Empire: Rogue Superpower and World Domination*, London: Pluto Press.

Bonney, N. (1982) 'Local Government and Political Development in Papua New Guinea', *Public Administration and Development*, 2, 113–127.

Bougainville Mine Workers Union (1989) Correspondence from Mathew Tukan, President, Bougainville Mine Workers Union, to the Honourable Rabbie Namaliu, Prime Minister, P. O. Box 6605, Boroko, National Capital District, 17 May.

Bougainville Revolutionary Army (1989) Correspondence from Francis Ona, Supreme Commander of the Bougainville Revolutionary Army, to Mr Rabbie Namaliu, Prime Minister of PNG, National Parliament, P. O. Box 6605, Boroko, PNG, 20 June.

Braithwaite, J. (1984) *Corporate Crime in the Pharmaceutical Industry*, London: Routledge and Kegan Paul.

—— (1988) 'White-Collar Crime, Competition, and Capitalism: Comment on Coleman', *The American Journal of Sociology*, 94(3), 627–632.

Braithwaite, J., Charlesworth, H., Reddy, P. and Dunn, L. (2010) *Reconciliation and Architectures of Commitment: Sequencing Peace in Bougainville*, Canberra: ANU E Press, <press.anu.edu.au/?p=57571>.

Bromby, R. (1990) 'Time for a Change', *Pacific Islands Monthly*, July, pp.23–24.

Brunton, B. (2001) 'Declaration of Brian Brunton', *Alexis Holyweek Sarei, et al. v Rio Tinto, plc. et al.*, Case No. 00-11695 MMM AIJx, United States District Court – Central District of California, Western Division.

Bukharin, N. (2003) *Imperialism and World Economy*, London: Bookmarks.

—— (2005) *Philosophical Arabesques*, London: Pluto Press.

Bullock, K. (1991) 'Australia and Papua New Guinea: Foreign and Defence Relations Since 1975', Research School of Pacific Studies (Australian National University) Working Paper No.227.

Callick, R. (1989a) 'First PNG Army Deaths', *Australian Financial Review*, 10 April, p.3.

—— (1989b) 'The Bougainville Minefield', *Australian Financial Review*, 26 May, p.1.

—— (1989c) 'Forces Lack of Discipline Even Unnerves Namaliu', *Australian Financial Review*, 20 June, p.8.

—— (1989d) 'Bougainville's Lessons for Pacific Leaders', *Islands Business*, August, pp.28–30.

—— (1989e) 'The Albatross that is Bougainville', *Australian Financial Review*, 7 November, p.13.

—— (1990a) 'Lloyd's Withdraws Bougainville Cover', *Australian Financial Review*, 25 January, p.8.

—— (1990b) 'Stench of War Likely to Linger on Bougainville for Years to Come', *Australian Financial Review*, 1 February, p.16.

—— (1990c) 'Bougainville: At Ground Zero', *Australian Financial Review*, 19 February, p.16.

—— (1990d) 'Battling for an Answer to Bougainville; Pacific Perspective', *Australian Financial Review*, 12 October, p.15.

—— (1991a) 'PNG Won Bougainville with Sanctions; Pacific Perspective', *Australian Financial Review*, 25 January, p.15.

—— (1991b) 'Many Losers in Bougainville Debacle; Pacific Perspective', *Australian Financial Review*, 12 March, p.15.

—— (1991c) 'Aust Ignorance Distorts the PNG Debate; Pacific Perspective', *Australian Financial Review*, 4 July, p.15.

—— (2010) 'Scholar and Mentor to Melanesia', *The Australia*, 26 May, p.28.

—— (2011) 'Battle Intensifies Over Bougainville Copper', *Weekend Australian*, 16 July, p.6.

Callinicos, A. (2007) 'Does Capitalism Need the State System?', *Cambridge Review of International Affairs*, 20(4), 533–549.

—— (2009) *Imperialism and Global Political Economy*, Cambridge: Polity.

Cammack, D. (2009) *Chronic Poverty in Papua New Guinea*, Background Paper for the Chronic Poverty Report 2008–09, Manchester: Chronic Poverty Research Centre.

Carruthers, D. S. (1990) 'Some Implications for Papua New Guinea of the Closure of the Bougainville Copper Mine', in May, R. J. and Spriggs, M. (eds) *The Bougainville Crisis*, Bathurst: Crawford House Press.

Cass, P. (1992) 'A Comparison of the Coverage of the Bougainville Civil War in the *Australian* and the *Times* of PNG', *Australian Journalism Review*, 14(2), 79–90.

Centre for Environmental Law and Community Rights, Friends of the Earth PNG, the Bismarck Ramu Group, Greenpeace Australia Pacific and the Forest Peoples Programme. (2011) *Request for Consideration under the Urgent Action/ Early Warning Procedure to Prevent Irreparable Harm to Indigenous Peoples' Rights in Papua New Guinea, 78th Session of the Committee on the Elimination of Racial Discrimination*, <www.forestpeoples.org/sites/fpp/files/publication/2011/03/png-cerd-2011-ew-ua-final.pdf>.

Claxton, K. (1998) *Bougainville 1988–98: Five Searches for Security in the North Solomons Province of Papua New Guinea*, Canberra: Strategic and Defence Studies Centre.

—— (2000) 'Violence, Internal Security and Security-Stakeholders in Papua New Guinea', in Dinnen, D. and Ley, A. (eds) *Reflections on Violence in Melanesia*, Leichardt: Hawkins Press and Asia Pacific Press.

Cohen, S. (2001) *States of Denial*, Cambridge: Polity.

Conley, T. (2001) 'The Re-Globalisation of the Australian Economy', *Policy, Organisation & Society*, 20(2), 199–231.

Connell, J. (1978) *Taim Bilong Mani: The Evolution of Agriculture in a Solomon Island Society*, Canberra: Australian National University.

—— (1979) 'The Emergence of a Peasantry in Papua New Guinea', *Peasant Studies*, 8(2), 103–137.

—— (1990) 'Perspectives on a Crisis (4)', in Polomka, P. (ed.) *Bougainville Perspectives on a Crisis*, Canberra: Strategic and Defence Studies Centre.

—— (1991) 'Compensation and Conflict: The Bougainville Copper Mine, Papua New Guinea', in Connell, J. and Howitt, R. (eds) *Mining and Indigenous Peoples in Australasia*, Sydney: Sydney University Press.

—— (1992) '"Logic is a Capitalist Cover-Up": Compensation and Crisis in Bougainville, Papua New Guinea', in Henningham, S., May, R. J. and Turner, L. (eds) *Resources, Development and Politics in the Pacific Islands*, Bathurst: Crawford House Press.

—— (1997) *Papua New Guinea: The Struggle for Development*, London: Routledge.

Cornelius, R. (1989) 'Proof of Evidence', *Bougainville Copper Limited v. Metals and Minerals Insurance Pte Limited, GRE Pacific Insurance Pty. Ltd., Taisho Marine & Fire Insurance Co. Ltd. and American Home Assurance Company*, Supreme Court of Victoria, No.CL220.

CRA – Conzinc Riotinto of Australia (1988) Memorandum from D. S. Carruthers, Chairman Bougainville Copper Limited, to Directors, Melbourne, 6 December.

—— (1989a) Correspondence from D. S. Carruthers, Group Executive, Conzinc Riotinto of Australia, to Sir Alistair Frame, Chairman of RTZ Ltd, 6 St Jame's Square, London, SW1Y 4JU, UK, 9 January.

—— (1989b) Memorandum from D. S. Carruthers to J. T. Ralph, 19 April.

—— (1989c) Correspondence from D. S. Carruthers, Group Executive, Conzinc Riotinto of Australia, to Sir Alisair [sic] Frame, RTZ Ltd., St James Square, London, 19 May.

—— (1989d) Memorandum from D. S. Carruthers, Chairman Bougainville Copper Limited, to Directors, Melbourne, 5 June.

—— (1990) 'Bougainville Update: The Economic Impact of Bougainville Copper', *CRA Gazette*, 25(6).

Darius, W. (1990a) 'Commercial Life on Bougainville Grinding to Halt', *Post-Courier*, 2 January, p.2.

—— (1990b) 'Rebels are on the Run in Buka – Ex-Commander', *Post-Courier*, 5 October, p.2.

De Gedare, D. (2000) 'Human Rights Violations in Papua New Guinea and in Bougainville, 1989–1997', in Rynkiewich, M. A. and Seib, R. (eds) *Politics in Papua New Guinea: Continuities, Changes and Challenges*, Goroka: Melanesian Institute.

Denoon, D. (1985) 'Capitalism in Papua New Guinea', *The Journal of Pacific History*, 20(3), 119–134.

—— (2000) *Getting Under the Skin: The Bougainville Copper Agreement and the Creation of the Panguna Mine*, Melbourne: Melbourne University Press.

DIB – Defence Intelligence Branch (1990) *An Intelligence Resume for Contingency Planning for North Solomons Province*, Port Moresby: Author.

Dinnen, S. (1994) 'Public Order in Papua New Guinea: Problems and Prospects', in Thompson, A. (ed.) *Papua New Guinea: Issues for Australian Security Planners*, Canberra: Australian Defence Studies Centre.

—— (2001) *Law and Order in a Weak State: Crime and Politics in Papua New Guinea*, Honolulu: University of Hawai'i Press.

Donaldson, M. (1980) 'Class Formation in Papua New Guinea: The Indigenous Bourgeoisie', *Journal of Australian Political Economy*, 7, 63–85.

Donaldson, M. and Good, K. (1981) 'The Eastern Highlands, Coffee and Class', in Denoon, D. and Snowden, C. (eds) *A Time to Plant and a Time to Uproot*, Boroko: Institute of Papua New Guinea Studies.

—— (1988) *Articulated Agricultural Development: Traditional and Capitalist Agricultures in Papua New Guinea*, London: Aldershot.

Dorney, S. (no date) 'Interview', In: *Pacific Project*.

—— (1998) *The Sandline Affair*, Sydney: ABC Books.

—— (2000) *Papua New Guinea: People, Politics and History Since 1975*, Sydney: ABC Books.

Downs, I. (1980) *The Australian Trusteeship: Papua New Guinea 1945–75*, Canberra: Australian Government Publishing Service.

Engels, F. (1969) *The Peasant War in Germany*, Moscow: Progress Publishers.

Evans, G. (1989) *Australia's Regional Security: Ministerial Statement by Senator the Hon. Gareth Evans QC, Minister for Foreign Affairs and Trade*, Canberra: Department of Foreign Affairs and Trade.

—— (1990) 'Australia and Papua New Guinea', in Anderson, D. (ed.) *The Papua New Guinea-Australia Relationship: Problems and Prospects*, Sydney: Pacific Security Research Institute.

—— (1993) 'Australia's Middle Power Diplomacy', The Inaugural Sir Zelman Cowen AIJA Annual Address on International Relations, Australian Institute of Jewish Affairs, Melbourne, 10 November.

—— (1997) 'The Labor Tradition: A View from the 1990s', in Lee, D. and Waters, C. (eds) *Evatt to Evans: The Labor Tradition in Australian Foreign Policy*, Sydney: Allen and Unwin.

Evans, G. and Grant, B. (1991) *Australia's Foreign Relations in the World of the 1990s*, Victoria: Melbourne University Press.

Evans, L. (1992) 'The Health and Social Situation on Bougainville', in Denoon, D. and Spriggs, M. (eds) *The Bougainville Crisis: 1991 Update*, Bathurst: Crawford House Press.

Ewing, G. (1989) 'Proof of Evidence', *Bougainville Copper Limited v. Metals and Minerals Insurance Pte Limited, GRE Pacific Insurance Pty. Ltd., Taisho Marine & Fire Insurance Co. Ltd. and American Home Assurance Company*, Supreme Court of Victoria, No.CL220.

Filer, C. (1990) 'The Bougainville Rebellion, the Mining Industry and the Process of Social Disintegration in Papua New Guinea', in May, R. J. and Spriggs, M. (eds) *The Bougainville Crisis*, Bathurst: Crawford House Press.

—— (1998) 'The Melanesian Way of Menacing the Mining Industry' in Zimmer-Tamakoshi, L. (ed.) *Modern Papua New Guinea*, Kirksville MO: Thomas Jefferson University Press.

—— (2011) 'The Political Construction of a Land Grab in Papua New Guinea', paper presented at the *International Conference on 'Global Land Grabbing'*, Institute of Development Studies (UK), 6–8 April.

Fitzpatrick, P. (1980) *Law and State in Papua New Guinea*, London: Academic Press.

Fletcher, L. and Webb, A. (2012) *Pipe Dreams: The PNG LNG Project and the Future Hopes of a Nation*, Sydney: Jubilee Australia.

Forster, M. (1992) 'The Bougainville Revolutionary Army', *The Contemporary Pacific*, 4(2), 368–372.

Foucault, M. (2003) '*Society Must be Defended': Lectures at the Collège de France 1975–76*, London: Penguin Books.

—— (2007) *Security, Territory, Population: Lectures at the Collège de France 1977–1978*, Basingstoke: Palgrave Macmillan.

Friedrichs, D. O. (2012) 'Resisting State Crime as a Criminological Project in the Context of the Arab Spring', in Stanley, E. and McCulloch, J. (eds) *State Crime and Resistance*, Abingdon: Routledge.

—— (2012) 'On Resisting State Crime: Conceptual and Contextual Issues', *Social Justice*, 36(3), 4–27.

Fulu, E., Warner, X., Miedema, S., Jewkes, R., Roselli, T. and Lang, J. (2013) *Why Do Some Men Use Violence Against Women and How Can We Prevent It? Quantitative Findings from the United Nations Multi-Country Study on Men and Violence in Asia and the Pacific*, Bangkok: UNDP, UNFPA, UN Women and UNV.

Garrett, J. (2011) 'BCL Rejects Allegations of Complicity in War on Bougainville', Radio Australia, 27 June, <www.radioaustralia.net.au/international/radio/onairhighlights/bcl-rejects-allegations-of-complicity-in-war-on-bougainville>.

Gewertz, D. B. and Errington, F. K. (1999) *Emerging Class in Papua New Guinea: The Telling of Difference*, Cambridge: Cambridge University Press.

Ghai, Y. (1997) 'Establishing a Liberal Political Order through a Constitution: The Papua New Guinea Experience', *Development and Change*, 28, 303–330.

Ghai, Y. and Regan, A. J. (2000) 'Bougainville and the Dialectics of Ethnicity, Autonomy and Separation', in Ghai, Y. (ed.) *Autonomy and Ethnicity: Negotiating Competing Claims in Multi-ethnic States*, Cambridge: Cambridge University Press.

Gibbon, P. and Neocosmos, M. (1985) 'Some Problems in the Political Economy of "African Socialism"', in Bernstein, H. and Campbell, B. K. (eds) *Contradictions of Accumulation in Africa: Studies in Economy and State*, London: Sage Publications.

Gillespie, R. (1992) *Inside Bougainville: Behind Papua New Guinea's Iron Curtain*, Melbourne: Asian Development Foundation.

—— (1993) *Krai Bilong Bougainville*, Port Kembla: Author.

—— (1996) 'Ecocide, Industrial Chemical Contamination and the Corporate Profit Imperative: The Case of Bougainville', *Social Justice*, 23(4), 109–125.

Good, K. (1986) *Papua New Guinea: A False Economy*, London: Anti Slavery Society.

Gramsci, A. (1971) *Selections from the Prison Notebooks*, London: Lawrence and Wishart.

Green, P. and Ward, T. (2000) 'State Crime, Human Rights, and the Limits of Criminology', *Social Justice*, 27(1), 101–115.

—— (2004) *State Crime: Governments, Violence and Corruption*, London: Pluto Press.

—— (2012), 'Civil Society, Resistance and State Crime', in Stanley, E. and McCulloch, J. (eds) *State Crime and Resistance*, Abingdon: Routledge.

Griffin, H. M. (2005) 'Sources on Pre-Mining Bougainville', in Regan, A. J. and Griffin, H. M. (eds) *Bougainville: Before the Conflict*, Canberra: Pandanus Books.

Griffin, J. (1990a) 'Bougainville is a Special Case', in May, R. J. and Spriggs, M. (eds) *The Bougainville Crisis*, Bathurst: Crawford House Press.

—— (1990b) '"Logic is a White Man's Trick": The Bougainville Rebellion', in Anderson, D. (ed.) *The PNG–Australian Relationship: Problems and Prospects*, Sydney: Pacific Security Research Institute.

—— (1995) 'Bougainville Corrigenda', *Eureka Street*, 5(2), 11.

—— (1996) 'Obituary: Bishop Gregory Singkai', *Eureka Street*, 6(8), 24.

—— (1997) 'We Have Shirked our Role in Troubled PNG', *The Australian*, 21 March, p.11.

—— (1998) 'Truth Casualties on Bougainville', *Eureka Street*, 8(2), 6.

Griffin, J. and Kawona, S. (1989) 'The Elections in North Solomons Province', in Oliver, M. (ed.) *Eleksin: The 1987 National Elections in Papua New Guinea*, Port Moresby: University of Papua New Guinea.

Griffin, J. and Togolo, M. (1997) 'North Solomons Province 1974–1990', in May, R. J., Regan, A. J. and Ley, A. (eds) *Political Decentralisation in a New State: The Experience of Provincial Government in Papua New Guinea*, Bathurst: Crawford House Publishing.

Griffin, J., Nelson, H. and Firth, S. (1979) *Papua New Guinea: A Political History*, Richmond: Heinemann Educational Australia.

Gross, E. (1978) 'Organizations as Criminal Actors', in Wilson, P. and Braithwaite, J. (eds) *Two Faces of Deviance: Crimes of the Powerless and Powerful*, Brisbane: University of Queensland Press.

Grossman, L. S. (1983) 'Rural Economic Differentiation, and Articulation in the Highlands of Papua New Guinea', *American Ethnologist*, 10(1), 59–76.

Gouy, J., Kapa, J., Mokae, A. and Levantis, T. (2010) 'Parting with the Past: Is Papua New Guinea Poised to Begin a New Chapter Towards Development?', *Pacific Economic Bulletin*, 25(1), 1–23.

Hannett, L. (1975) 'The Case for Bougainville Secession', *Meanjin Quarterly*, 34(3), 286–293.

Harvey, D. (1982) *The Limits to Capital*, Oxford: Blackwell.

—— (2003) *The New Imperialism*, Oxford: Oxford University Press.

—— (2010) *The Enigma of Capital and the Crises of Capitalism*, London: Profile Books.

Havini, Moses (1990) 'Human Rights Violations and Community Disruptions', in May, R. J. and Spriggs, M. (eds) *The Bougainville Crisis*, Bathurst: Crawford House Press.

Havini, Marilyn (1995) *A Compilation of Human Rights Abuses Against the People of Bougainville: 1989 – 1995*, Vol.1, Sydney: Bougainville Freedom Movement.

—— (1997) 'Questions and Answers', in *Women Speak Out on Bougainville: Forum Papers*, Neutral Bay: Women for Bougainville.

—— (2003) 'Journey into Exile', in Sirivi, J. T. and Havini, M. T. (eds) *As Mothers of the Land*, Canberra: Pandanus Books.

Hawke, R. (1990) 'Speech', State Function Room, Parliament House, Port Moresby, 3 September.

Hawksley, C. (2006) 'Papua New Guinea at Thirty: Late Decolonisation and the Political Economy of Nation-Building', *Third World Quarterly*, 27(1), 161–173.

—— (2007) 'Constructing Hegemony: Colonial Rule and Colonial Legitimacy in the Eastern Highlands of Papua New Guinea', *Rethinking Marxism*, 19(2), 195–207.

Hegarty, D. (2009) 'Governance at the Local Level in Melanesia – Absent the State', *Commonwealth Journal of Local Governance*, 3, < www.gdn-oceania.org/ Portals/83/david_hegarty_paper.pdf>.

Hermkens, A. K. (2011) 'Mary, Motherhood, and Nation: Religion and Gender Ideology in Bougainville's Secessionist Warfare', *Intersections: Gender and Sexuality in Asia and the Pacific*, 25, <intersections.anu.edu.au/issue25/hermkens.htm>.

—— (2013) 'Like Moses Who Led His People to the Promised Land: Nation- and State-Building in Bougainville', *Oceania*, 83(3), 192–207.

Hiambohn, W. (1988a) 'BCL Shuts Down After New Attack', *Post-Courier*, 6 December, p.1.

—— (1988b) 'Tohian Orders His Men: Shoot to Kill', *Post-Courier*, 7 December, p.1.

—— (1989a) 'Cabinet Sends Troops to Guard Key Installations', *Post-Courier*, 22 March, p.2.

—— (1989b) 'Three More Deaths in Buin Shoot-Out', *Post-Courier*, 23 March, p.2.

—— (1989c) 'Soldiers Under Specific Orders to Flush Out Ona', *Post-Courier*, 28 March, p.2.

—— (1989d) 'Industry Wants All Mineral Rights to Remain With State', *Post-Courier*, 4 April, p.2.

—— (1989e) 'Militants May Be Getting Foreign Help', *Post-Courier*, 10 April, p.2.

—— (1989f) 'Bougainville Group Alleges Atrocity', *Post-Courier*, 19 April, p.1.

—— (1989g) 'Huge BCL Stake is To Be Offered in NSP Peace Bid', *Post-Courier*, 28 April, p.2.

—— (1989h) 'Murder of Minister Puts Back Signing', *Post-Courier*, 12 September, pp.1–2.

—— (1989i) 'Dotaona Replaced as Security Chief', *Post-Courier*, 16 October, p.1.

—— (1990a) 'Level of Goods, Services Fall', *Post-Courier*, 9 February, p.2.

—— (1990b) 'Ona: I Will Surrender if Violence Goes On', *Post-Courier*, 20 March, p.1.

—— (1990c) 'Whew! Made it: Namaliu Survives his First Two Years and Eyes the Future', *Pacific Islands Monthly*, August, pp.15–17.

—— (1990d) 'Buka Death Toll Now 23', *Post-Courier*, 4 October, p.1.

Hirst, P. Q. (1975) 'Marx and Engels on Law, Crime and Morality', in Taylor, I., Walton, P. and Young, J. (eds) *Critical Criminology*, London: Routledge and Kegan Paul.

Howie-Willis, I. (2010) 'An Inspirational Teacher and Activist', *Canberra Times*, 11 June, p.12.

Hriehwazi, A. (1989a) 'Saboteurs Strike Non-Company Targets', *Post-Courier*, 18 January, p.2.

—— (1989b) 'Surrender or Die', *Post-Courier*, 20 January, p.1.

—— (1989c) 'Bougainville Comes to a Standstill', *Post-Courier*, 21 March, p.1.

—— (1989d) 'Dotaona Tightens Control on Province', *Post-Courier*, 30 June, p.2.

—— (1989e) 'Premier, Minister Bashed Up', *Post-Courier*, 3 July, pp.1–2.

—— (1989f) 'Mine Restart Lasts for Less Than a Day', *Post-Courier*, 6 September, p.1.

—— (1989g) 'Another Soldier Dies in Explosives Accident', *Post-Courier*, 2 October, p.2.

—— (1990a) 'Ceasefire!', *Post-Courier*, 1 March, p.1.

—— (1990b) 'Government Imposes Blockade on Islands', *Post-Courier*, 3 May, p.2.

—— (1990c) 'Bishop Singkai Pleads for Lifting of Blockade', *Post-Courier*, 4 May, p.2.

Iadicola, P. (2011) 'Do Empires Commit State Crime', in Rothe, D. L. and Mullins, C. W. (eds) *State Crime: Current Perspectives*, London: Rutgers University Press.

Ilyenkov, E. V. (1982) *The Dialectics of the Abstract and the Concrete in Marx's Capital*, Moscow: Progress Publishers.

Jennings, P. and Claxton, K. (2013) *A Stitch in Time: Preserving Peace on Bougainville*, Canberra: Australian Strategic Policy Institute, < www.aspi.org.au/publications/ special-report-a-stitch-in-time-preserving-peace-on-bougainville/SR59_ bougainville.pdf>.

Jessop, B. (2007) *State Power*, Cambridge: Polity Press.

Joint Standing Committee on Foreign Affairs, Defence & Trade (1990) *Australia's Relation with Papua New Guinea*, Transcript, Canberra: Australian Government Publishing Service.

—— (1999) *Bougainville: The Peace Process and Beyond*, <parlinfo.aph.gov.au/ parlInfo/search/display/display.w3p;query=Id:committees%2Fcommjnt% 2Fmo000188.sgm%2F0009>.

Joku, F. A. (1989) 'BCL to Stay on Despite Violence', *Post-Courier*, 13 April, p.1.

Jopling, S. (1989) 'Proof of Evidence', *Bougainville Copper Limited v. Metals and Minerals Insurance Pte Limited, GRE Pacific Insurance Pty. Ltd., Taisho Marine & Fire Insurance Co. Ltd. and American Home Assurance Company*, Supreme Court of Victoria, No.CL220.

Jubilee Australia (2013) 'Testimonies: Not On My Watch Campaign', *Jubilee Australia Website*, < www.jubileeaustralia.org/2013/campaigns/notonmywatch/ testimonies>.

Kaputin, J. R. (1992) *Crisis in the North Solomons Province: Report of the Special Committee*, Port Moresby: Department of the Prime Minister.

Kauzlarich, D. and Kramer, R. C. (1998) *Crimes of the American Nuclear State: At Home and Abroad*, Boston: Northeastern University Press.

Kemelfield, G. (1990) 'A Short History of the Bougainville Ceasefire Initiative', in May, R. J. and Spriggs, M. (eds) *The Bougainville Crisis*, Bathurst: Crawford House Press.

—— (1992) 'Reflections on the Bougainville Conflict: Underlying Causes and Conditions for a Resolution', in Denoon, D. and Spriggs, M. (eds) *The Bougainville Crisis: 1991 Update*, Bathurst: Crawford House Press.

Kiely, R. (2010) *Rethinking Imperialism*, Basingstoke: Palgrave Macmillan.

King, H. F. (1978) *The Discovery and Development of the Bougainville Copper Deposit*, Melbourne: Conzinc Riotinto of Australia.

Kolma, F. (1991) 'Triumph of Justice', *Pacific Islands Monthly*, November, pp.8–9.

Kramer, R. C. and Michalowski, R. J. (1991) 'State-Corporate Crime', paper prepared for American Society of Criminology Meeting, Baltimore, Maryland, 7–12 November 1990, revised: September 1991.

Kramer, R. C., Michalowski, R. J. and Kauzlarich, D. (2002) 'The Origins and Development of the Concept and Theory of State-Corporate Crime', *Crime & Delinquency*, 48(2), 263–282.

Lacher, H. (2006) *Beyond Globalization: Capitalism, Territoriality and the International Relations of Modernity*, Oxford: Routledge.

Lasslett, K. (2010a) 'Crime or Social Harm? A Dialectical Perspective', *Crime, Law and Social Change*, 54(1), 1–19.

—— (2010b) 'Scientific Method and the Crimes of the Powerful', *Critical Criminology*, 18(3), 211–228.

—— (2010c) 'Winning Hearts and Mines: The Bougainville Crisis 1988-1990', in Jackson, R., Murphy E. and Poynting S. (eds) *Contemporary State Terrorism: Theory and Practice*, Abingdon: Routledge.

—— (2012a) 'Power, Struggle and State Crime: Researching through Resistance', *State Crime*, 1(1), 126–148.

—— (2012b) 'State Crime by Proxy: Australia and the Bougainville Conflict', *British Journal of Criminology*, 52(4), 705–723.

—— (2012c) 'State Terror and the Bougainville Conflict', in Lasslett, K. (ed.) *State Crime Testimony Project*, <www.statecrime.org/testimonyproject>.

Lawson, S. (1992) *Ethnonationalist Dimensions of Internal Conflict: The Case of Bougainville Secessionism*, Canberra: Peace Research Centre.

Lebowitz, M. A. (2003) *Beyond Capital: Marx's Political Economy of the Working Class*. Basingstoke: Palgrave Macmillan.

—— (2009) *Following Marx: Method, Critique, and Crisis*, Chicago: Haymarket Books.

Liria, Y. A. (1993) *Bougainville Campaign Diary*, Victoria: Indra Publishing.

—— (2001) 'Declaration of Yauka Aluambo Liria', *Alexis Holyweek Sarei, et al. v Rio Tinto, plc. et al.*, Case No. 00-11695 MMM AIJx, United States District Court – Central District of California, Western Division.

Loewenstein, A. (2013) *Profits of Doom*, Melbourne: Melbourne University Press.

Lukács, G. (1974) *Conversations with Lukács*, London: Merlin Press.

—— (1978) *The Ontology of Social Being*, Vol.2, London: Merlin Press.

Lummani, J. (2005) 'Post-1960s Cocoa and Copra Production in Bougainville', in Regan, A. J. and Griffin, H. M. (eds) *Bougainville: Before the Conflict*, Canberra: Pandanus Books.

Mackenzie, S. and Green, P. (2008) 'Performative Regulation: A Case Study in how Powerful People Avoid Criminal Labels', *British Journal of Criminology*, 48 (2), 138–153.

MacQueen, N. (1993) 'An Infinite Capacity to Muddle Through? A Security Audit for Papua New Guinea', in Sutton, P. and Payne, A. (eds) *Size and Survival: The Politics of Security in the Caribbean and the Pacific*, London: Frank Cass and Company.

MacWilliam, S. (1988) 'Smallholdings, Land Law and the Politics of Land Tenure in Papua New Guinea', *Journal of Peasant Studies*, 16(1), 77–109.

—— (2005) 'Post-War Reconstruction in Bougainville: Plantations, Smallholders and Indigenous Capital', in Regan, A. J. and Griffin, H. M. (eds) *Bougainville: Before the Conflict*, Canberra: Pandanus Books.

Maketu, B. T. (1988) *Defence in Papua New Guinea: Introductory Issues*, Canberra: Strategic and Defence Studies Centre.

Marfleet, P. (2013) 'Mubarak's Egypt – Nexus of Criminality', *State Crime*, 2(2), 112–134.

Marx, K. (1973) *Grundrisse: Foundations of the Critique of Political Economy*, Harmondsworth: Penguin Books Ltd.

—— (1975) *Early Writings*, Harmondsworth: Penguin Books.

—— (1976) *Capital*, Vol.1, Harmondsworth: Penguin Books.

—— (1981) *Capital*, Vol.3, Harmondsworth: Penguin Books.

—— (1995) *Value, Price and Profit*, <www.marxists.org/archive/marx/works/1865/value-price-profit/index.htm>.

Marx, K. and Engels, F. (1956) *The Holy Family or Critique of Critical Critique*, London: Lawrence and Wishart.

Marx, K. and Engels, F. (1973) *The Revolutions of 1848: Political Writings*, Vol.1, Harmondsworth: Penguin Books.

Marx, K. and Engels, F. (1982) *Selected Correspondence*, Moscow: Progress Publishers.

Masiu, R. (2014) 'O'Neill Gives Green Light for Repeal of Mining Act', *Post-Courier*, 30 January, p.4.

May, R. J. (1990) 'Political Implications of the Bougainville Crisis for Papua New Guinea', in May, R. J. and Spriggs, M. (eds) *The Bougainville Crisis*, Bathurst: Crawford House Press.

—— (1993) *The Changing Role of the Military in Papua New Guinea*, Canberra: Strategic and Defence Studies Centre.

—— (2004) *State and Society in Papua New Guinea: The First Twenty-Five Years*, Canberra: ANU E Press, <epress.anu.edu.au/sspng>.

McCasker, A. W. (1966) 'Economic Development in Papua and New Guinea', *Australian Territories*, 6(3), 2–13.

McKillop, R. and Firth, S. G. (1981) 'Foreign Intrusion: The First Fifty Years', in Denoon, D. and Snowden, C. (eds) *A Time to Plant and a Time to Uproot: A History of Agriculture in Papua New Guinea*, Boroko: Institute of Papua New Guinea Studies.

Mészáros, I. (2001) *Socialism or Barbarism*, New York: Monthly Review Press.

—— (2011) *Social Structures and Forms of Consciousness: Dialectic of Structure and History*, New York NY: Monthly Review Press.

Michalowski, R. (1985) *Order, Law and Crime*, New York NY: Random House.

—— (2009) 'Power, Crime and Criminology in the New Imperial Age', *Crime, Law and Social Change*, 51(3-4), 303–325.

—— (2010) 'Keynote Address: Critical Criminology for a Global Age', *Western Criminology Review*, 11(1), 3–10.

Mirinka, R. (2004) 'Community Development and BOCBIHP', in Sirivi, J. T. and Havini, M. T. (eds) *As Mothers of the Land: The Birth of the Bougainville Women for Peace and Freedom*, Canberra: Pandanus Books.

Mitchell, D. D. (1976) *Land and Agriculture in Nagovisi, Papua New Guinea*, Boroko: Institute of Applied Social and Economic Research.

—— (1982) 'Frozen Assets in Nagovisi', *Oceania*, 53(1), 56–66.

Momis, J. (1987a) Correspondence from Fr John Momis, Member for Bougainville, to Paul Quodling, Managing Director Bougainville Copper Limited, Panguna, North Solomons Province, 4 May.

—— (1987b) Correspondence from Fr John Momis, Member for Bougainville, to Paul Quodling and Robert Cornelius, Outgoing and Incoming Managing Director Bougainville Copper Limited, Panguna, North Solomons Province, 25 May 1987.

—— (2001) 'Declaration of John Momis', *Alexis Holyweek Sarei, et al. v Rio Tinto, plc. et al.*, Case No. 00-11695 MMM AIJx, United States District Court – Central District of California, Western Division.

—— (2011) 'Speech to the PNG Australia Business Forum', Madang, 16 May.

—— (2013) 'Speech to the House of Representatives', Buka, 13 January.

Moore, C. and Kooyman, M. (eds) (1998) *A Papua New Guinea Political Chronicle 1967– 1991*, Bathurst: Crawford House Publishing.

Morauta, L. (1986) 'Law and Order in Papua New Guinea: A Tenth Anniversary Report', in Morauta, L. (ed.) *Law and Order in a Changing Society*, Canberra: Australian National University.

Morgan, M. (2005) 'Cultures of Dominance: Institutional and Cultural Influences on Parliamentary Politics in Melanesia', Discussion Paper 2005/2, Canberra: Research School of Pacific and Asian Studies, Australian National University, <www.cdi.anu.edu.au/.AP/2004-05/D_P/05_02_dp_morgan[1].pdf>.

Moulik, T. K. (1977) *Bougainville in Transition*, Canberra: Australian National University.

Mullins, C. W. (2009) '"He Would Kill me with his Penis": Genocidal Rape in Rwanda as a State Crime', *Critical Criminology*, 17(1), 15–33.

Mullins, C. W. and Rothe, D. L. (2008) *Blood, Power and Bedlam: Violations of International Criminal Law in Post-Colonial Africa*, New York NY: Peter Lang.

Namaliu, R. (1989) *Report on the State of Emergency Bougainville Province*, Port Moresby: Government Printer.

—— (1990) 'Transcript of Joint News Conference', Travelodge Hotel, Port Moresby, September 3.

—— (1995) 'Politics, Business and the State in Papua New Guinea', *Pacific Economic Bulletin*, 10(2), 61–65.

Nangoi, B. (1989a) 'Booby Traps Order Under a Probe', *Post-Courier*, 22 September, p.1.

—— (1989b) 'Bougainville South is "Out of Control"', *Post-Courier*, 12 December, p.1.

Nelson, H. (2005) 'Fighting for Her Gates and Waterways: Changing Perceptions of New Guinea in Australian Defence', Discussion Paper 2005/3, Canberra: State, Society and Governance in Melanesia, Australian National University.

Nisira, P. (2014) 'Interview', In: *Bougainville on the Brink*, Journeyman Pictures, <www.journeyman.tv/66710/short-films/bougainville-on-the-brink-hd.html>.

North Solomons Provincial Government (1987) Correspondence from Joseph C. Kabui MPA, Premier North Solomons Province, to Mr Bob Cornelius, Managing Director Bougainville Copper Limited, Building 36, Panguna, North Solomons Province, 7 December.

—— (1989) *Provincial Select Committee Report on the Bougainville Crisis*, Arawa: Author.

NPLA – (New) Panguna Landowners Association (1987a) Correspondence from Perpetua Serero, Chairlady Panguna Landowners Association, to General Manager, Personnel Department, Bougainville Copper, Panguna, 2 September.

—— (1987b) Correspondence from Perpetua Serero, Chairlady Land Owners Association, to Mr Bob Cornelius, Managing Director Bougainville Copper Limited, Building 36, Panguna, North Solomons Province, 23 October.

——(1987c) Correspondence from Perpetua Serero, Chairlady Panguna Landowners Association, to the Chairman Bougainville Copper Limited, GPO Box 2028-S., Melbourne,Victoria, 3001, Australia, 1 December.

—— (1988a) 'Petition to the National Government and Bougainville Copper Limited', 11 March.

—— (1988b) Correspondence from Perpetua Serero, Chairlady, Panguna Landowners Association, and Francis Ona, Secretary, Panguna Landonwers Association to the Managing Director, Bougainville Copper LTD., Panguna, 5 April.

——(1988c) Correspondence from Perpetua Serero, Chairlady Panguna Landowners Association, and Francis Ona, Secretary Panguna Landowners Association to the Minister for Minerals and Energy, the National Government, Port Moresby, 5 April.

——(1988d) Correspondence from Perpetua Serero, Chairlady Panguna Landowners Association, and Francis Ona, Secretary Panguna Landonwers Association to Mr Joseph Kabui, Premier, North Solomons Provincial Government, North Solomons Province, 5 April.

—— (1988e) 'Log of Claims', 24 October.

—— (1988f) Correspondence from Panguna Landowners Association to Minerals and Energy as Well as Environmental Departments of the National Government, 25 October.

—— (1988g) Correspondence from Perpetua Serero, Chairlady Panguna Land Owners Association, to Mr Bob Cornelius, Managing Director Bougainville Copper Limited, Building 36, Panguna, North Solomons Province, 18 November 1988.

—— (1988h) 'The Main Tactics to be Highlighted in the Speech by Members of Panguna Land Owners Association', 10 December.

Numapo, J. (2013) *Commission of Inquiry into the Special Agriculture and Business Leases: Final Report*, Port Moresby: Commission of Inquiry into the Special Agricultural and Business Leases.

O'Callaghan, M.L. (1989) 'Squad of Police Rushed to Riots: PNG', *Sydney Morning Herald*, 21 March, p.11.

—— (1990a) 'Govt Seeks Early Cease-Fire; PNG', *Sydney Morning Herald*, 15 February, p.9.

—— (1990b) 'Rebels in PNG Agree to Ceasefire', *Sydney Morning Herald*, 1 March, p.1.

Ogan, E. (1972) *Business and Cargo: Socioeconomic Change among the Nasioi of Bougainville*, Canberra: Australian National University.

—— (1990) 'Perspectives on a Crisis (5)', in Polomka, P. (ed.) *Bougainville Perspectives on a Crisis*, Canberra: Strategic and Defence Studies Centre.

—— (1999) 'The Bougainville Conflict: Perspectives from Nasioi', Discussion Paper 99/3, Canberra: State, Society and Governance in Melanesia, Australian National University.

—— (2005) 'Snapshots from Nasioi, 1963–2000', in Regan, A. J. and Griffin, H. M. (eds) *Bougainville: Before the Conflict*, Canberra: Pandanus Books.

Ogan, E. and Wesley-Smith, T. (1992) 'Papua New Guinea: Changing Relations of Production', in Robillard, A. B. (ed.) *Social Change in the Pacific Islands*, London: Kegan Paul International.

Okole, H. (1990) 'The Politics of the Panguna Landowners' Association', in May, R. J. and Spriggs, M. (eds) *The Bougainville Crisis*, Bathurst: Crawford House Press.

—— (2005) 'The "Fluid" Party System of Papua New Guinea', *Commonwealth and Comparative Politics*, 43(3), 362–381.

Oliver, D. (1991) *Black Islanders: A Personal Perspective of Bougainville 1937–1991*, Melbourne: Hyland House Publishing.

O'Malley, P. (1987) 'Marxist Theory and Marxist Criminology', *Crime and Social Justice*, 29, 70–87.

Ona, F. (1989) 'Communique', 29 November.

—— (1990a) 'Perspectives on a Crisis(1)', in Polomka, P. (ed.) *Bougainville: Perspectives on a Crisis*, Canberra: Strategic and Defence Studies Centre.

—— (1990b) 'Declaration of Independence – Republic of Bougainville', in Polomka, P. (ed.) *Bougainville: Perspectives on a Crisis*, Canberra: Strategic and Defence Studies Centre.

OPLA – (Old) Panguna Landowners Association (1987) Correspondence from Michael Pariu, Executive Committee, Panguna Landowners Association, to Mr J. Auna, General Manager, Personnel Services, Bougainville Copper Limited, Panguna, 7 October.

Panguna Management Consultative Committee (2011) Meeting Minutes, Conference Room – ABG Administration, 10 November.

Papua New Guinea National Parliament (1989) *Draft Hansard*, Port Moresby: National Parliament.

—— (1990) *Draft Hansard*, Port Moresby: National Parliament.

Papuan Oil Search Ltd (1989) 'Bougainville and BCL – A Review & Comparison with Iagifu-Hedinia', Board Briefing Notes, 31 July.

Patel, I. (2013) 'The Second Anniversary of the Arab Spring', < statecrime.org/online_article/the-second-year-anniversary-of-the-arab-spring/ >.

Pearce, F. (1976) *The Crimes of the Powerful*, London: Pluto Press.

Permanent Parliamentary Committee on National Emergency (1989a) *Statement No.2: Report of the Permanent Parliamentary Committee on National Emergency*, Port Moresby: Government Printer.

—— (1989b) *Statement No.3: Report of the Permanent Parliamentary Committee on National Emergency*, Port Moresby: Government Printer.

PNG Department of Defence (1989) *Defence Report 1988*, Boroko: Author.

—— (1990) *Defence Report 1989*, Boroko: Author.

—— (1991) *Defence Report 1990*, Boroko: Author.

PNG Mine Watch (2013) '"Not Credible": AusAID Mining Adviser Defends Rio Tinto Against War Crimes Allegation', *PNG Mine Watch Blog*, 28 November, < ramumine.wordpress.com/2013/11/28/not-credible-ausaid-mining-adviser-defends-rio-tinto-against-war-crimes-allegations/ >.

PNG National Government (1988) Correspondence from Rabbie L. Namaliu, CMG, MP, Prime Minister of Papua New Guinea, to R. J. Cornelius, Managing Director Bougainville Copper Limited, Panguna, North Solomons Province, 10 December 1988.

—— (1989a) Meeting Minutes, Parliament 'B' Wing Conference Room, 25 April.

—— (1989b) Correspondence from Rabbie L. Namaliu, CMG, MP, Prime Minister of Papua New Guinea, to R. J. Cornelius, Managing Director Bougainville Copper Limited, P. O. Box 1354, Arawa, North Solomons Province, 19 May.

—— (1990) Correspondence from Rabbie L. Namaliu, CMG, MP, Prime Minister of Papua New Guinea, to Mr D. S. Carruthers, Chairman Bougainville Copper Limited, Floor 35, 55 Collins St., Melbourne, Victoria, 5 February.

Poulantzas, N. (1978) *State, Power, Socialism*. London: Verso.

Public Accounts Committee (2003) *Report of the Public Accounts Committee on the Parliamentary Services*, Waigani: National Parliament of Papua New Guinea.

—— (2006a) *Public Accounts Committee Report to Parliament on the Inquiry into the Department of Lands and Physical Planning*, Waigani: National Parliament of Papua New Guinea.

—— (2006b) *Public Accounts Committee Report to Parliament on the Inquiry into the Office of the Public Curator*, Waigani: National Parliament of Papua New Guinea.

—— (2007) *Public Accounts Committee Report to Parliament on the Inquiry into the Sepik Highway, Roads and Bridges Maintenance and Other Infrastructure Trust Account*, Waigani: National Parliament of Papua New Guinea.

Quodling, P. (1991) *Bougainville: The Mine and the People*, Sydney: The Centre for Independent Studies.

Rea, S. (1988) 'Troops on Standby as Cabinet Meets', *Post-Courier*, 8 December, p.1.

—— (1989a) 'Soliders to Step Up Action', *Post-Courier*, 11 April, p.1.

—— (1989b) 'Forces Will Move in to Get Militants', *Post-Courier*, 9 June, p.1.

—— (1989c) 'Diro Admits He Ordered the Use of Booby Traps', *Post-Courier*, 25 September, p.1.

—— (1990a) 'Province Approves Plan to Move Out 1500 Workers', *Post-Courier*, 27 February, p.2.

—— (1990b) 'Split in BRA!', *Post-Courier*, 24 September, p.1.

Regan, A. J. (1996) *The Bougainville Conflict: Origins and Development, Main 'Actors', and Strategies for its Resolution*, Port Moresby: University of Papua New Guinea Faculty of Law.

—— (1997) 'The Papua New Guinea Policy-Making Environment as a Window on the Sandline Controversy', in Dinnen, S., May, R. J. and Regan, A. J. (eds) *Challenging the State: the Sandline Affair in Papua New Guinea*, Canberra: National Centre for Development Studies.

—— (1998) 'Causes and Course of the Bougainville Conflict', *The Journal of Pacific History*, 33(3), 269–285.

—— (1999) 'Submission – Bougainville: The Peace Process and Beyond', in Parliament of the Commonwealth of Australia, Jointing Standing Committee on Foreign Affairs and Trade, 39th Parliament, Foreign Affairs Sub-Committee, *Submissions – Inquiry into the Bougainville Peace Process, Volume 2, Submissions Numbers 25–30*, Canberra: Parliament of the Commonwealth of Australia.

—— (2000a) 'Traditional Leaders and Conflict Resolution in Bougainville: Reforming the Present by Re-writing the Past?', in Dinnen, D. and Ley, A. (eds) *Reflections on Violence in Melanesia*, Leichardt: Hawkins Press and Asia Pacific Press.

—— (2000b) 'Interview', In: Report Claims 20,000 People Died During Bougainville Crisis, *The World Today*, ABC Local Radio, 21 November.

—— (2002) 'Bougainville: Beyond Survival', *Cultural Survival*, 26(3), 20–24.

—— (2003) 'The Bougainville Conflict: Political and Economic Agendas', in Ballentine, K. and Sherman, J. (eds) *The Political Economy of Armed Conflict: Beyond Greed and Grievance*, London: Lynne Rienner Publishing.

—— (2005) 'Identities Among Bougainvilleans', in Regan, A. J. and Griffin, H. M. (eds), *Bougainville: Before the Conflict*, Canberra: Pandanus Books.

—— (2006) 'Development and Conflict in Papua New Guinea', Unpublished Paper.

—— (2010) *Light Intervention: Lessons from Bougainville*, Washington DC: United States Institute of Peace Press.

—— (2013) 'Bougainville: Conflict Deferred?', in Aspinall, E., Jeffrey, R. and Regan, A. J. (eds) *Diminishing Conflicts in Asia and the Pacific: Why Some Subside and Other's Don't*, Abingdon: Routledge.

Rogers, C., Bleakley, R., Ola, W. and CARE Integrated Community Development Project Team (2011) *Rural Poverty in Remote Papua New Guinea: Case Study of Obura-Wonenara District*, Canberra: Crawford School of Economic and Government, Australian National University.

Rogers, T. A. (2002) *The Papua New Guinea Defence Force: Vanuatu (1980) to Bougainville (1990)*, Unpublished PhD, Canberra: Australian National University.

Rosenberg, J. (1994) *The Empire of Civil Society*, London: Verso.

Rothe, D. L. (2009) 'Introduction: Resisting State Criminality', *Social Justice*, 36(3), 1–4.

Rynkiewich, M. A. (2000) 'Big-man Politics: Strong Leadership in a Weak State', in Rynkiewich, M. A. and Seib, R. (eds) *Politics in Papua New Guinea: Continuities, Changes and Challenges*, Goroka: Melanesian Institute.

Saffu, Y. (1998a) 'January–December 1987', in Moore, C. and Kooyman, M. (eds) *A Papua New Guinea Political Chronicle 1967–1991*, Bathurst: Crawford House Publishing.

—— (1998b) 'January-December 1989', in Moore, C. and Kooyman, M. (eds) *A Papua New Guinea Political Chronicle 1967 – 1991*, Bathurst: Crawford House Publishing.

—— (1998c) 'January–December 1990', in Moore, C. and Kooyman, M. (eds) *A Papua New Guinea Political Chronicle 1967–1991*, Bathurst: Crawford House Publishing.

Sagir, B. (2005) 'Traditional Leadership and the State in Bougainville: A Background Paper' < pidp.org/pibn/pidp/its/sagir.htm >.

Senge, F. (1988) 'How Wingti was Toppled', *Pacific Islands Monthly*, August, pp.10–13.

—— (1991) 'Calendar of Fear', *Pacific Islands Monthly*, April, pp.10–12.

Seriotase, R. (1991) 'Interview', In: Blood on the Bougainvillea, *Four Corners*, ABC Television, Sydney, 24 June.

Sharp, N. (1997) *Bougainville – Blood on our Hands: Australia's Role in PNG's War*, Sydney: AID/WATCH.

Singirok, J. (2001) 'Declaration of General Singirok', *Alexis Holyweek Sarei, et al. v Rio Tinto, plc. et al.*, Case No. 00-11695 MMM AIJx, United States District Court – Central District of California, Western Division.

Sirivi, J. T. (2004) 'Running the Blockade', in Sirivi J. T. and Havini, M. T. (eds) *As Mothers of the Land: The Birth of the Bougainville Women for Peace and Freedom*, Canberra: Pandanus Books.

Slapper, G. and Tombs, S. (1999) *Corporate Crime*, Essex: Pearson Education Limited.

Smith, R. (1990) 'Bougainville and National Unity', in Polomka, P. (ed.) *Bougainville: Perspectives on a Crisis*, Canberra: Strategic and Defence Studies Centre.

Snow, D. (1991) 'Blood on the Bougainvillea', *Four Corners*, ABC Television, Sydney, 24 June.

Somare, M. (2001) 'Draft Declaration of Michael Somare' *Alexis Holyweek Sarei, et al. v Rio Tinto, plc. et al.*, Case No. 00-11695 MMM AIJx, United States District Court – Central District of California, Western Division.

Spriggs, M. (1990) 'Bougainville December 1989 – January 1990: A Personal History', in May, R. J. and Spriggs, M. (eds) *The Bougainville Crisis*, Bathurst: Crawford House Press.

—— (1992a) 'Bougainville Update: August 1990 to May 1991', in Denoon, D. and Spriggs, M. (eds) *The Bougainville Crisis: 1991 Update*, Bathurst: Crawford House Press.

—— (1992b) 'Bougainville Update: May to October 1991', in Denoon, D. and Spriggs, M. (eds) *The Bougainville Crisis: 1991 Update*, Bathurst: Crawford House Press.

Standish, B. (1994) 'Papua New Guinea: The Search for Security in a Weak State', in Thompson, A. (ed.) *Papua New Guinea: Issues for Australian Security Planners*, Canberra: Australian Defence Studies Centre.

—— (2007) 'The Dynamics of Papua New Guinea's Democracy: An Essay', *Pacific Economic Bulletin*, 22(1), 135–157.

Stanley, E. and McCulloch, J. (2012a) 'Resistance to State Crime' in Stanley, E. and McCulloch, J. (eds) *State Crime and Resistance*, Abingdon: Routledge.

—— (eds) (2012b) *State Crime and Resistance*, Abingdon: Routledge.

Strathern, A. (1984) *A Line of Power*, London: Tavistock Publications.

—— (1993) 'Violence and Political Change in Papua New Guinea', *Pacific Studies*, 16(4), 41–60.

Tanis, J. (2002) 'In Between: Personal Experiences in the 9-Year Long War on Bougainville' <ips.cap.anu.edu.au/sites/default/files/Tanis-Gray.pdf>.

—— (2005) 'Nagovisi Villages as a Window on Bougainville in 1988', in Regan, A. J. and Griffin, H. M. (eds) *Bougainville: Before the Conflict*, Canberra: Pandanus Books.

Taylor, P. (2011) 'Speech to the Australian PNG Business Council', Madang, 17 May.

Teschke, B. (2003) *The Myth of 1648: Class, Geopolitics, and the Making of Modern International Relations*, London: Verso.

Thompson, H. and MacWilliam, S. (1992) *The Political Economy of Papua New Guinea*, Wollongong: Journal of Contemporary Asia Publishers.

Thomson, B. (2011) 'Blood and Treasure', *Dateline*, SBS Television, 26 June, <www.sbs.com.au/dateline/story/about/id/601246/n/Blood-and-Treasure>.

Tohian, P. (1989a) *Second Report on the State of Emergency Bougainville Province*, Port Moresby: Government Printer.

—— (1989b) *Fourth Report on the State of Emergency Bougainville Province*, Port Moresby: Government Printer.

—— (1990) *The Sixth Report on the Bougainville State of Emergency to National Parliament*, Port Moresby: Government Printer.

Tombs, S. (2012) 'State-Corporate Symbiosis in the Production of Crime and Harm', *State Crime*, 1(2), 170–195.

Tombs, S. and Whyte, D. (2002) 'Unmasking the Crimes of the Powerful', *Critical Criminology*, 11(3), 217–236.

—— (eds) (2003) *Unmasking the Crimes of the Powerful: Scrutinizing States and Corporations*, New York NY: Peter Lang.

—— (2007) *Safety Crimes*, Devon: Willan Publishing.

Toohey, P. (2013) 'Bougainville Copper Mine in PNG Shut in 1989 on Stock Market', *News.com.au*, 4 June, <www.news.com.au/finance/business/bougainville-copper-mine-in-png-shut-in-1989-on-stock-market/story-fnda1bsz-1226657261349>.

Treadgold, M. L. (1978) *The Regional Economy of Bougainville: Growth and Structural Change*, Canberra: Australian National University.

Trotsky, L. (2005) *The History of the Russian Revolution*, London: Pathfinder.

Tunim, M. K. (2003) 'Where is Kaea?', in Sirivi, J. T. and Havini, M. T. (eds) *As Mothers of the Land*, Canberra: Pandanus Books.

Turner, M. (1990) *Papua New Guinea: The Challenge of Independence*, Harmondsworth: Penguin Books.

Umbrella Panguna Landowners Association (no date) *Project Formulation Document*.

—— (2007) *The Opportunity Presented by BCL as a Going Concern*, 21 March.

—— (2010) *BCL Landowners Evaluation*, 7 January.

Vernon, D. (2005) 'The Panguna Mine', in Regan, A. J. and Griffin, H. M. (eds) *Bougainville: Before the Conflict*, Canberra: Pandanus Books.

Ward, T. and Green, P. (2000) 'Legitimacy, Civil Society, and State Crime', *Social Justice*, 27(4), 76–93.

Wehner, M., and Denoon, D. (eds) (2001) *Without a Gun: Australians' Experience Monitoring Peace in Bougainville, 1997-2001*, Canberra: Pandanus Books.

Wesley-Smith, T. (1989) 'Pre-Capitalist Modes of Production in Papua New Guinea', *Dialectical Anthropology*, 14, 307–321.

—— (1990) 'The Politics of Access: Mining Companies, the State, and Landowners in Papua New Guinea', *Political Science*, 42(2), 1–19.

Wesley-Smith, T. and Ogan, E. (1992) 'Copper, Class, and Crisis: Changing Relations of Production in Bougainville', *The Contemporary Pacific*, 4(2), 245–267.

Wiley, B. (1992) 'Bougainville: A Matter of Attitude', *The Contemporary Pacific*, 4(2), 376–78.

Wolfers, E. P. (1992) 'Politics, Development and Resources: Reflections on Constructs, Conflict, and Consultants', in Henningham, S. and May, R. J. (eds) *Resources, Development and Politics in the Pacific Islands*, Bathurst: Crawford House Press.

Wood, E. M. (2002) *The Origin of Capitalism: A Longer View*, London: Verso.

—— (2003) *Empire of Capital*, London: Verso.

Woodman, S. (1994) 'The Ghost of Kokoda: The Role of Papua New Guinea in Australia's Strategic Outlook', in Thompson, A. (ed.) *Papua New Guinea: Issues for Australian Security Planners*, Canberra: Australian Defence Studies Centre.

Young, T. R. (1981) 'Corporate Crime: A Critique of the Clinard Report', *Contemporary Crises*, 5(3), 323–336.

Zale, D. (1997) 'Women and War: Life Issues, Refugees, Peace and Justice', in *Women Speak Out on Bougainville: Forum Papers*, Neutral Bay: Women for Bougainville.

Index

Rio Tinto, 12, 22, 87–8, 107, 117, 202,
    209, *see also* Bougainville Copper
    Limited, Conzinc Riotinto of
    Australia
Road Mining Tailings Leases Trust
    Fund, 210–1
Rothe, Dawn, 17, 18
Royal Papua New Guinea
    Constabulary, 42–3, 77, 83, 93, 109
    'destructions', 95–6
    mobile squads, 68, 77–8, 81, 88, 90,
    94
    Rapid Deployment Unit, 42, 68

Sabumei, Ben, Minister for Defence,
    115, 134, 139–40
Serero, Perpetua, 48–9, 59–60, 64, 66,
    70, 83–4, 106–7
Singkai, Gregory, 113
Singko, James, 89, 137
state
    and capital, 123–4, 139, 182, 183
    and class struggle, 74, 181–2, 185–6
    and crisis, 124
    and governmentality, 5–8, 40, 139,
    183
    origins of the capitalist state 5
    and violence, 2;
state-corporate crime, 15, 185–6, 207–8
    and the Bougainville conflict, 15
    and empiricism, 16–20
    the integrated theoretical model of
    state-corporate crime, 18
state crime
    and civil society, 195

and class struggle, 11, 186
and contradictions of capitalism, 10,
    179–80
definition, 10, 207
and empire, 207
and empiricism, 16–20, 179, 184
integrated theory of international
    criminal law violations, 17–8
and Marxism, 2, 178–90, 184–9
methodological challenges, 21–2
ontological status 2
see also resistance, state-corporate
    crime, state crime studies
state crime studies, 189–90
Strathern, Andrew, 38

Taylor, Allan, Australian High
    Commissioner, 102
Taylor, Peter, Chairman of Bougainville
    Copper Limited, 191–2, 203
Teschke, Benno, 5
Thomson, Brian, 202
Tohian, Paul, Police Commissioner of
    Papua New Guinea, 82, 83, 90–1,
    137
Tombs, Steve, 15, 16
Trotsky, Leon, 26–7
Tsiamalili, Peter, North Solomons
    Administrative Secretary, 75, 211

Vernon, Don, 52, 209

Ward, Tony, 10, 195
Whyte, David, 16
Wood, Ellen Meiksins, 4–5, 6

www.ingramcontent.com/pod-product-compliance
Lightning Source LLC
Chambersburg PA
CBHW032124020426
42334CB00016B/1067